MEN OF STEEL, WOMEN OF WONDER

ISSUE 04

DEFENDER OF INNOCENTS

ANDRIANNA CAMPBELL

MEN OF STEEL, WOMEN OF WONDER

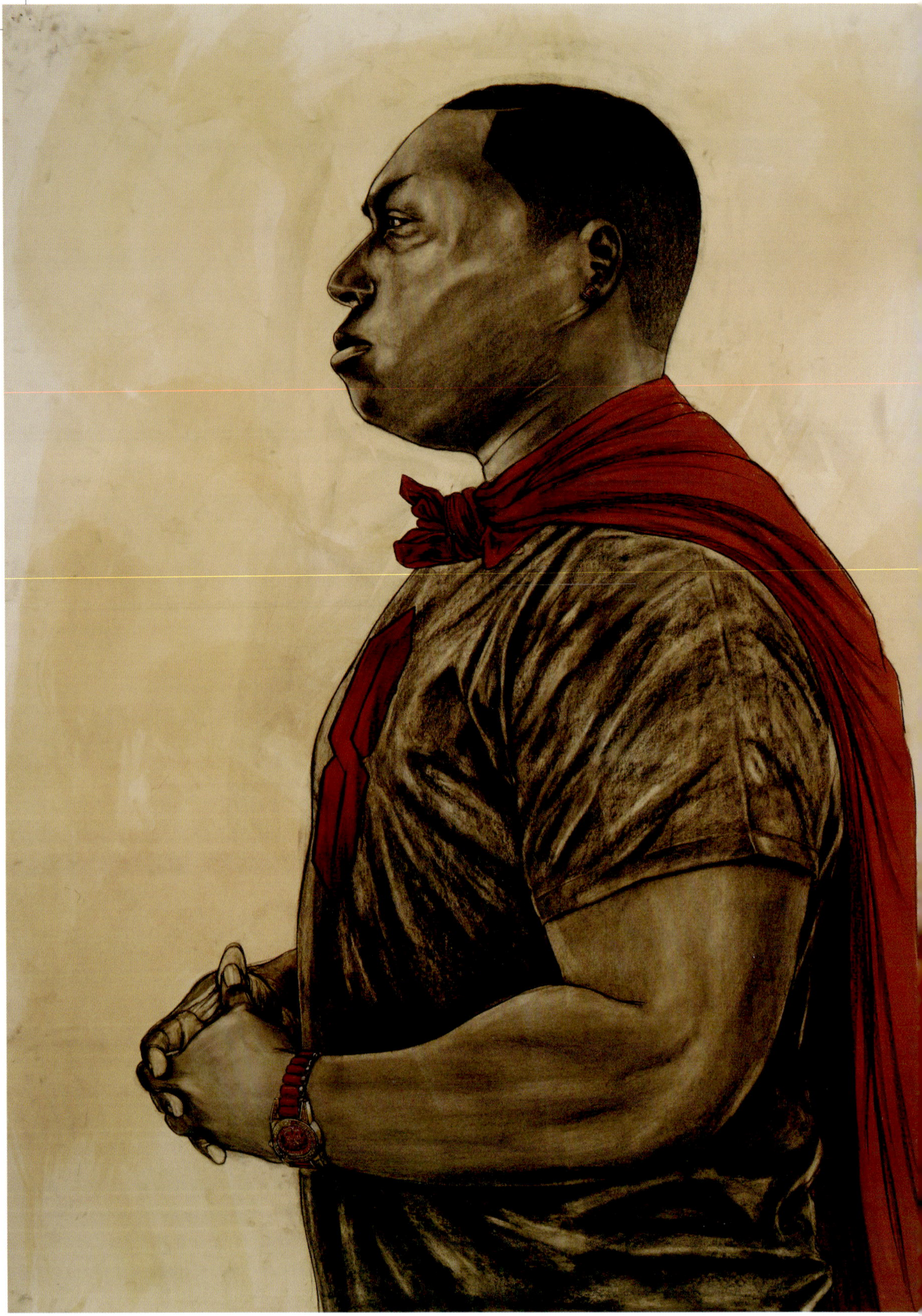

Superheroes

Dreaming Utopia in Art

ANDRIANNA CAMPBELL

In Andy Warhol's *Superman* of 1961, a hovering caped superhero blows a triangular cone of white air, which generates a gust of wind, picks up the smoky dust on the ground, and billows it out to two corners of the canvas. At the top edge, his cape and his thought bubble are cut off by the black outline of the panel. Warhol chose to slightly obscure the words in the thought bubble making them almost indecipherable. The words reflect on the unseen action obscured by the cloud of smoke, "Good! A mighty puff of my super-breath extinguished the forest fire!" Most of the detail and activity take place in the upper half of the canvas, and without the text we would not understand the murky action in the lower half of the painting. To further punctuate the visual-textual interplay, both Superman's body and the big red letters PUFF! dangle midair, positioned as the focal points of this early painting using the comic hero as subject.[1]

In Warhol's *Superman*, we immediately identify the subject by his blue leotard, red cape, and boots—after all it could be no one else—and yet conspicuously out of view is the emblazoned yellow *S*; thus the colors in the painting are primarily red, white, and blue, which are the colors found on the flag of the United States of America. The clear color associations of Superman with America—and for many superheroes such as Wonder Woman and Captain America—pinpoint the contradictions inherent in superheroes as embodiments of culture. Moreover, for the popularity of superheroes to flourish, they must also be fighters against strongmen, corruption, fascism and enforcers of the dream of a better society for all. It is as Chris Gavaler writes: "Comic book superheroes express the paradox that democratic utopianism can be defended only through anti-democratic means."[2] The allure of the

Robert Pruitt, *SUP*, 2018. Conte charcoal on coffee-stained paper. Courtesy of the artist and the Koplin Del Rio Gallery.

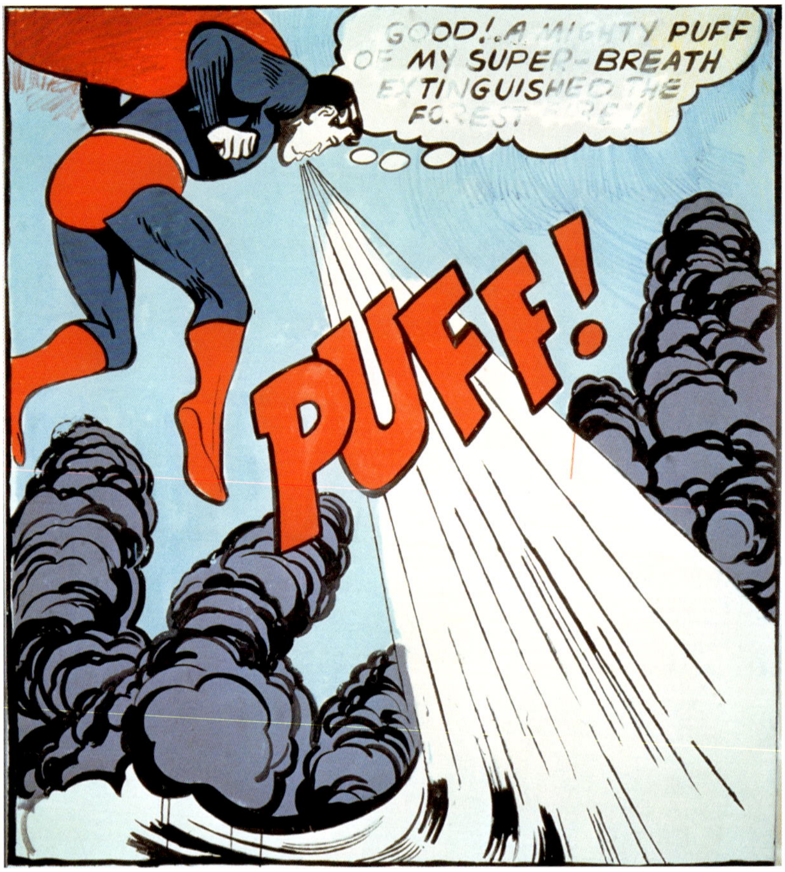

Andy Warhol, *Superman*, 1961. Synthetic polymer paint and crayon on canvas. Private collection.

superhero rests on the strength and will of a select few, who balance democratic values and in whom we place a trust that they may couple moral efficacy and agency in a manner that so few of us are able.[3]

Are they of the nation (as in its governance) or inclusive of its communities (as in population)? Are they defenders of the rule of law, tantamount in any democracy? Or are they above the law, vigilantes, or strongmen capable of operating outside of the judiciary? And finally does their claim to protect the innocent mean that they are protected under the Good Samaritan laws by their very intention of helping those injured or in harm's way? The answer to all of these questions is yes. For the iconic image of the superhero endures by the very promise of a continuation of all of these themes.

Warhol's *Superman* is an early example of an artist engaging with comics, a form of popular visual culture, which could also serve as the subject in high art.[4] When Warhol began appropriating, it was as

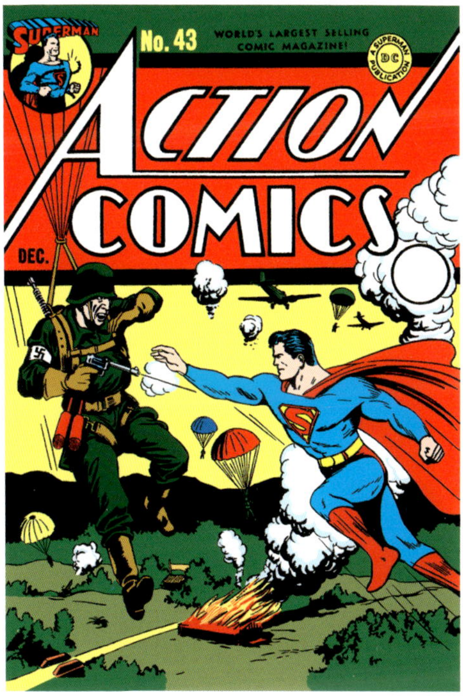

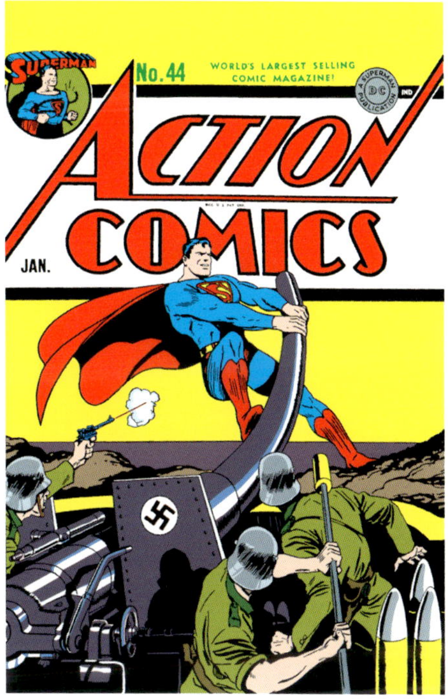

Benjamin Buchloh writes, "[to] create conditions in which mass culture and high art would be forced into an increasingly tighter embrace."[5] That tighter embrace was predicated on instantaneous recognition of the subject stemming from how popular Superman became in the two decades before Warhol made this painting.

The first comic to feature Superman, *Action Comics* #1, premiered in June of 1938. It should be of no surprise then that the Golden Age of comics emerged in the United States in the lead up to World War II and continued in its aftermath. As is commonly referenced, two Jewish high school students, writer Jerry Siegel and artist Joe Shuster created Superman in the wake of the rising fascism that they saw in Europe.[6] Early covers of the comic saw Superman fighting Nazis. On the cover of *Action Comics* #43, he takes a direct shot from a Nazi parachutist; on the cover of *Action Comics* #44, he bends a tank gun while engaging three German troops. Originally envisioned as "Champion of the Oppressed," Superman initially fought corruption in government and housing policy, but as World War II continued, Siegel and Shuster put him in service of defending American values and the Allied front on the covers of the early comics. Later the "Champion of the Oppressed"

← Fred Ray, cover of *Action Comics* #43, December 1941. © DC Comics.

↑ Fred Ray, cover of *Action Comics* #44, January 1942. © DC Comics.

Rostam was immortalized by the famous tenth century AD *poet Ferdowsi, in the Shahnameh (Book of Kings). A legacy which has remained alive and vigorous, cherished by Iranians for centuries, the epic of Shahnameh depicts a fantastical world, a fairyland where the first man who was an Iranian king rules and the prowess of various early heroes magnifies the Persian legacy.*

Rostam, the National Hero of Persia, closely resembles the notion of Hollywood's Superheroes. He had a costume, a Hood, a super fantastic horse, and a gallery of Archenemies, magical connections, and godlike friends, unprecedented powers, and a strong tendency to combat threats against Humanity. Who else resembles Rostam but Superman, hence the use of his emblem.

—SIAMAK FILIZADEH

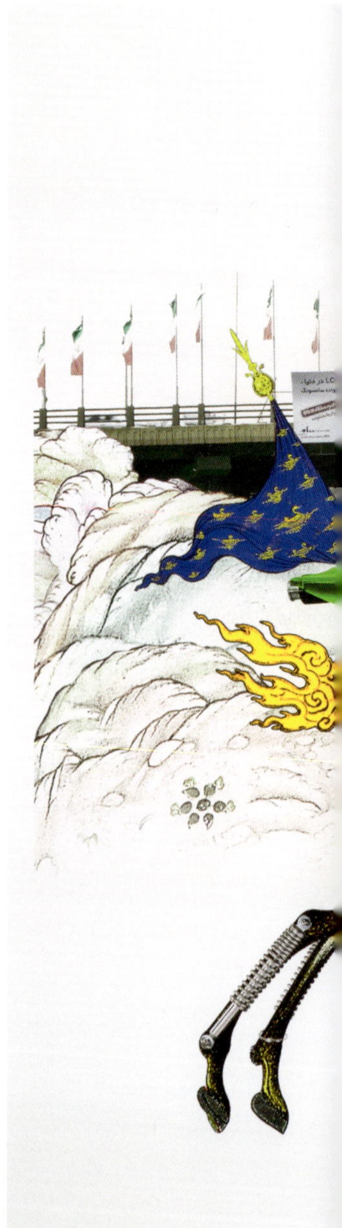

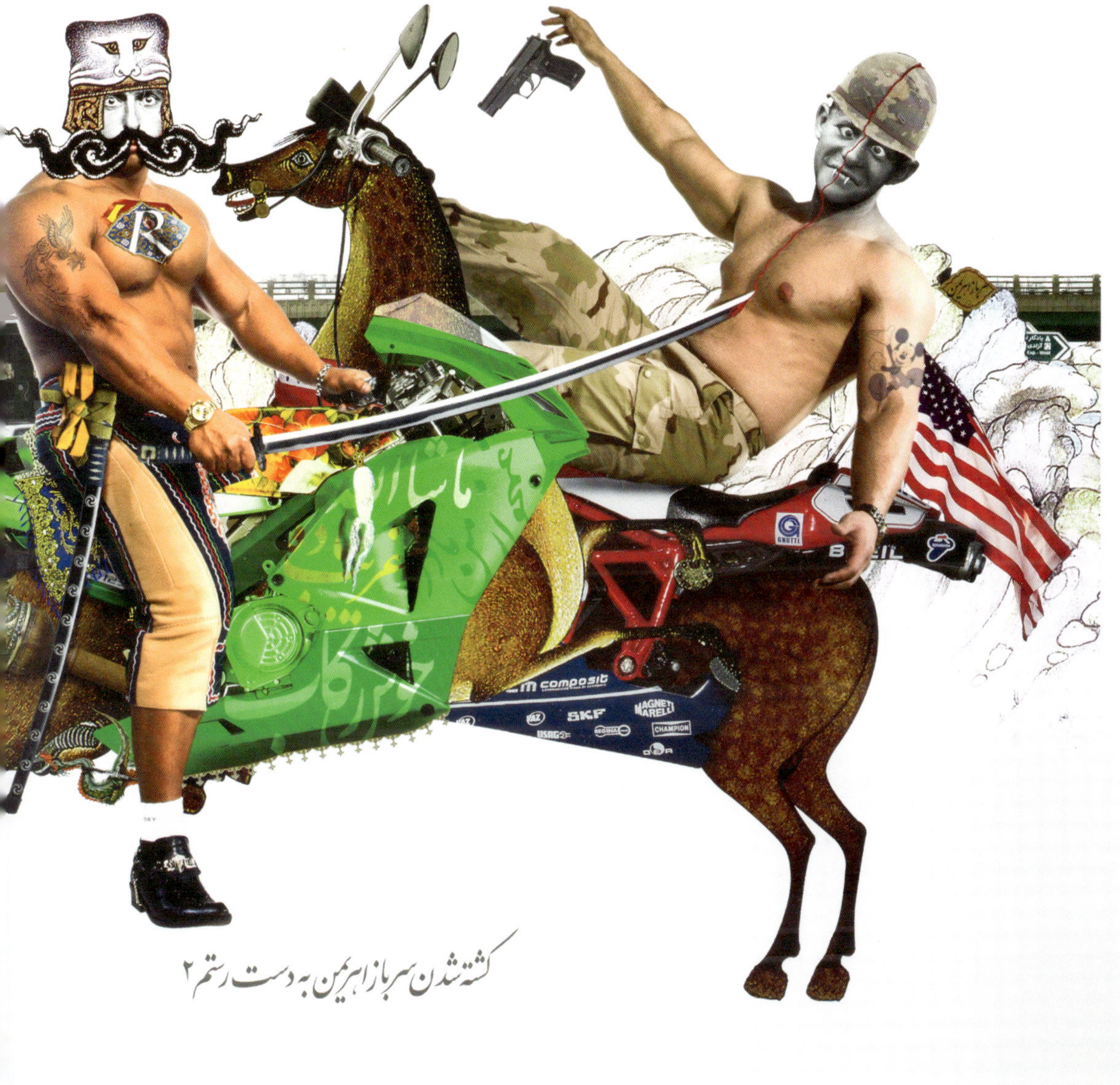

Siamak Filizadeh, *The Soldiers of Evil are Killed by Rostam II*, Rostam II series, 2009. Digital print on canvas. Los Angeles County Museum of Art. Purchased with funds provided by the Karl Loring Trust and Art of the Middle East.

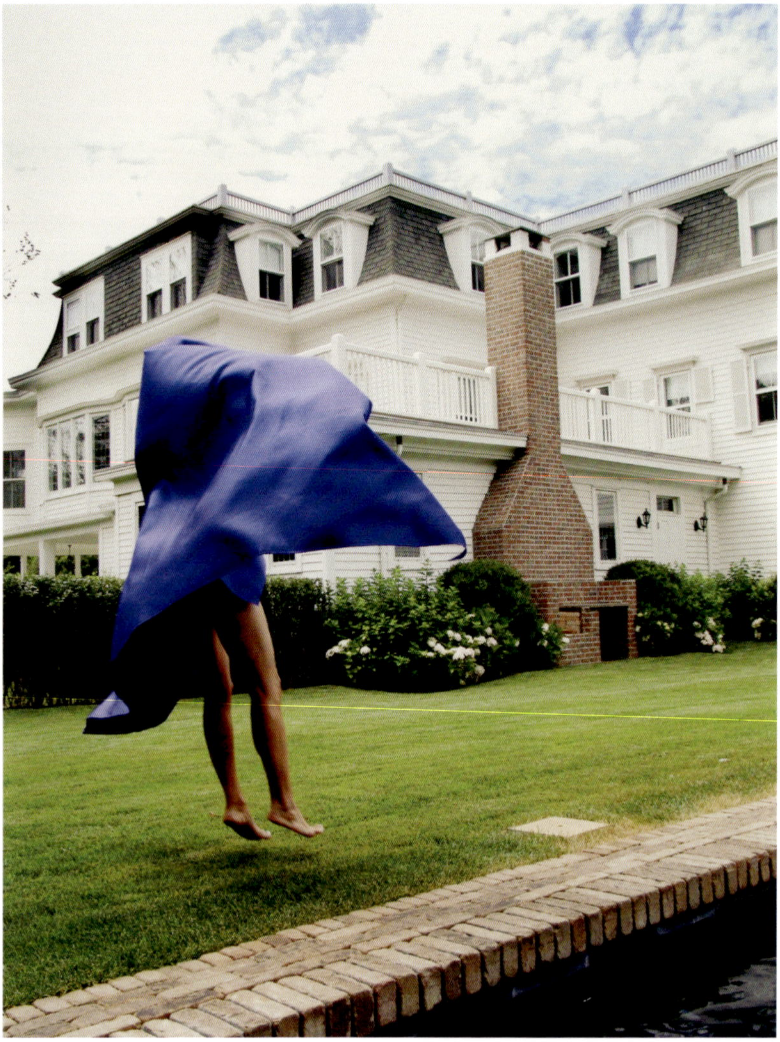

↑ Aphrodite Désirée Navab, *Landing* from *Super East/West Woman*, 2002–8. Archival chromogenic prints. Collection of the artist.

→ Aphrodite Désirée Navab, *Object of Curiosity* from *Super East/West Woman*, 2002–8. Archival chromogenic prints. Collection of the artist.

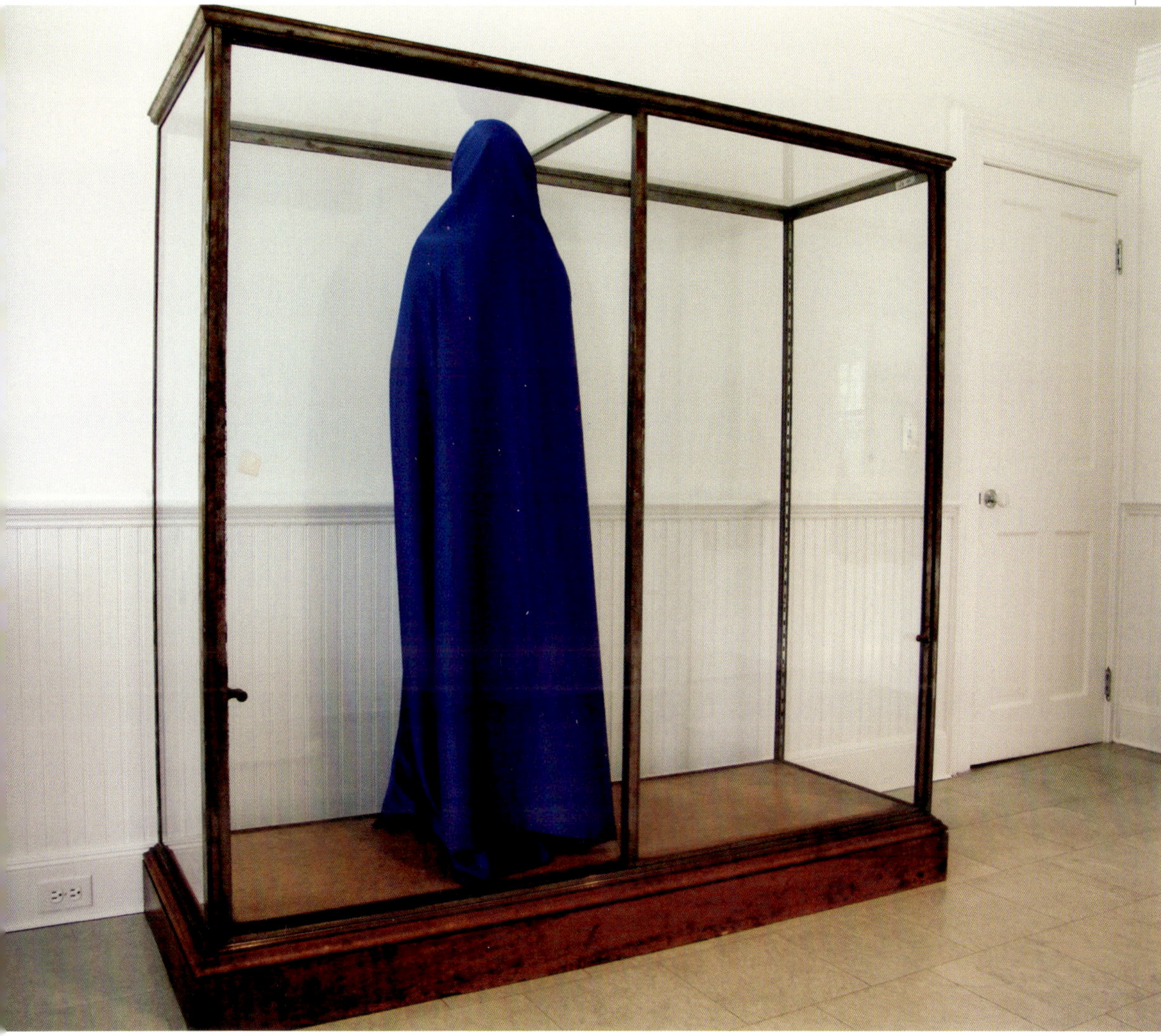

I first saw Superman *in 1978, when I was seven years old with my family in Isfahan, Iran. The metaphor of flight left a profound impression on me. Particularly, his cape reminded me of the* chador *(Farsi for hejab) that my grandmother, Haj-khanom, wore. When the 1978–79 Islamic revolution began, we fled Iran as a family and never returned. I was never able to see my grandparents again. I identified with his irreparable loss of family and homeland. Years later in my art, I transformed the Superman of my childhood into a* Super East-West Woman *whose chador turns into a cape of agency.*

—APHRODITE DÉSIRÉE NAVAB

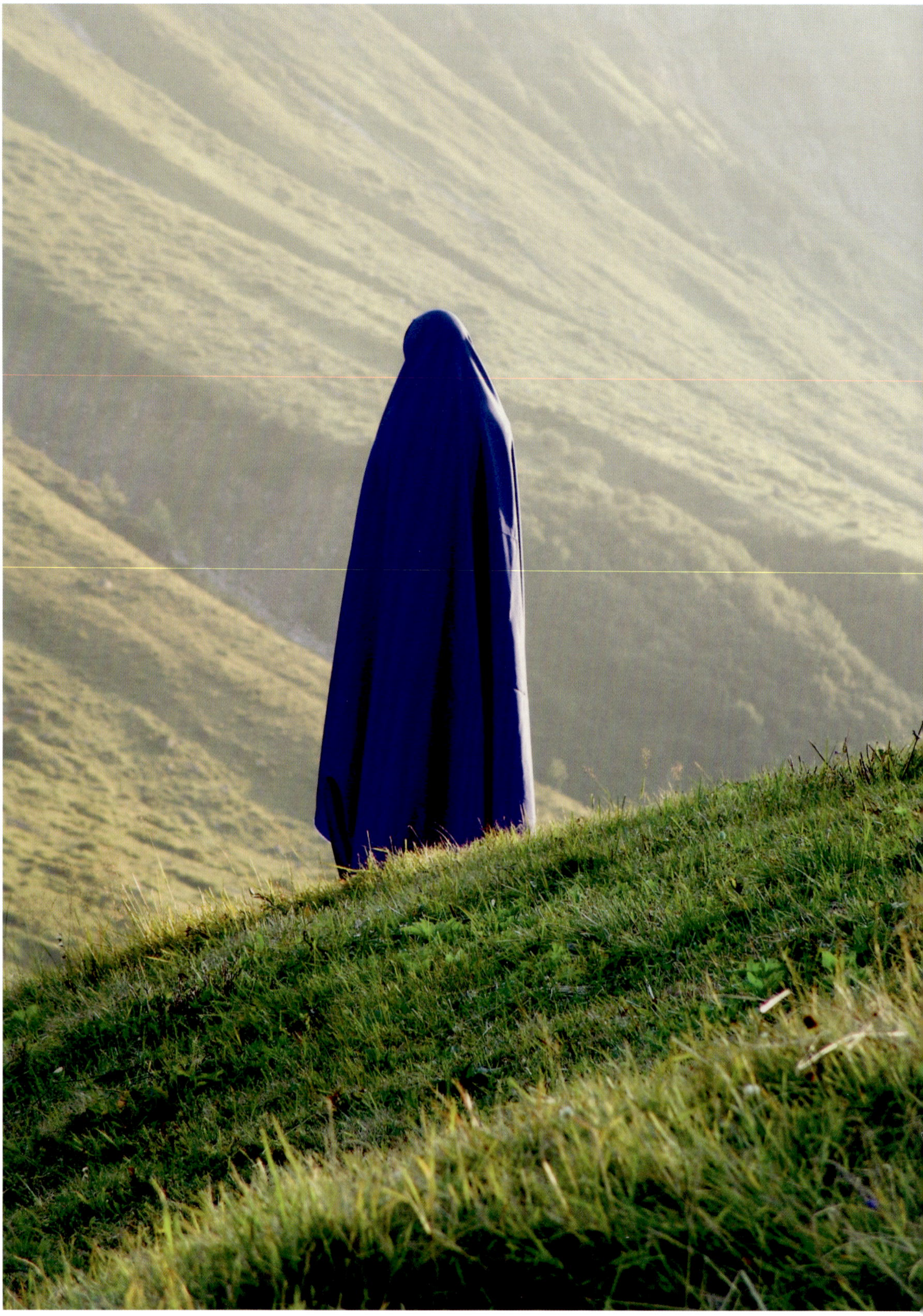

image would shift in the post-war period to the Superman we know today who dedicates himself to "truth, justice and the American way."[7] In the 1950s, the American way broadly implied democracy and a rule of governance, so rather than fight for the working class or against foreign enemies, he battled the KKK and other hate groups at home.

Superheroes as Immigrants

Few countries in their founding documents claim an identity founded on the value of immigration.[8] For the Founding Fathers, the desire to sculpt a culture out of many had to be inscribed on the Great Seal of the United States: "E pluribus unum" or "Out of many one." The Latinate had older origins, but as a part of the design for the seal, John Adams, Benjamin Franklin, and Thomas Jefferson conceived it and adopted it for the Continental Congress in 1782. Furthermore, a few of our most iconic superheroes were foreign born. Superman is from the planet Krypton and Wonder Woman hails from Paradise Island (later renamed Themyscira) in the Mediterranean.[9]

It is this theme of immigration that Dulce Pinzón picks up in her photograph *Noe Reyes from Puebla works as a delivery person in Brooklyn, New York. He sends $500 a week*. In the photograph, a young man on a bicycle wears an ill-fitting Superman costume. From the large red-and-yellow escutcheon *S* on his chest to his red boots and to his cape waving behind him in the wind, he is outfitted as Superman. Yet we are not fooled for a minute; unlike the suspension of disbelief necessary to accept the succession of movie stars who have played the Man of Steel (from Christopher Reeve to Henry Cavill) and who comport themselves

Aphrodite Désirée Navab, *World Summit* from *Super East/West Woman*, 2002–8. Archival chromogenic prints. Collection of the artist.

as the hetero-masculine figure of Superman, Reyes seems quite young. We know that Reyes is in costume, and in his bicycle basket he carries take-out food in familiar red warmers.

Pinzón makes no attempt to cast a Mexican square-jawed Superman. Instead, the title of the photograph proclaims that Reyes is from Puebla in Mexico and even more precisely, that the five hundred dollars he sends home is indubitably a sizeable percentage of his meager earnings. Reyes is one of many everyday heroes, who are often not recognized in their day-to-day activities in our towns and cities. Akin to Siegel and Shuster's Clark Kent, Reyes is a worker, an everyman, and perhaps even closer in resemblance to Siegel, himself, who worked as a deliveryman in 1933. Instead of wearing a delivery boy's attire, however, the iconic costume explicates Reyes's internal character. Pinzón situates the exemplary nature of superbeings as interchangeable with the ethical qualities of immigrants in a series of photographs of workers dressed as superheroes.

The theme of immigration in Pinzón's photograph aligns with what Enrique Chagoya has termed a "reverse anthropology" in his own paintings. Despite cries for white nationalism in the United States, Chagoya's work counters white nativist claims by pointing out that Mesoamerican and indigenous populations are the true natives of the Americas. For instance, in Chagoya's *Crossing I* (1994), the painting emulates the aesthetic of an Aztec codex whose beige paper resembles animal skin. Like Chagoya's acrylic and oil on paper, Pre-Columbian codices featured illustrative and written accounts of historic and mytho-historic events. In a fictionalized depiction, *Crossing I* documents the contact between a pilgrim, an early European settler, and the Aztec god of rain, Tlaloc.[10]

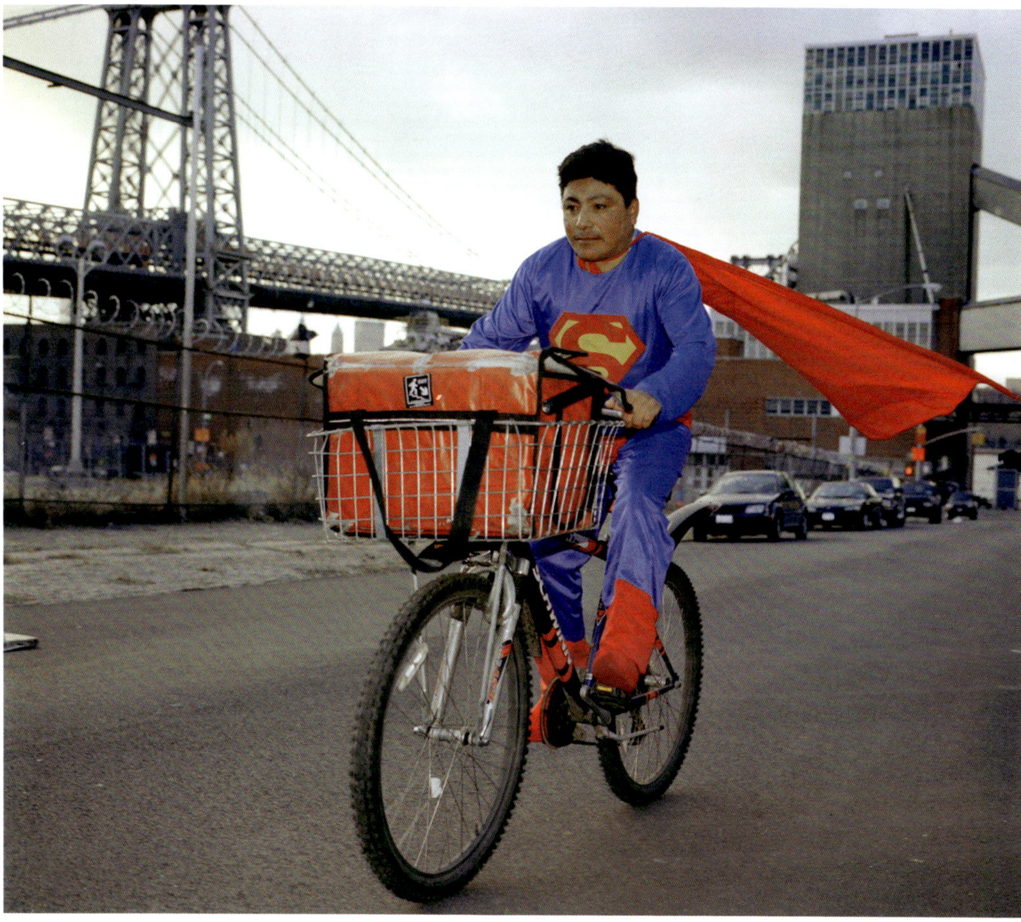

Though *Crossing I* prominently depicts a pilgrim who travelled to the Americas and who certainly interacted with Northeast coast Native Americans, they most likely did not make it south to Mexico. In the painting, the pilgrim's hat flies off his head as he opens his black doublet. Tugging his shirt open, he reveals his Superman costume beneath, and he is none other than Clark Kent, who is often depicted thus. Because Kent's body has been truncated at the waist, and Tlaloc is shown full figured, they are relatively the same height. In the bombastic language of Superman, Kent addresses Tlaloc, who stands stiffly holding the lightning rod with which he is often associated. The two speech bubbles are adjacent to Superman's face: "I don't know what hole you crawled out of or where you came from—but I'm sending you back!" The presumptive text, with its assumption of a xenophobic attitude, is in the pompous style of comic dialogue. As Superman confronts Tlaloc, the rain god is conspicuously silent. Of course, the irony of *Crossing I* is that Tlaloc

Dulce Pinzón, *Noe Reyes from Puebla works as a delivery person in Brooklyn, New York. He sends $500 a week,* 2005–2010. Archival c-print from analog image. Collection of the artist.

The Real Story of The Superheroes *began after 9-11. I saw how much attention the media was paying to people that helped rebuild New York and the nation but was forgetting the more invisible ones, the immigrants.*

I was working as a Union Organizer and saw the need to recognize the labor and achievements of Latino immigrants that worked, paid taxes, had the lowest paying jobs, but somehow managed to send money back to their communities.

I got inspired by the work I was doing and the rebirth of the superhero concept. When I was visiting my family in Mexico I saw Superman and Wonder Woman costumes in a market and the whole concept came to me. **—DULCE PINZÓN**

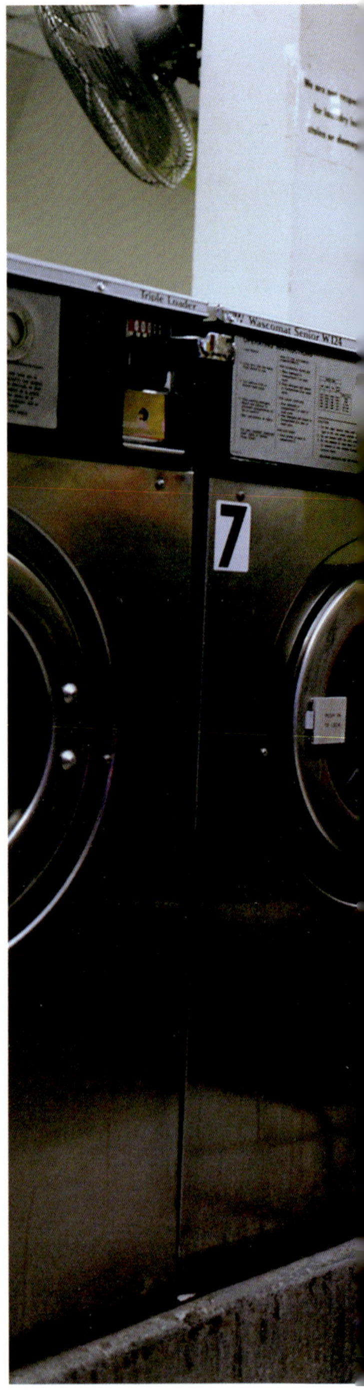

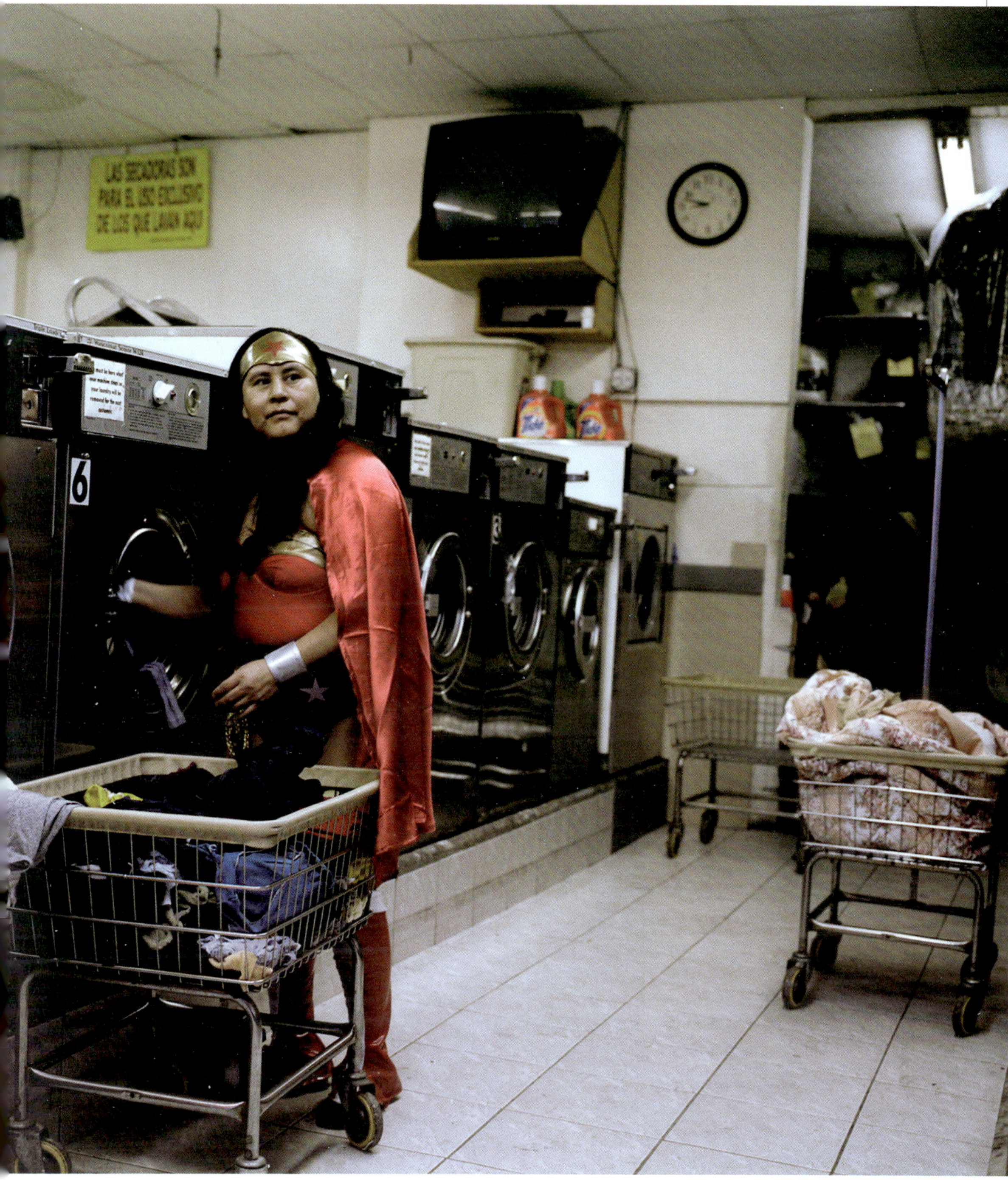

Dulce Pinzón, *Maria Luisa Romero from Puebla works in a laundromat in Brooklyn, New York. She sends $150 a week*, 2005–2010. Archival c-print from analog image. Collection of the artist.

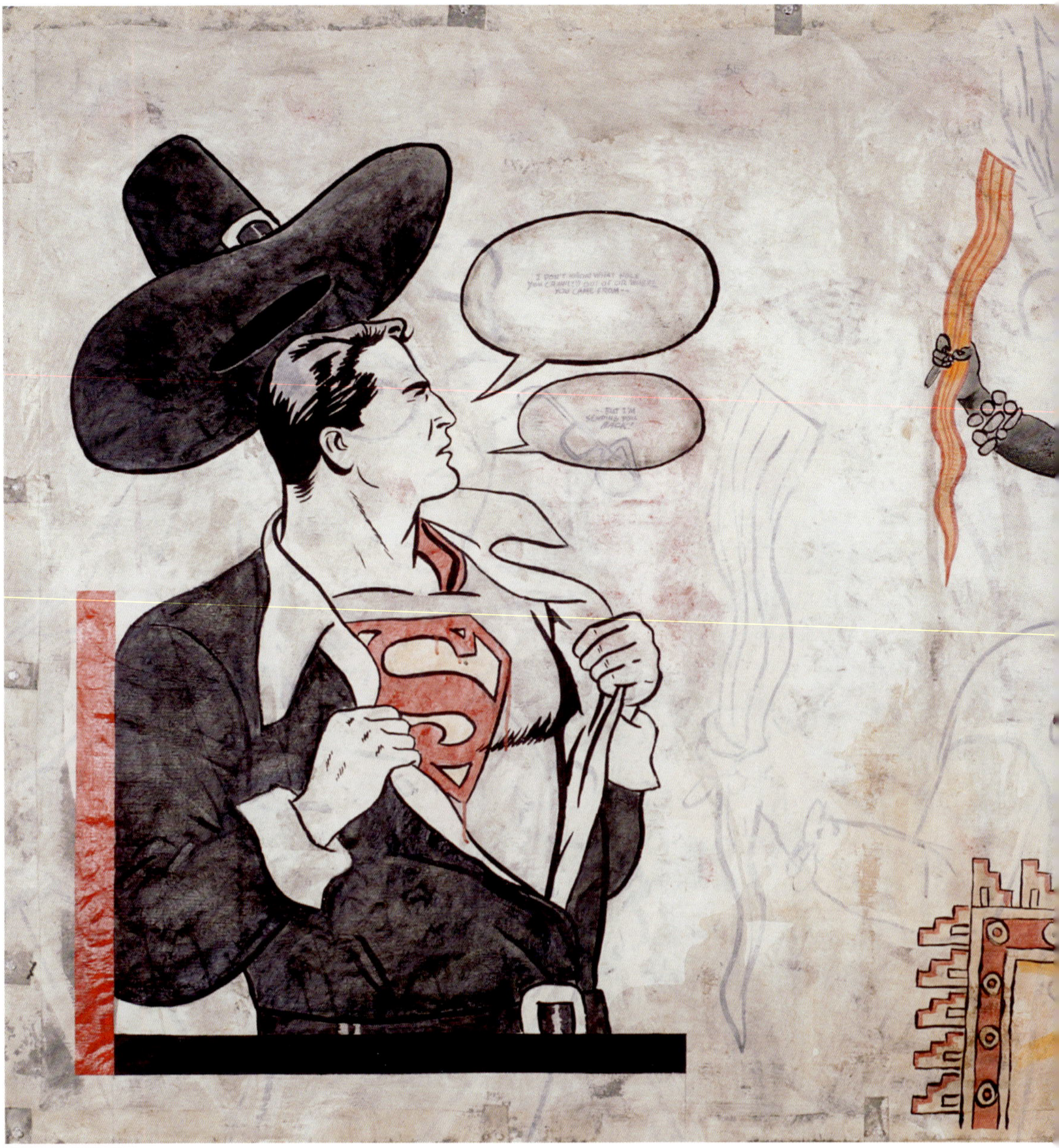

Enrique Chagoya,
Crossing I (Cruce I),
1994. Acrylic and water based oil on handmade Mexican Amate paper (handmade paper from the Amate tree). From the collection of Julia L. Lanigan.

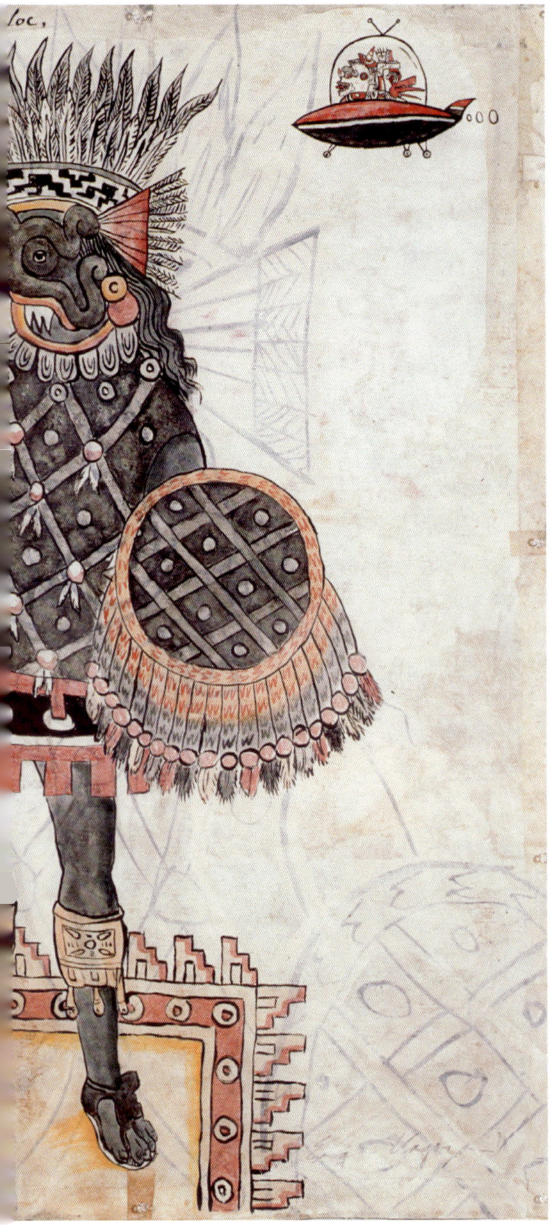

In this work Superman is the perfect alien from out of space confronting Tlaloc, the Aztec God of Rain. These two characters become symbolic proxies for the collision between the earlier European colonizers of North America and the Native Americans. I hope people see the paradox within the fact that the first "illegal aliens" to arrive in North America were the Spanish Conquistadors and the Pilgrims, who did not have any passports and were acting against the law of the land of hundreds of Indigenous Nations. In this sense the contemporary undocumented immigrants aren't different than the first ones (with good and bad qualities). We should not dehumanize them.

—ENRIQUE CHAGOYA

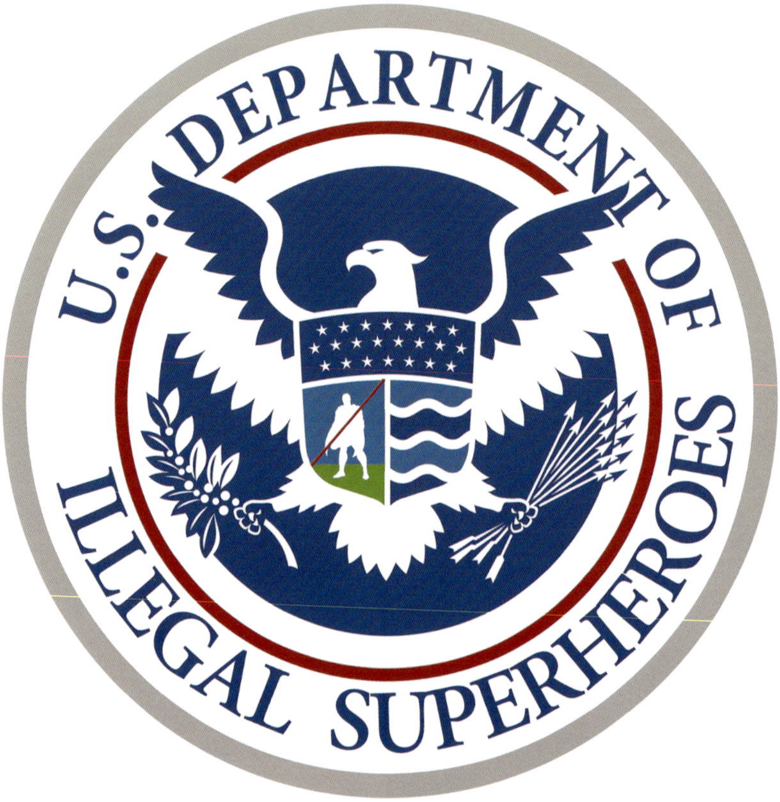

↑ US Department of Illegal Superheroes, ICE DISH Seal, 2012.

→ Roger Shimomura, *American vs. American #2*, circa 2012. Acrylic on canvas. Courtesy of the artist.

Superman and Wonder Woman, ICE DISH fugitives who have committed crimes on multiple occasions, are subject to deportation at any time in consistence with federal law. As other agencies expand operations, working to meet demand for additional detention space through facilities such as Little Rock Air Force Base or Casa Padre, a former Wal-Mart in Texas, ICE DISH remains committed with parallel rigor. Through Operation: Pilgrim's Pride, named after a company who assisted ICE in Arkansas ten years ago, ICE DISH ERO intends to apprehend these criminals in a joint effort with Fugitive Operations and with support from Crystal Bridges.

—ICE DISH SPOKESWOMAN ANAÏS BIGOTE

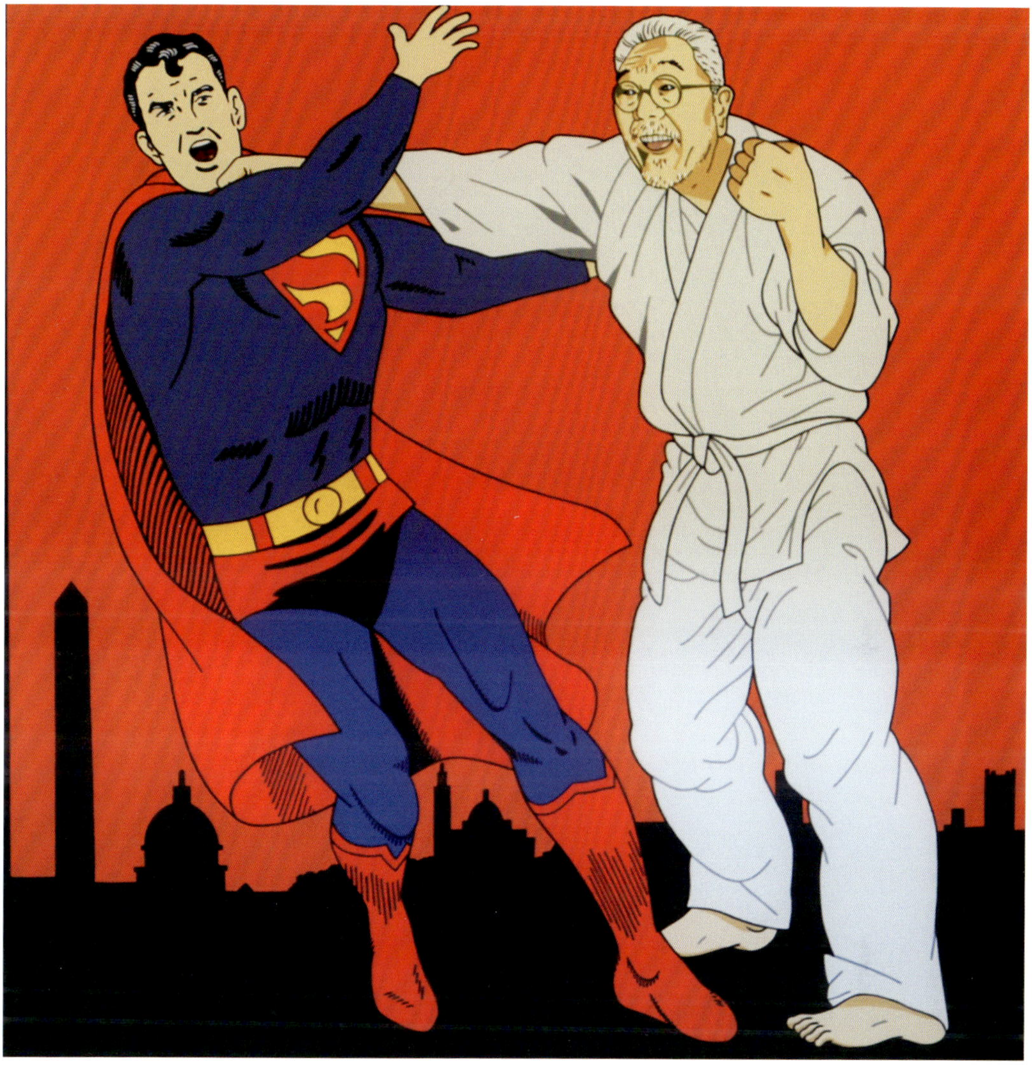

According to Action Comics, *Superman crash landed in Kansas in 1938, one year before I was born and 31 years before I landed in the same state. It is said too that Superman, like my family, was of the Methodist faith. We all seem to have been brought up under a patriarchal and political social structure, which taught a belief that this was truth, justice, and the American way. This system was eventually exposed to be more equal for some than others. Finally we began to call it, more accurately,* White Privilege. —**ROGER SHIMOMURA**

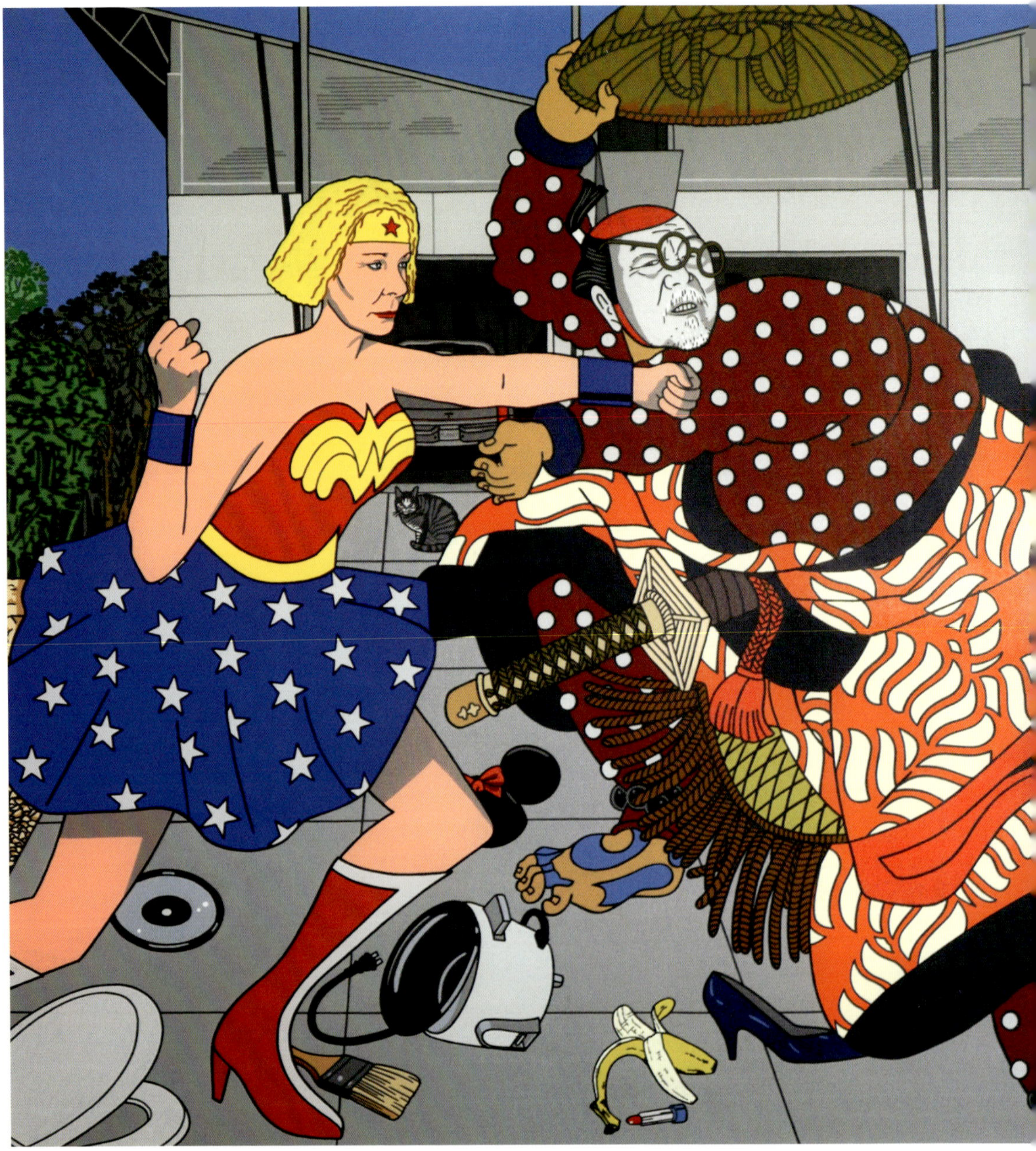

Roger Shimomura,
American vs. American,
2010. Acrylic on canvas.
The Art of Emprise,
Emprise Bank,
Wichita, KS.

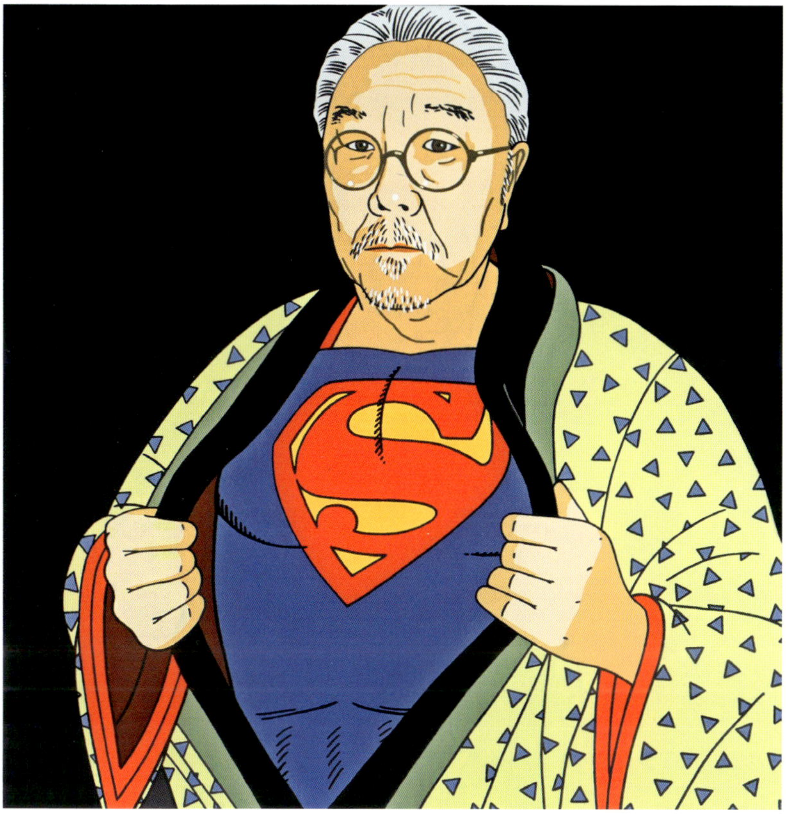

is indigenous to the Americas, whereas both the pilgrim and Superman are the true interlopers. Chagoya's "reverse anthropology" exposes certain sociocultural hypocrisies by inventing and juxtaposing events from our visual landscape that upset our firmly held beliefs. If anthropology is the study of *anthropo*, that which it means to be human—the scientific research of our origins and cultural developments, then Chagoya allows us to examine not only spoken assumptions but also iconographic ones.

For many artists, American superheroes provide the perfect paradigm from which to beg the question of who is American. Roger Shimomura's *American vs. American* (2010) shows an unconventionally blonde Wonder Woman grabbing a Japanese ukiyo-e character by the beard. A toilet and a rice cooker litter the scene, and we are witness to the struggle between two Americans—but only one (with European features)—is readily understood as such. This tension also bubbles to the surface in Shimomura's *American in Disguise* from 2012, which shows the artist opening his kimono to reveal the *S* on his chest. His countenance is sad and forlorn as he is forced to assert his true nationality in costume because his outward racial features pigeonhole him as a foreigner.

Roger Shimomura, *American in Disguise*, 2012. Acrylic on canvas. Collection of the Hallie Ford Museum of Art, Willamette University, Maribeth Collins Art Acquisition Fund, 2014.031.

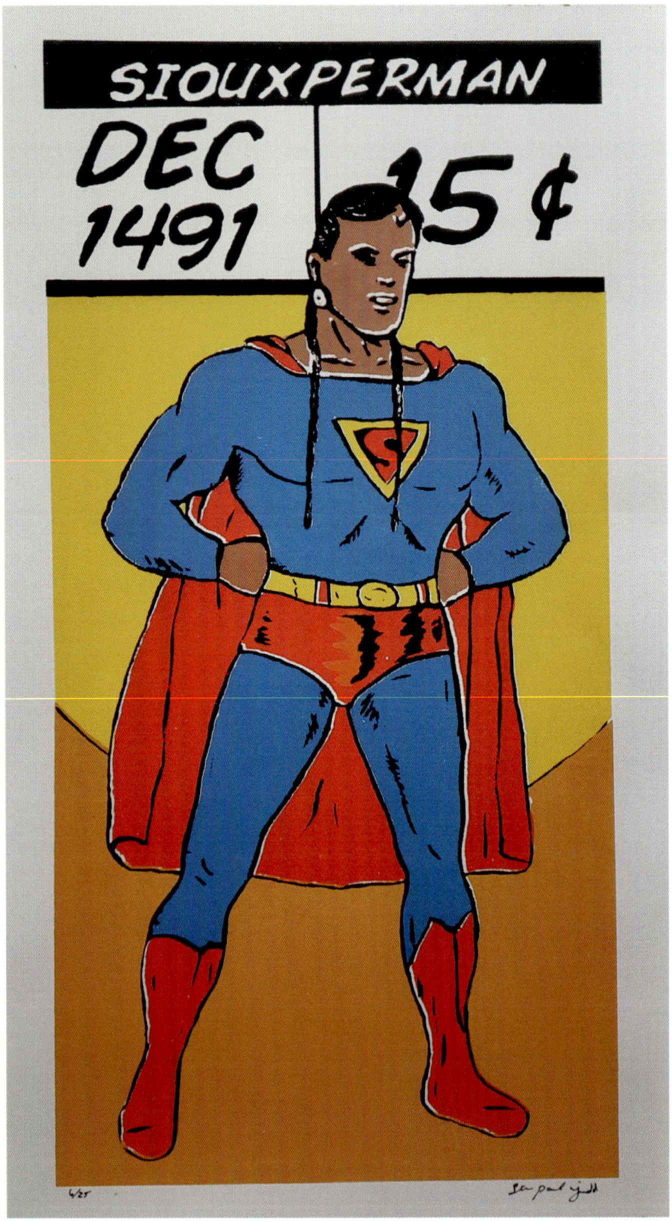

Steven Paul Judd, *Siouxperman*, 2014. Serigraph. Edition 25. Courtesy of the artist.

I first started my primary education on the Choctaw reservation in Mississippi. Although we were all native students, we still liked movies just like any other little kid in US. When I saw characters I liked in movies, I would act them out when I got home. Pretending I was Indiana Jones cracking a bull whip, or my favorite, Superman, flying through the air. I even made my own cape out of a plastic

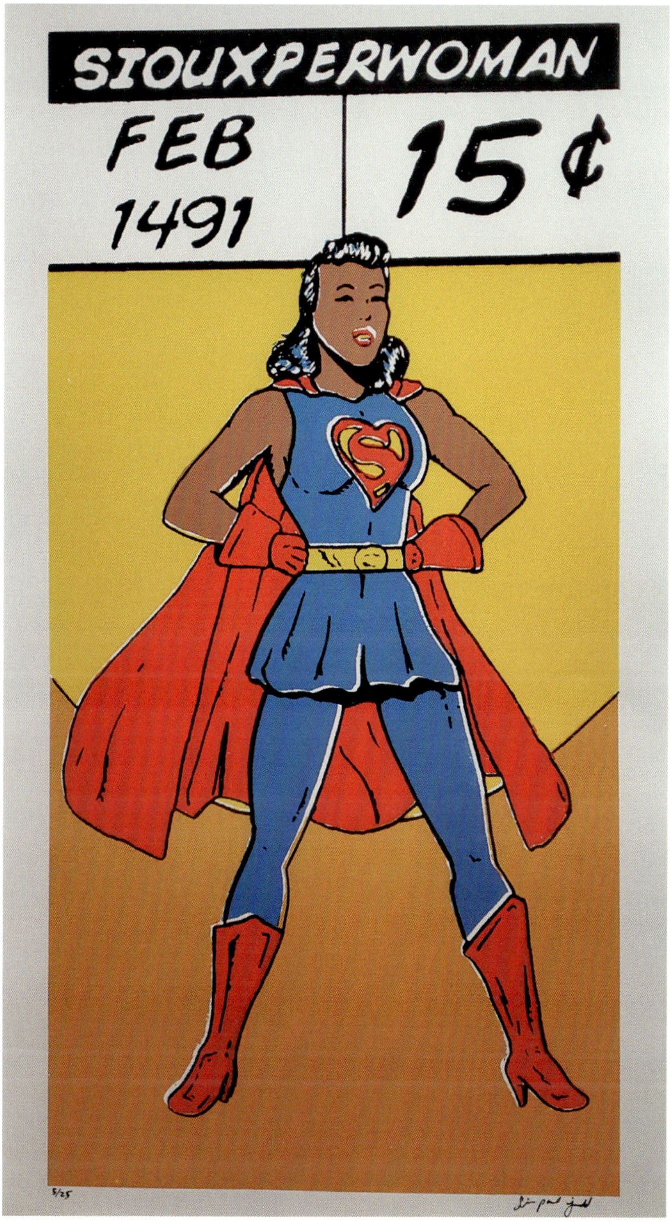

tarp. But as a child none of the images I saw of "superheroes" looked like me or anyone in my family. I'd pretend I was Superman, but in my world Superman had brown skin, or he had braids. Now that I'm older I like to make images of Superman that the seven-year-old me (or any native kid) can see and pretend it's him without having to change the skin color in my imagination.

—STEVEN PAUL JUDD

Steven Paul Judd, *Siouxperwoman*, 2014. Serigraph. Edition 25. Courtesy of the artist.

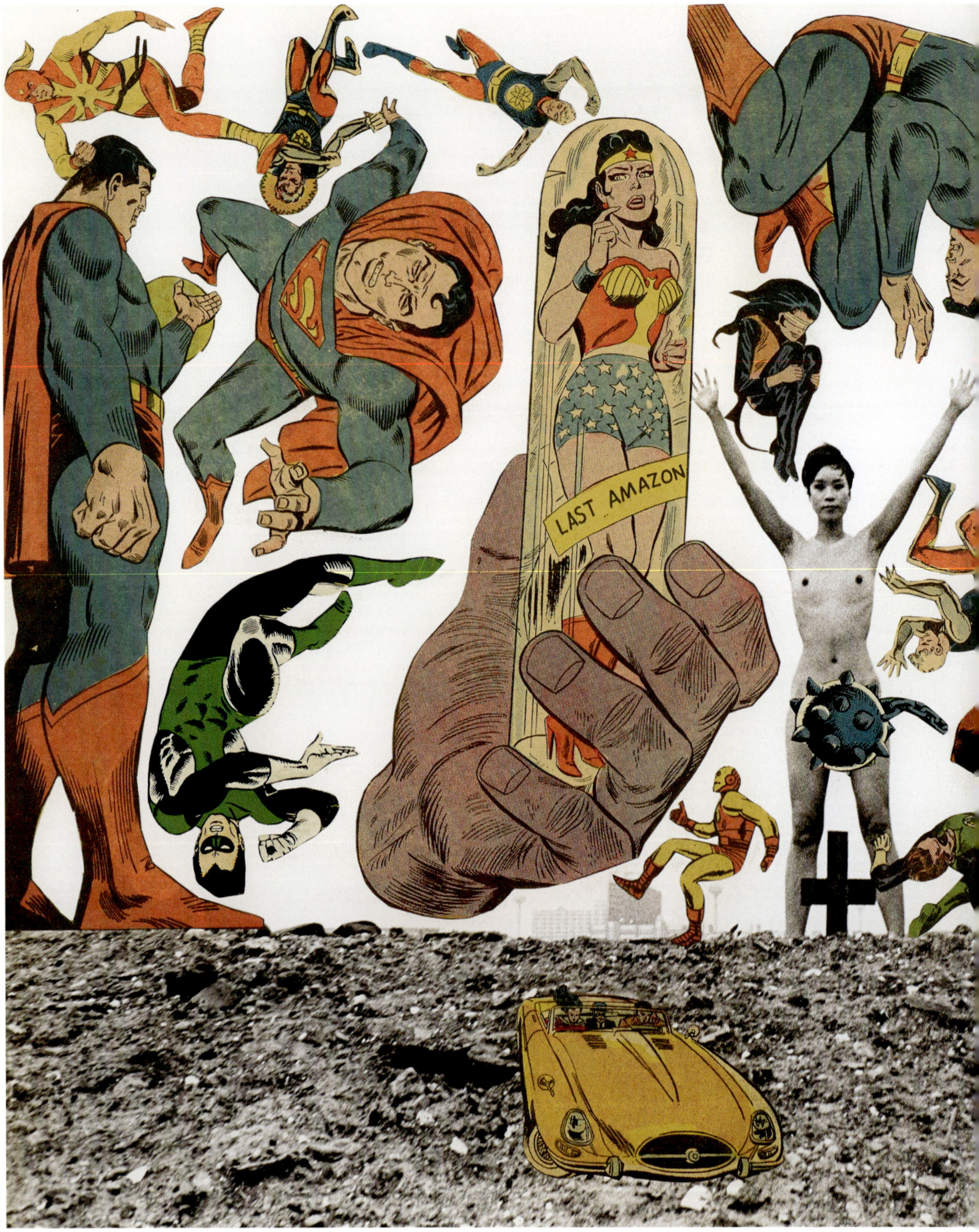

Keiichi Tanaami, *Comic Strip*, 1967. Collage and photography. Collection Walker Art Center, Minneapolis, T. B. Walker Acquisition Fund, 2015.

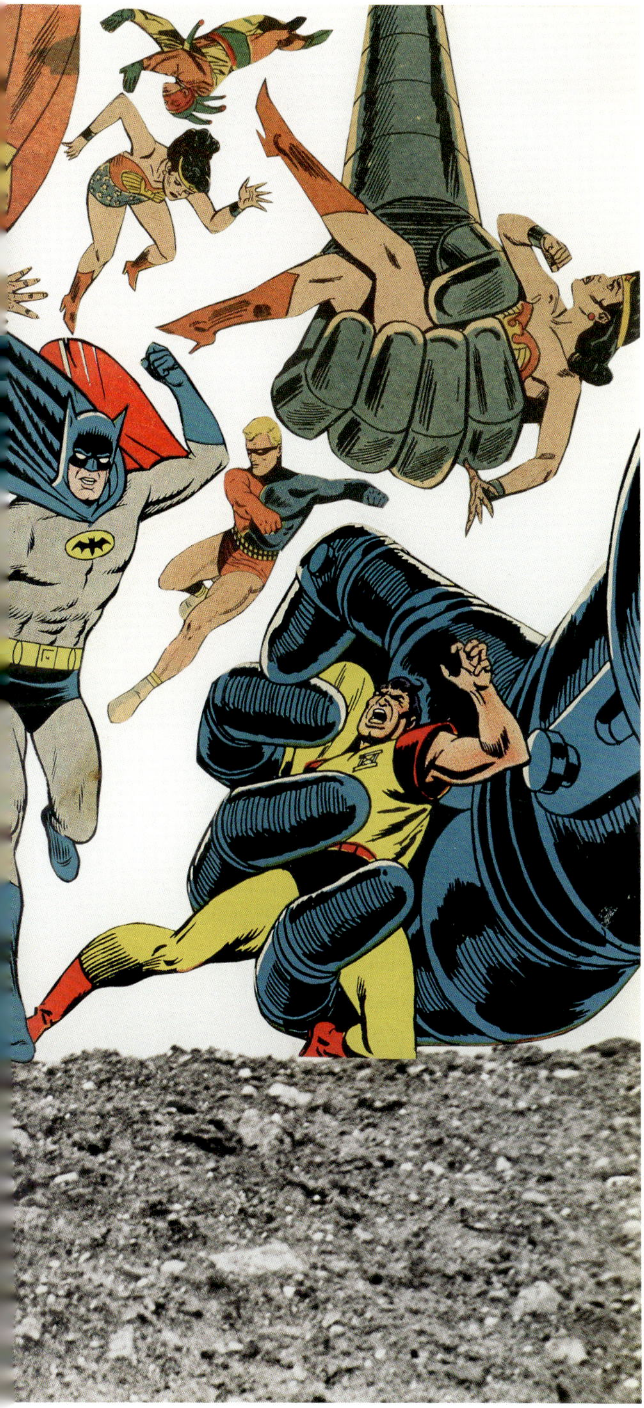

My generation experienced World War II during our childhood, and in the aftermath of the war, with the rise of American democracy, we grew up with American comics and movies and so forth.

This work depicts the advent of the American superheroes on the burnt-out landscape of Tokyo, where nothing remained.

There is an expression in Japanese called "Hadaka ikkan." It means to start from absolutely nothing, or literally, to be completely naked. This was Japan after the war.

—KEIICHI TANAAMI

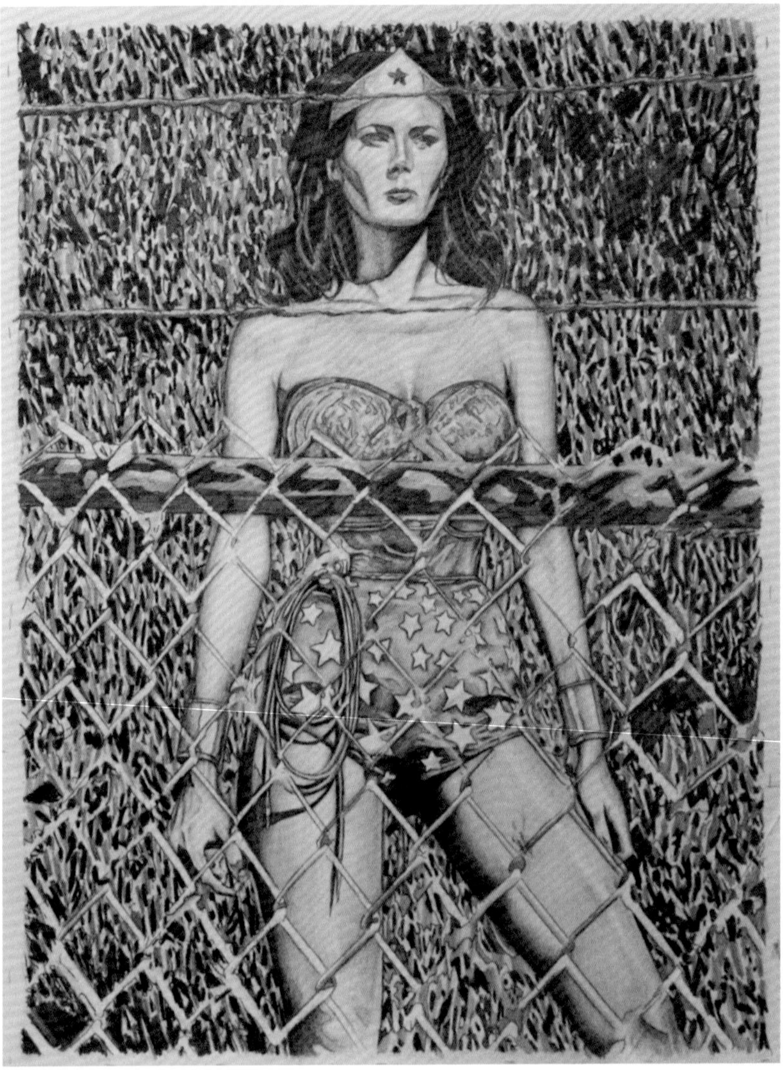

↑ Vincent Ramos, *Barbed Wire, Chain Link, & the Lasso of Truth*, 2016. Graphite and carbon on paper. Courtesy of the artist.

→ Vincent Ramos, *March Against Dick*, 2016. Graphite and carbon on paper. Courtesy of the artist.

Women as Superheroes

Returning to Shimomura's blonde Wonder Woman, it is notable that Superheroes in the Golden Age of comics were predominately male. Yet it is no surprise that the advent and fast success of Superman would bring about a super woman. Created by the American psychologist William Moulton Marston (under the name Charles Moulton), Wonder Woman is often positioned as a female version of Superman. Tellingly, her original name was Suprema. Very quickly she became a ubiquitous character in popular culture as well as in fine art. Whether she is at the center of a bedlam of a fight scene, such as in Jacky Tsai's *Golden Fortune Tree* (2017), or looking forlorn from behind a chain-link fence in Vincent Ramos's *Barbed Wire, Chain Link, & the Lasso of Truth* (2016), Wonder

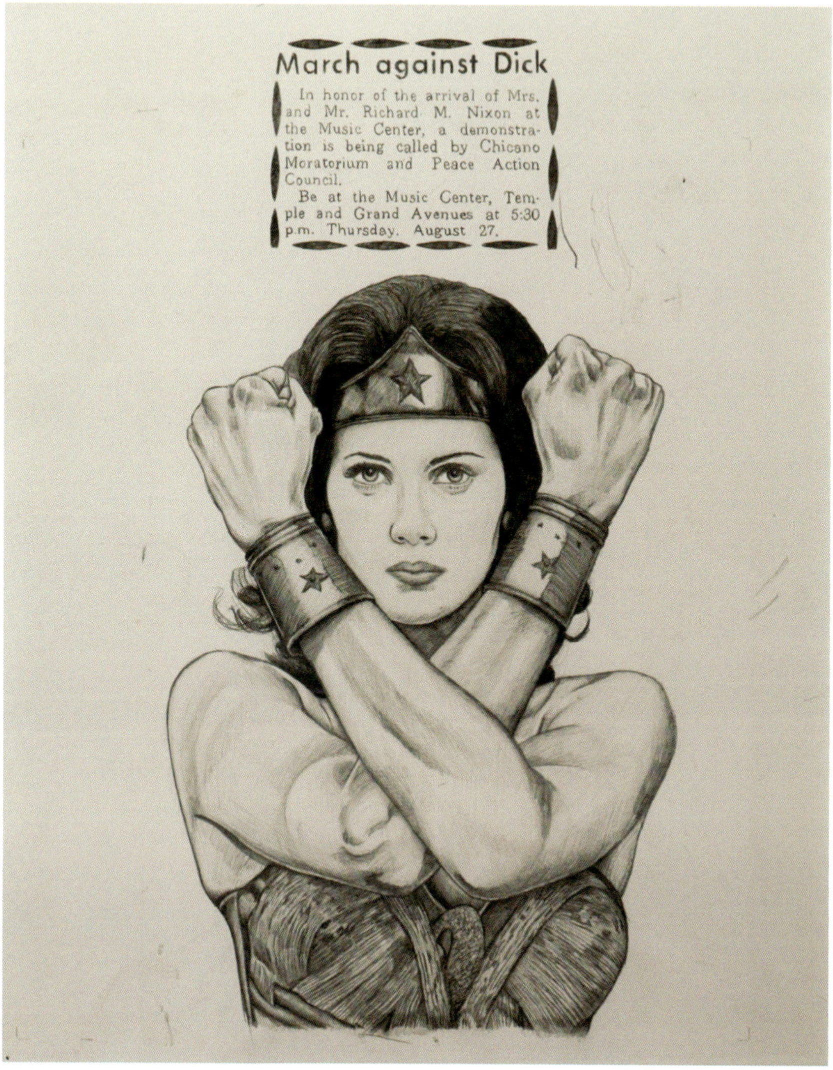

My interest in Wonder Woman lies less in the character and more in the specific individual who portrayed her on television—actress Lynda Carter. She is of Mexican ancestry (like myself) and since my 1970s/80s childhood, this fact has not been lost on me. In both pieces, I was thinking about the dual mirror-like political landscapes of the 1970s and today. The drawn references to the Nixon presidency, to barbed wire and chain link fences, is in stark contrast to Wonder Woman's/Carter's presence as a strong female and cultural symbol devoid of boundaries, and representative, within these works, of both political dissent and resistance.

—VINCENT RAMOS

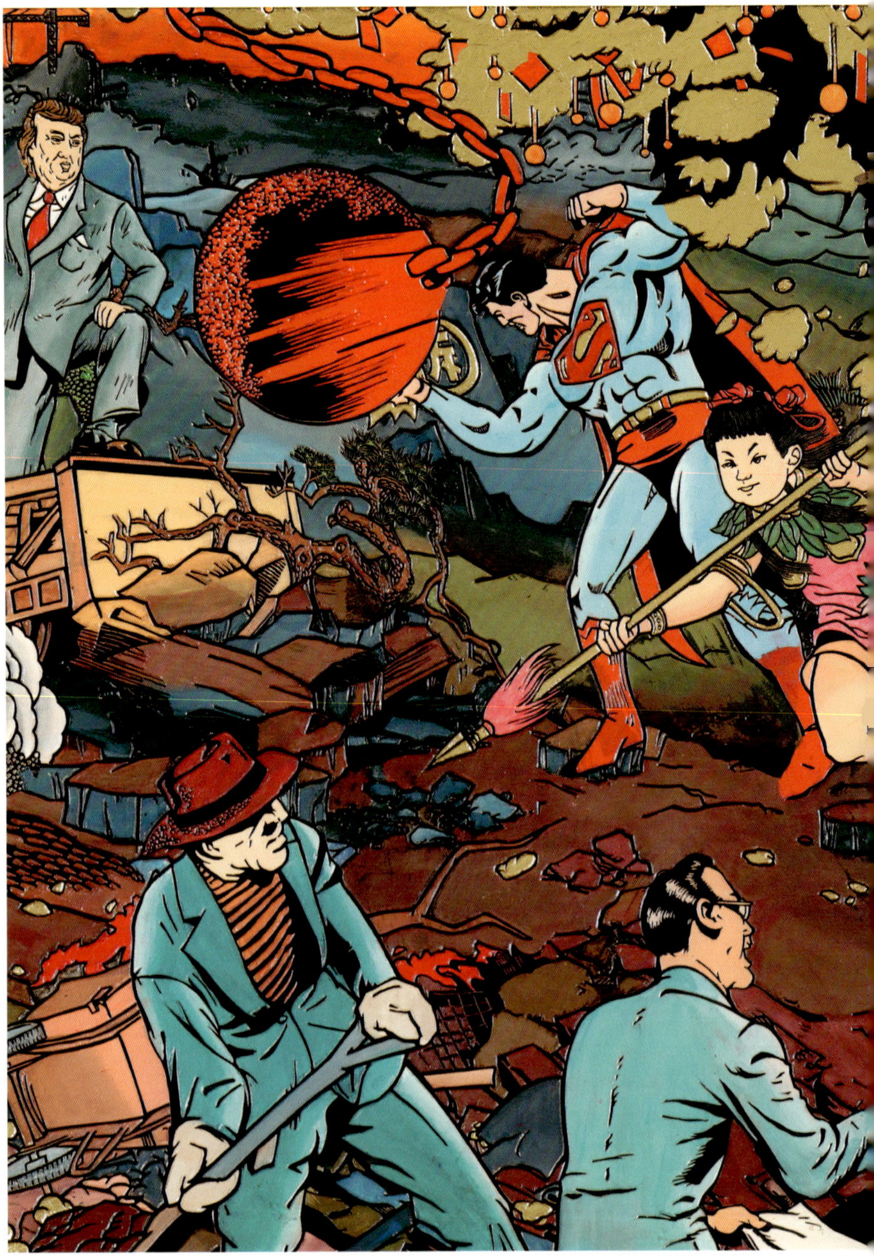

Instead of coming from the conventional symbols such as power, superheroes in my works are deemed to be the medium of the conversation between traditional eastern ideology and present multicultural life. I play with their flaws and obsessions, which are also ours, because I tend to create a rather ambiguously playful

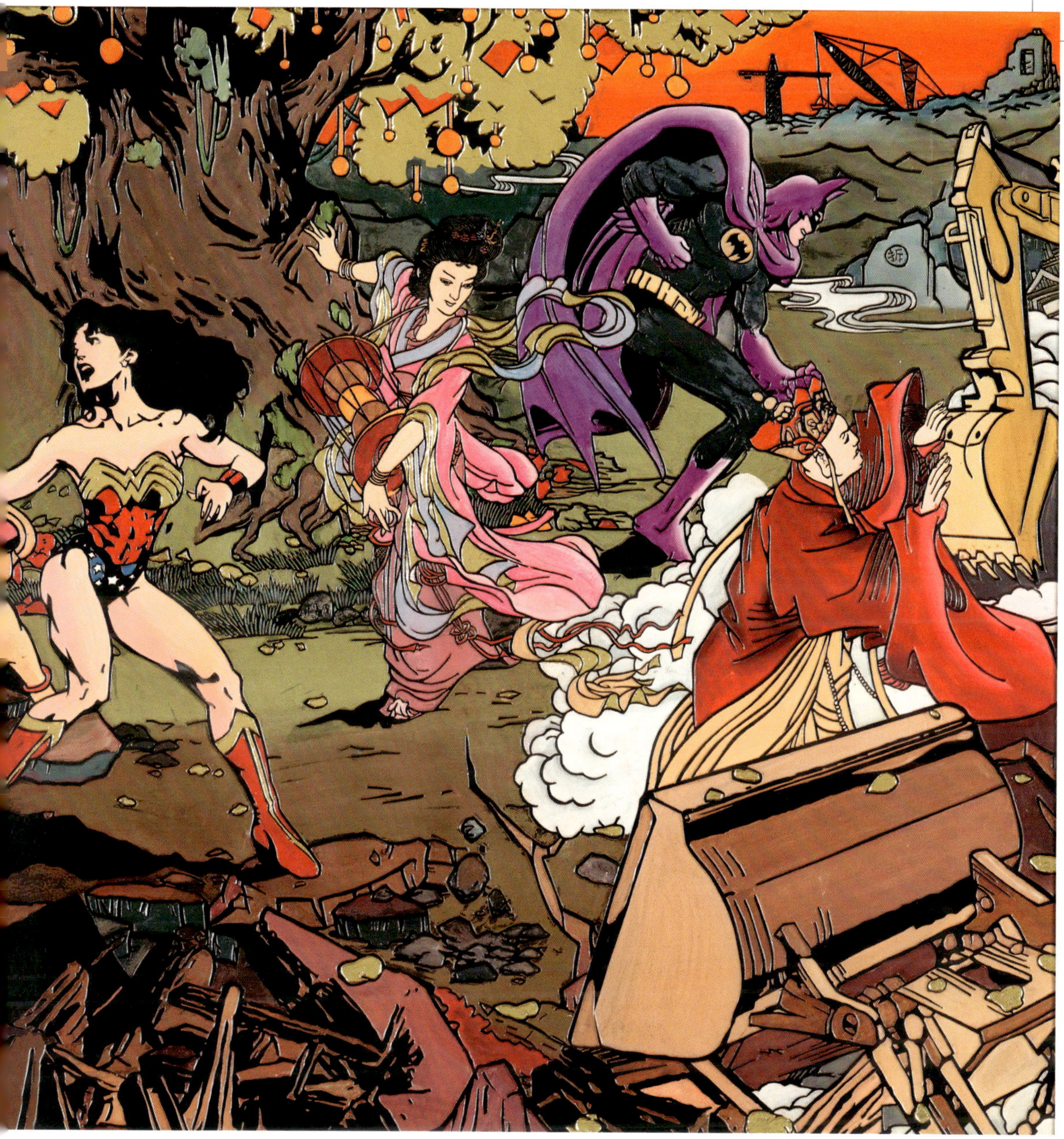

vibe for myself to respond to the issues of people's social lives that I perceived. They remind me of where I am, where my art comes from, and how I witness and experience the cultural clash between the east and the west. **—JACKY TSAI**

Jacky Tsai, *Golden Fortune Tree*, 2017. Lacquer carving on wood panel. Collection of the artist.

Woman's bare legs, tall boots, and bathing suit cut costume meant that she was a sex symbol as well as a hero.

There is a way in which her hypersexualized femininity and dress is seemingly at odds with her crime-fighting mandate. Is this the most comfortable costume for battling villains? It seems likely that Emma Amos's *Tightrope* (1994) addresses this concern. In the painting, a woman in a loose-fitting Wonder Woman costume walks on a tightrope high above a large crowd carrying a T-shirt decorated with bare breasts and fruit. Her baggy clothes and the strange T-shirt draw attention to the precariousness of balancing the daring feats of Wonder Woman with the sex appeal symbolized by the nude breasts and the fecundity that fruit usually refers to in art.

One of the most iconic depictions of Wonder Woman is Dara Birnbaum's *Technology/Transformation: Wonder Woman* (1978–79), which navigates through appropriated footage and text the sexual power that female superheroes are so often required to emanate. In the video Birnbaum collects scenes from the then on-air television show in which the actress Lynda Carter played Wonder Woman. The video begins with nearly thirty seconds of explosions before Wonder Woman begins to spin, trapping her in a repetitive loop of explosion and transformation between her civilian self, Diana Prince, and the superhero Wonder Woman. Akin to the use of the loop, other scenes depend not on narrative as do the comic books and television program but rather on the structural use of repetition, action, and reversal of footage. Though these structural techniques were being used in the 1970s in art films, *Technology/Transformation: Wonder Woman* is one of the earliest examples of an artist using television footage in their work.

Emma Amos, *Tightrope*, 1994. Acrylic on linen with Kente borders. Courtesy of the artist and Ryan Lee Gallery, New York.

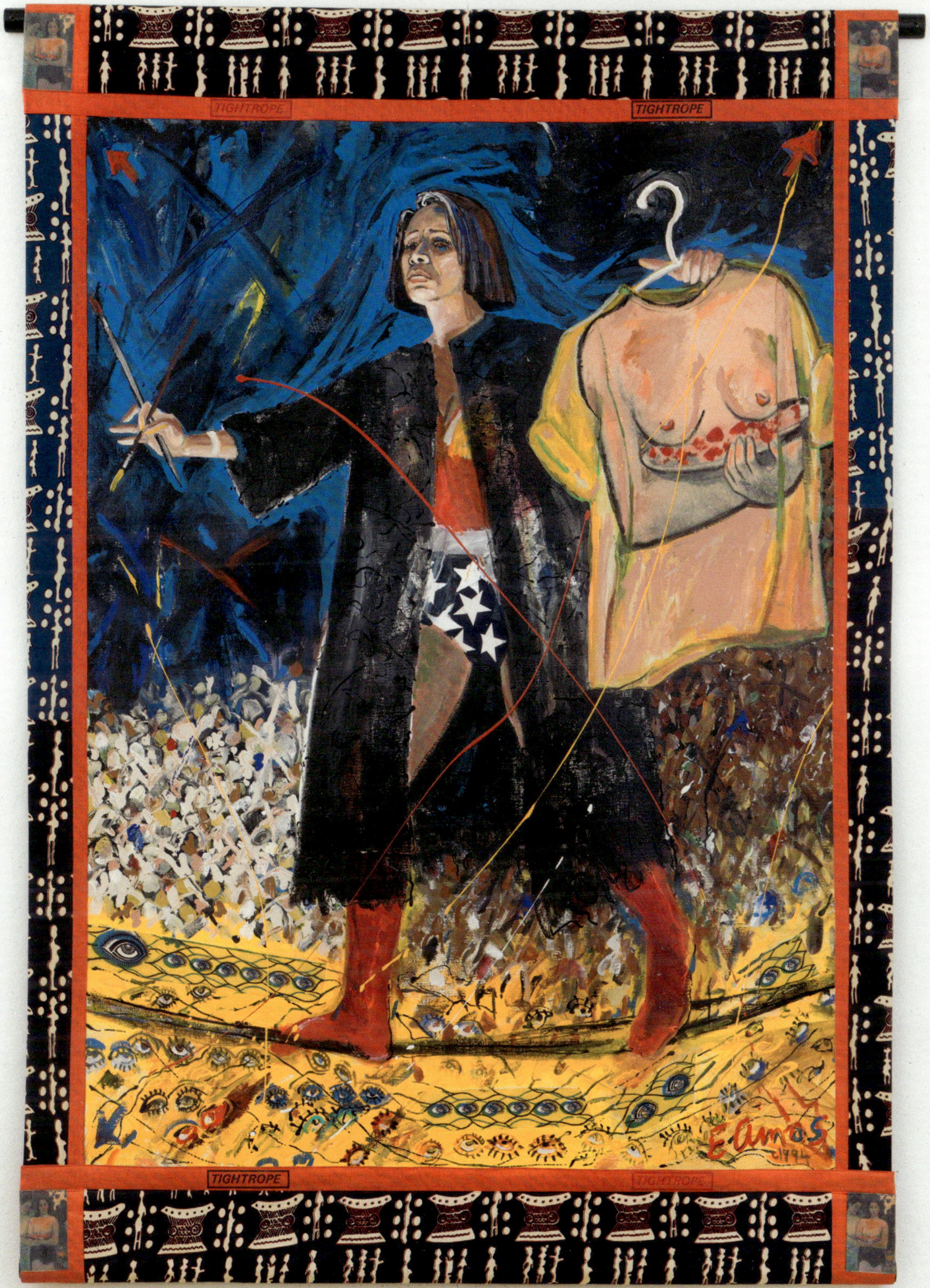
TIGHTROPE
TIGHTROPE
TIGHTROPE
TIGHTROPE
E Amos
1994

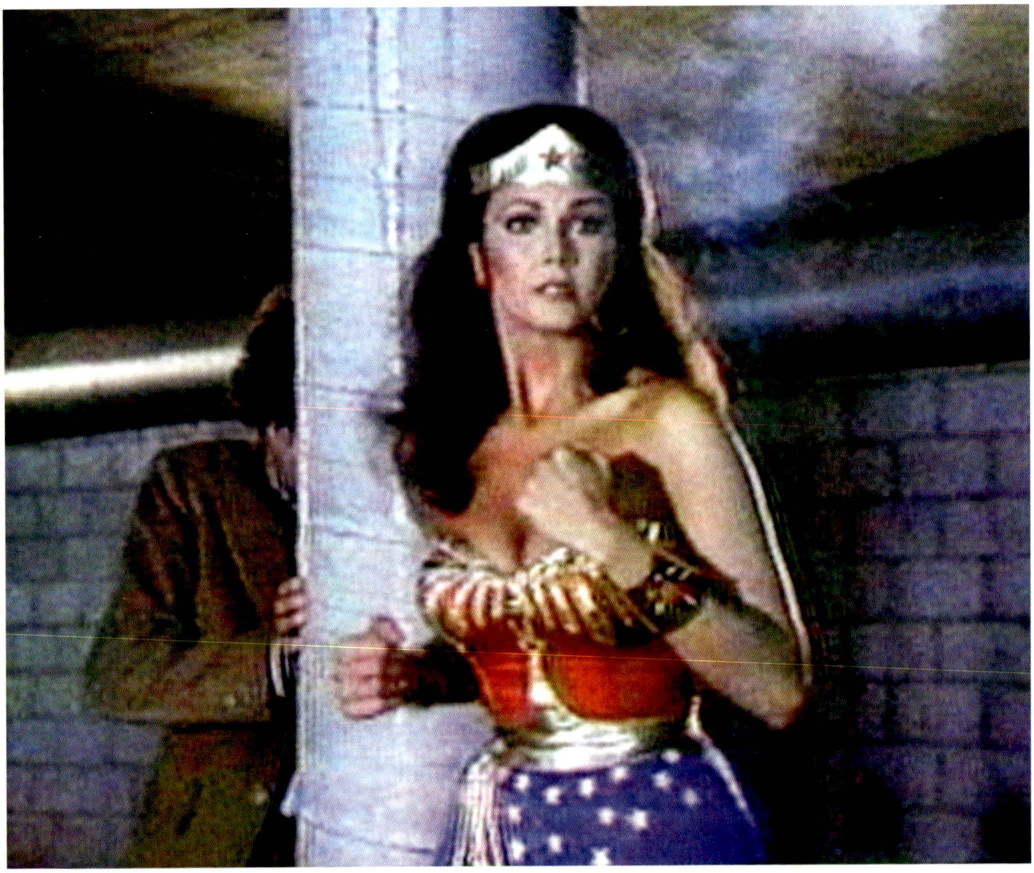

For instance, over halfway through the video, a blue screen with scrolling text appears. Akin to Marcel Duchamp's *Anémic Cinéma* (1926), the text—rather than moving images—becomes the subject of the video. Through scrolling upward, it forces the engagement of the viewer as a reader and thereby interrupts what Christian Metz deems the mesmerizing quality of watching moving images.[11] Text inverts the medium of video because it makes it an active medium (more akin to reading a comic) instead of a more passive medium such as film. It brings *Technology/Transformation: Wonder Woman* back to the original source material: comics. Birnbaum's text begins with a series of *I*s, which reminds the spectator of their subject position as a viewer in relation to Wonder Woman in the video. Then the *I*s scroll upward, and some of these lines appear: *I am Wonder, Wonder Woman, Get us out from Under Wonder Woman, I want to take you down, Said I want to take you*

Dara Birnbaum, *Technology/Transformation: Wonder Woman*, 1978. Videos. Collection of the artist.

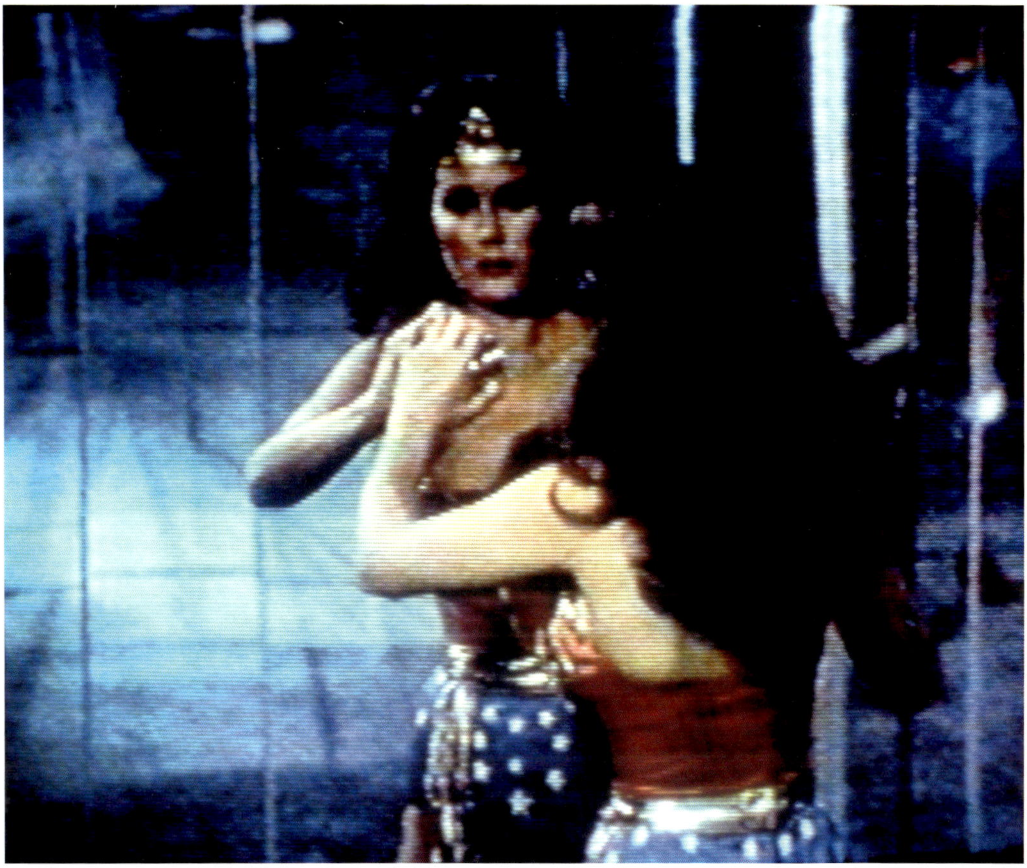

*With regard to super-heroes, I think there exists a crisis of identity. I knew this from the very beginning—as expressed in my work "Technology/ Transformation: Wonder Woman," ©1978/9. Here the viewer is exposed to a dualistic view of woman: you either heroicize her or you underrate her as a secretary. The abbreviated narrative—running, spinning, saving a man—allows the underlying theme to surface '*Real *becomes* Wonder *in order to "do good" (be moral) in an (a) (im)moral society.' And what place did you create for me? Where am I between the two? That burst of light says I'm a secretary, I'm a Wonder Woman, I'm a secretary, I'm a Wonder Woman, and there's nothing in-between. And the in-between is the reality we need to live in.*

—DARA BIRNBAUM

down, Show you all the powers that I possess, Shake thy Wonder Maker.[12] The words convey a poetic rhythm. Taken from the dance song "Wonder Woman in Discoland," the double entendre play of the words alludes to how Wonder Woman's strength originates in her sexual prowess.

Birnbaum's *Technology/Transformation: Wonder Woman* had a direct influence on Sarah Hill's *They Wonder* (2014/2015), a performance where the artist dresses in a hand-crafted Wonder Woman costume. Hill relates, "During the performance *They Wonder*, I repeatedly spin around and around in circles. I am interested in the continuous action of spinning and getting no-where, falling down and getting back up. This specific action of spinning comes from Dara Birnbaum's *Technology/Transformation: Wonder Woman* (1978)."[13] Hill goes on to tie their performance to questions of sexual identity: "Comic Books have always revealed themes and characters that can be identified as queer, the majority of superheroes always live two lives, one as hero and one as civilian."[14] Hill's performance, though staged in the open, recalls what Hill sees as a shared pattern of secrecy between superheroes living in disguise and queer individuals throughout the twentieth century who had to live in the closet after the designation of homosexuality as a medical defect.

Hill's performance as Wonder Woman is a process of constant outing, as Birnbaum's video highlighted the process of constant transformation between Diana Prince and Wonder Woman. Perhaps the performativity of outing as an ongoing process strangely relates to characteristic apparel. For instance, Eve Sedgwick quotes an ACT UP T-shirt that reads, "I am out, therefore I am," in order to reflect on how the T-shirt does not merely identify the wearer as out, but rather involves its wearer in a constant *performance* of outing oneself and thus

The Waitresses, *Wonder Waitress* vignette, April 1978. Documentary photograph, 7-day, site-specific, Conceptual Performance Art. © The Waitresses – Jerri Allyn & Anne Gauldin. Photographer Maria Karras.

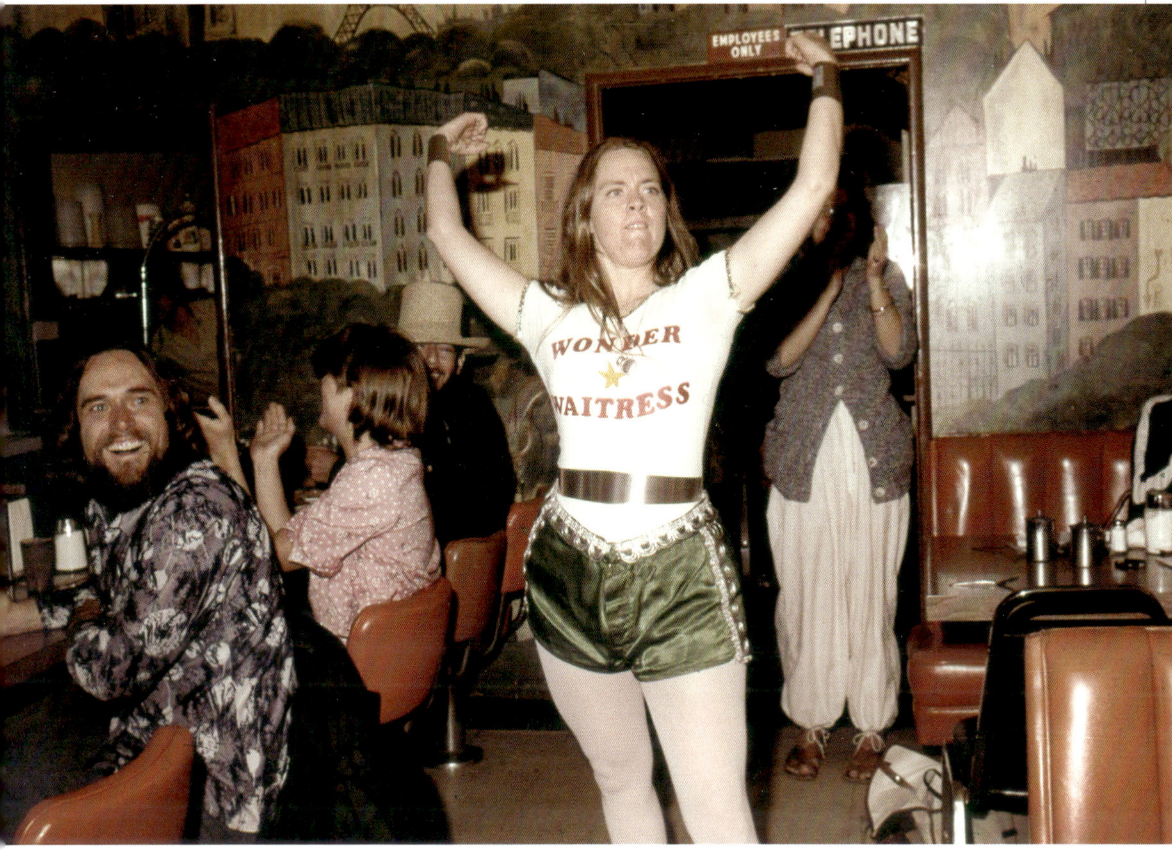

WHY NOT entertain a vision of strong women who governed their own "Paradise Island"—

And aimed for peace around the globe during the very real violence of World War II?

The Waitresses are still in love—

with both the imaginative 1978 star—

And the evidence of female rulers on the isle of Lesbos.

Half of The Waitresses are dykes and regale in the legendary tidbits that confirm warrior Amazons.

WHY NOT Women of Wonder, given the rise of the #MeToo movement, striving to end the very real violence that continues against women today?

Waitresses are still in need.

—JERRI ALLYN FOR THE WAITRESSES

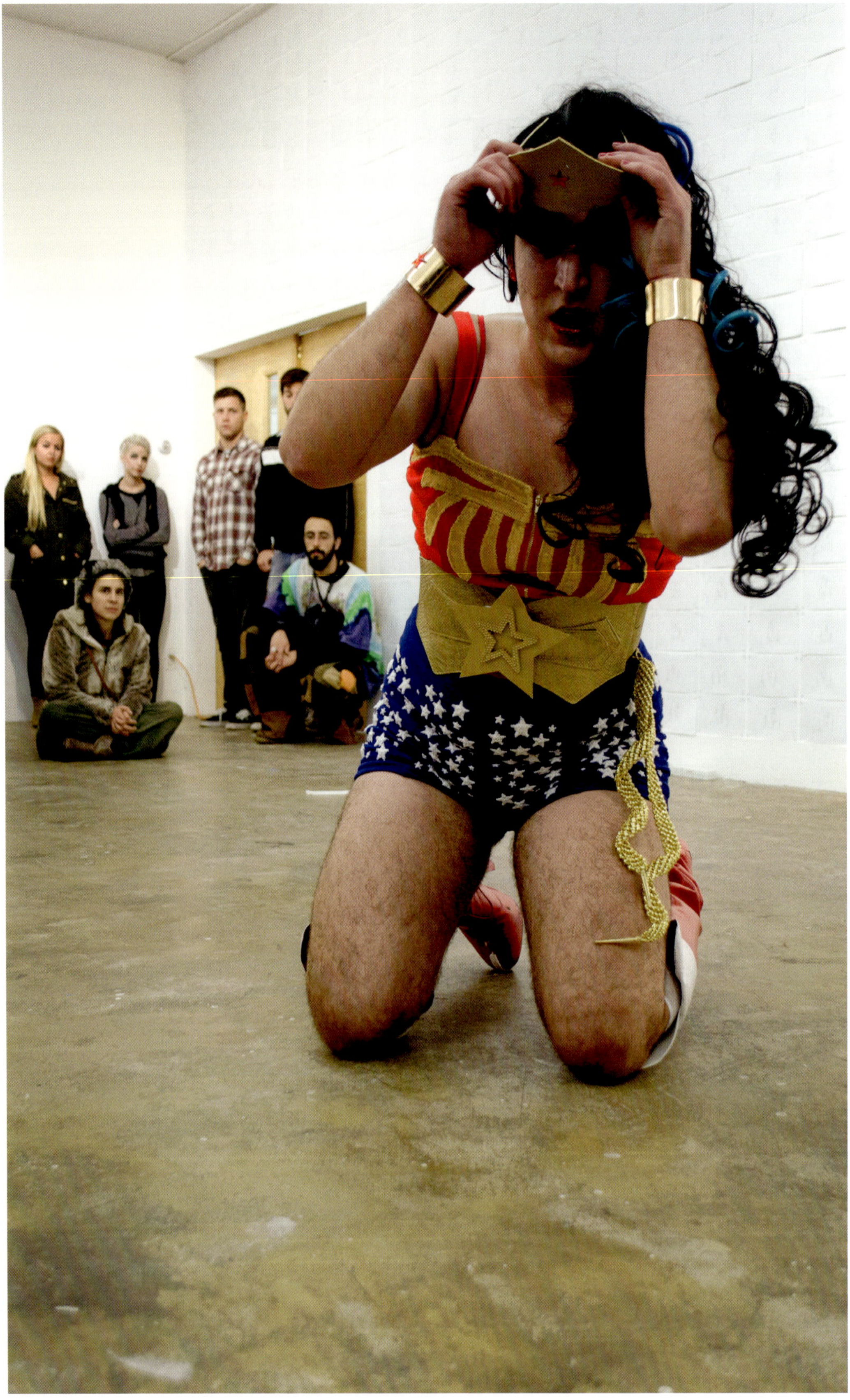

The visual catalyst for They Wonder *is Dara Birnbaum's video* Technology/Transformation: Wonder Woman *(1978) that appropriates the 1970's television show with Lynda Carter as Wonder Woman. In this way, the performance is already working through an image of Wonder Woman that has been mediated by another artist. Birnbaum's video loops in a technological repetition.* They Wonder *turns this technological transformation into a physical one. Unlike the limitless strength of a superhero's body, the performance tests the limits of corporeal endurance that lead to physical exhaustion. In this way* They Wonder *pushes Birnbaum's critique of Wonder Woman beyond the gender binary.*

—SARAH HILL

Sarah Hill, *They Wonder*, 2015. Public Communication: Performing Knowledge of the Body. Suplex, BLUE orange Contemporary, Houston, Texas.

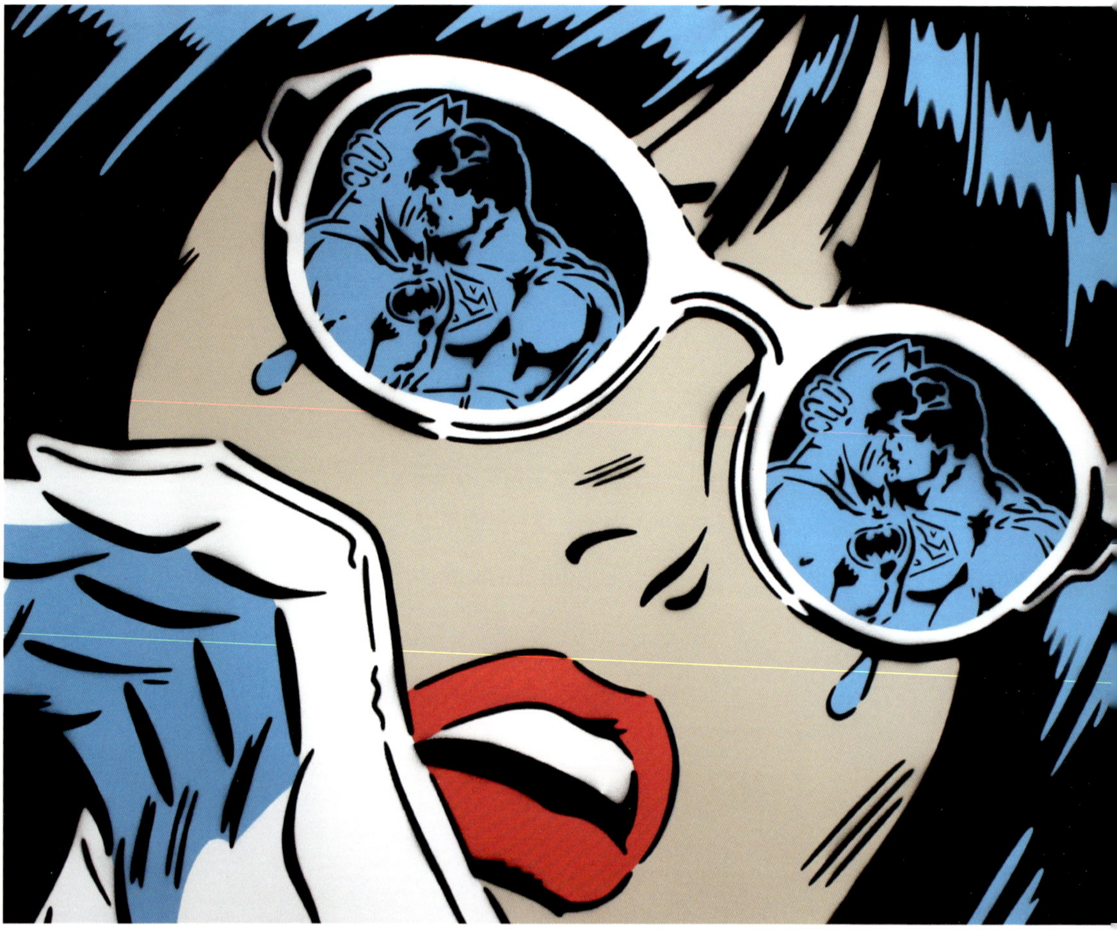

Superman represents the true alpha male. The modern day god disguised as a mild-mannered man. This juxtaposition always fascinated me. Is everyone I see walking down the street using a disguise to hide their true feelings, strengths, and weaknesses? How many of us wish we had the strength of a god to break free from the facades we cower behind? Maybe the biggest show of strength is the ability to be ourselves, free from fear of judgement and persecution, and to live life on our own terms. Superheroes can inspire us to break free from the shadows and become the hero we are all capable of being.

—RICH SIMMONS

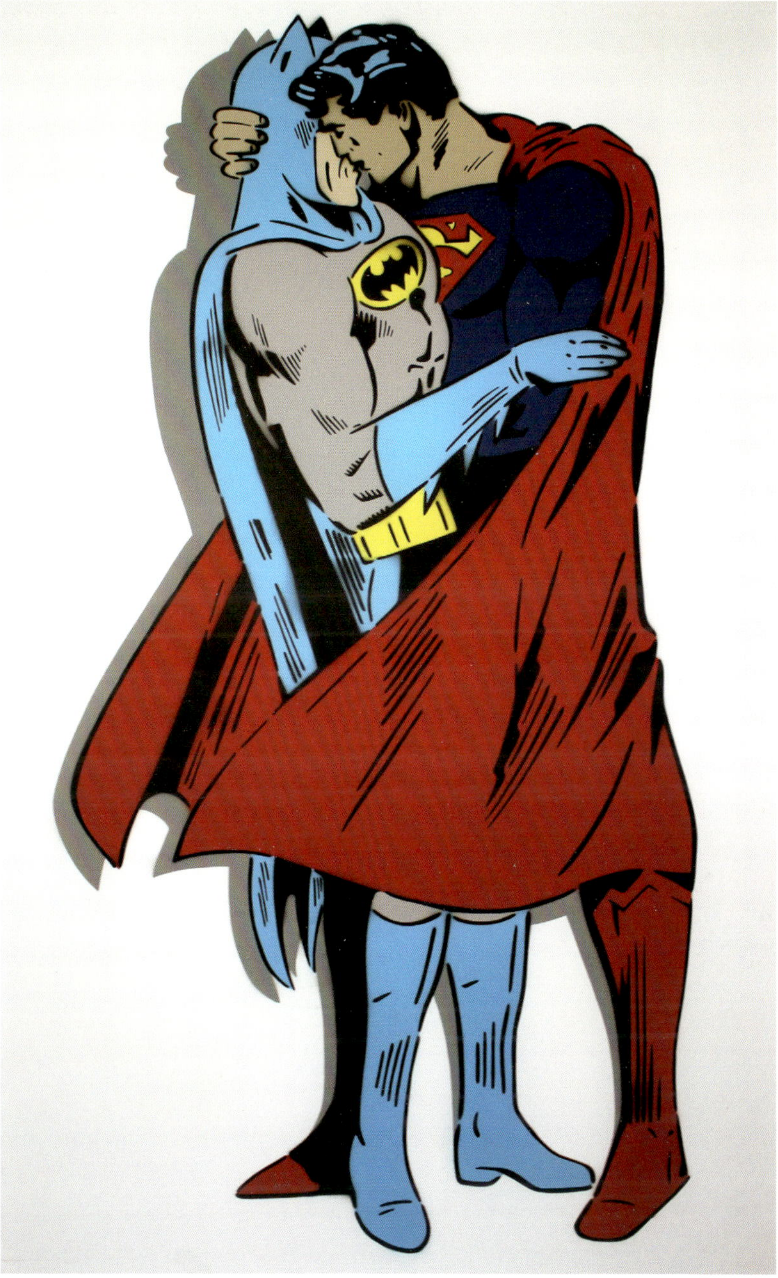

↑ Rich Simmons, *Between the Capes*, 2014. Mixed media. Collection of the artist and Oliver Cole Gallery–Miami.

← Rich Simmons, *Blue Reflections*, 2016. Mixed media. Collection of the artist and Oliver Cole Gallery–Miami.

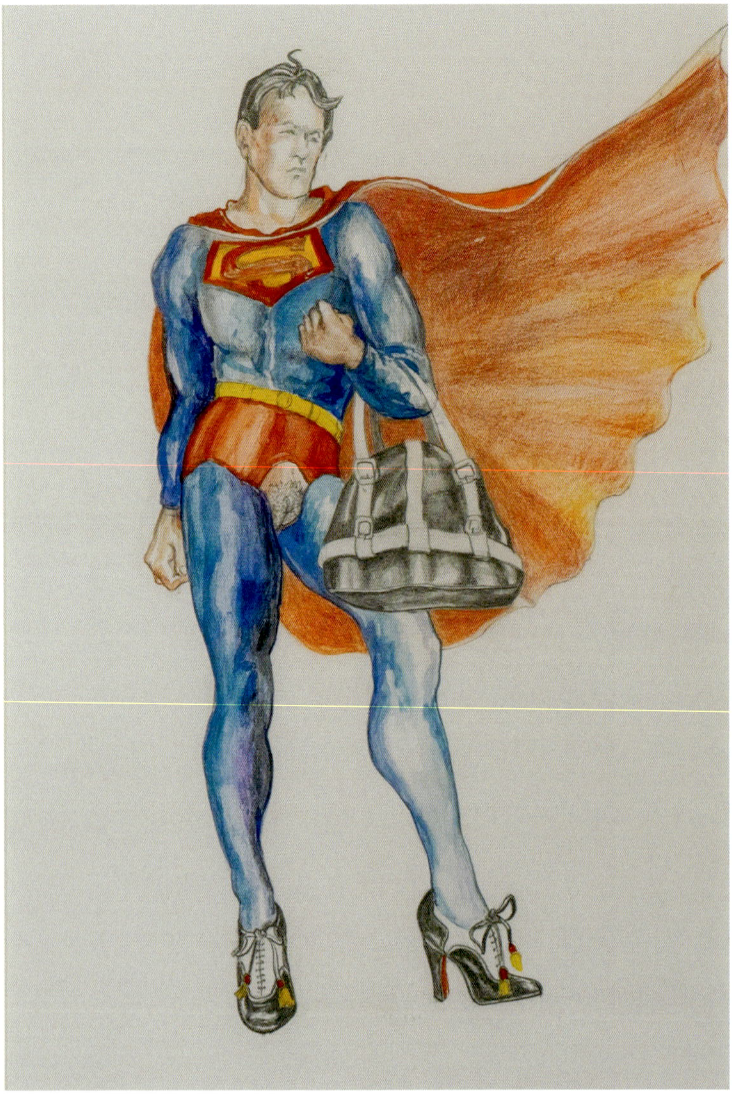

In 1971 I had a show at Motif Editions Gallery in London, which explored sexuality, equality, fixed identities, and politics. I decided to use humor and Comic Book Heroes as a metaphor for the then current politics and issues of the time. The Vietnam War, etc. A lot of this is instinctive and I don't think I quite understood what I was producing or the effect it would have; it made perfect sense to me but the show was closed down by the police, who said they didn't mind the images of the Women but that the way I had depicted the men was disgusting.

—MARGARET HARRISON

becoming the true self. [15] In an analogous manner, superheroes are so often in the process of coming out by using an obvious costume change, not necessarily as queer but as beings far superior in strength and acuity to regular humans; it is a revelation of a being that would otherwise be frightening because of their power. Only their disguises prevent them from being outliers in normative populations.

The artist Renée Cox, aware that there are few African American superheroes, addresses this scarcity of representation of African Americans in general and African American women in particular by creating her own superhero, Rajé. [16] Resembling Wonder Woman and having clear associations with Wonder Woman's twin sister Nubia, (who DC Comics introduced in February of 1973), Rajé wears a red, black, green, and yellow costume. In one particular photograph, *The Liberation of Lady J and UB*, Rajé frees the well-known African American brands Aunt Jemima and Uncle Ben. Rather than showing the two figures as we know them—a Mammy figure and an Uncle Tom-like house slave, respectively—Cox depicts them in racy superhero costumes like Rajé's own. Their bodies are fit and ready for action. Their names have been changed to *Lady J and UB*, and all three figures seem poised to battle, standing with the graphics of their boxes behind them. Cox's invention of a black superhero is predicated on eradicating the stereotyped portrayals of blacks in popular visual culture. Rajé liberates two of them, mirroring Siegel and Shuster's intertwinement of Superman with themes of liberation that we see in the interwar and postwar periods. Comic heroes show us how our established champions may change and evolve with the cultural moment, and where there is a lack, artists create new heroes altogether.

Margaret Harrison, *The Healthier Choice*, 2007. Watercolor and drawing materials. Courtesy of the artist and Ronald Feldman Gallery, New York.

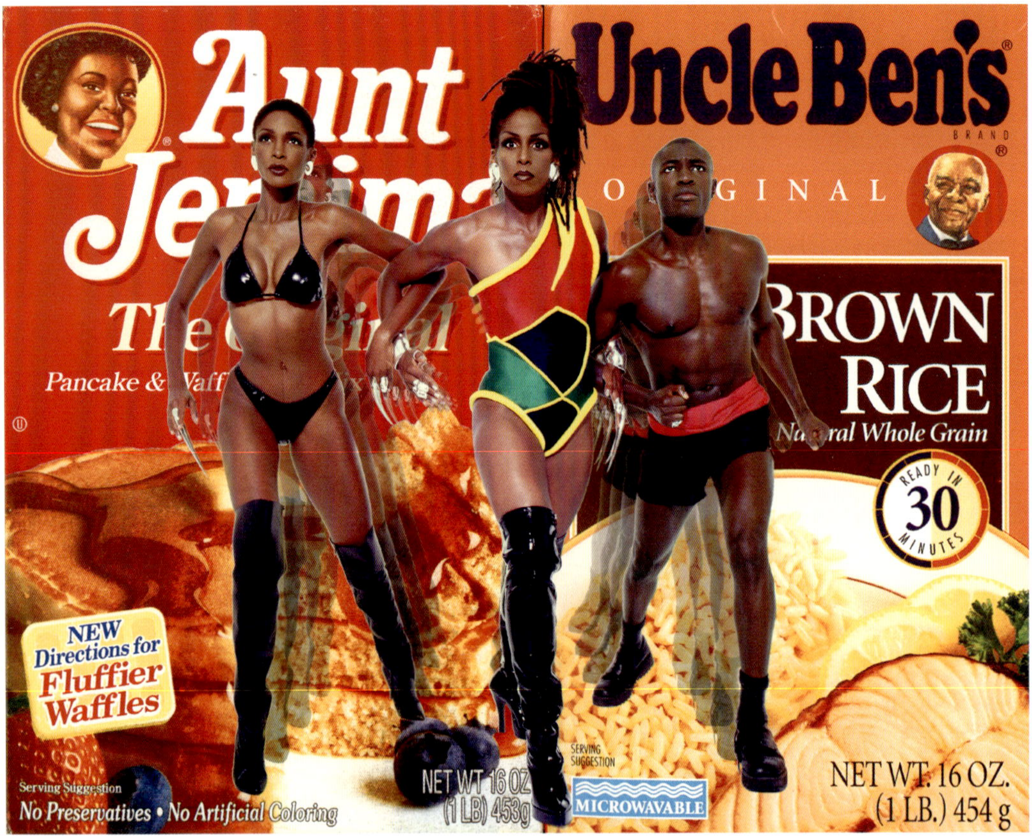

↑ Renée Cox, *Liberation of Lady J and UB*, 1998. Dye destruction print, Diasec mounted. Courtesy of the artist.

→ Renée Cox *Eruption*, (from the Rajé Series), 1998. Cibachrome print. Courtesy of the artist.

Artists of a diverse group of backgrounds embrace the superhero, but these themes—though so neatly divided in this essay into culture, race, gender, and sexuality—are far more intersectional. *The Great White Way, 22 Miles, 5 Years, 1 Street* (2001–2006), Pope.L's ambitious work, tackles how variegated these issues could be, inclusive of able bodies. Pope.L, wearing a capeless Superman costume with a skateboard strapped to his back, crawled the busy Broadway thoroughfare from the Statue of Liberty to the Bronx. Because of the pain of crawling on one's hands and knees, he often could only endure six or so blocks before stopping. In many ways Pope.L's crawl is not *about* a black man dressed as Superman but could be interpreted as a commentary on homelessness, the plight of the handicapped, or even on the process of immigration. To start the crawl at the Statue of Liberty, which was the entryway into the United States for so many, up through the university

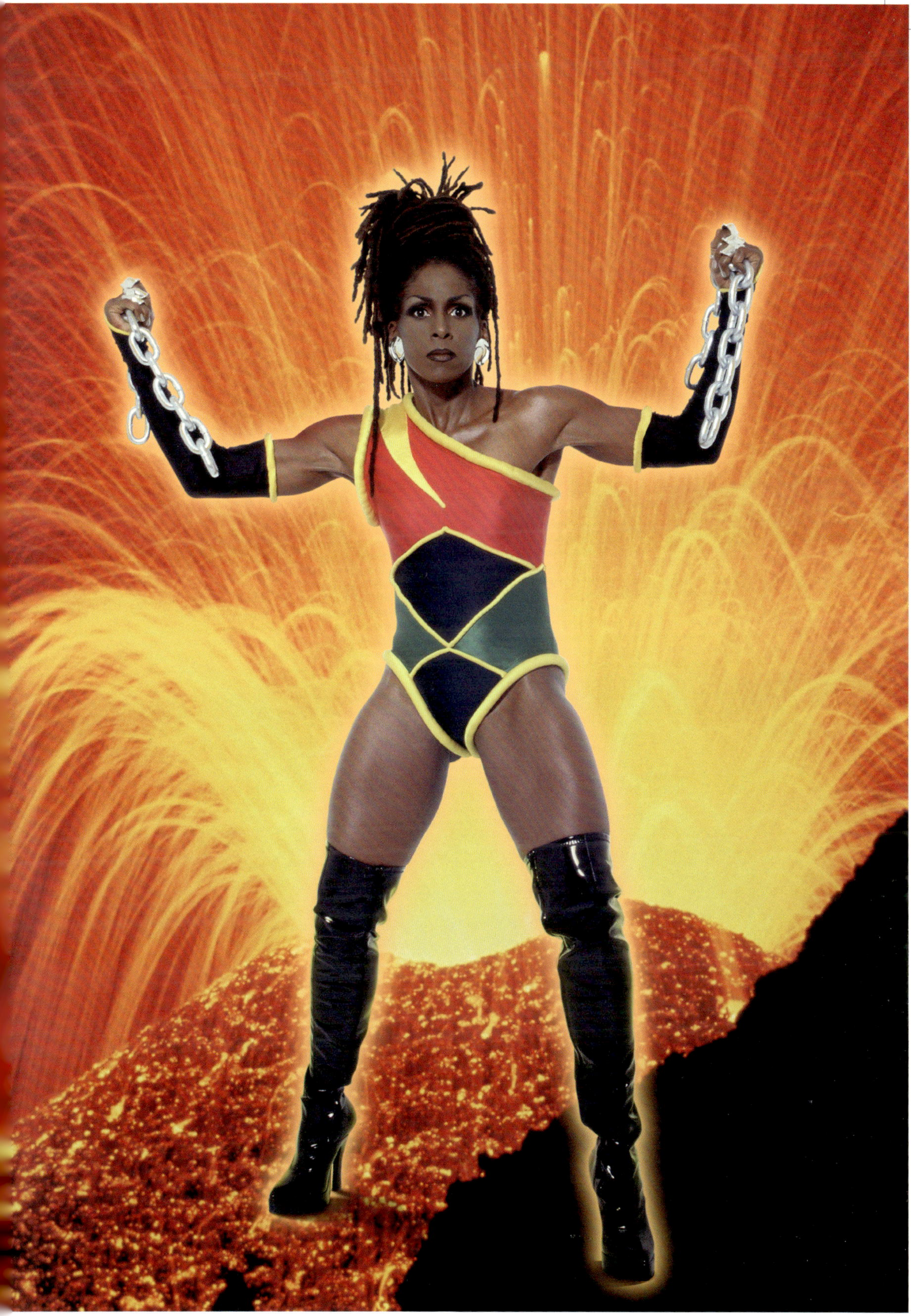

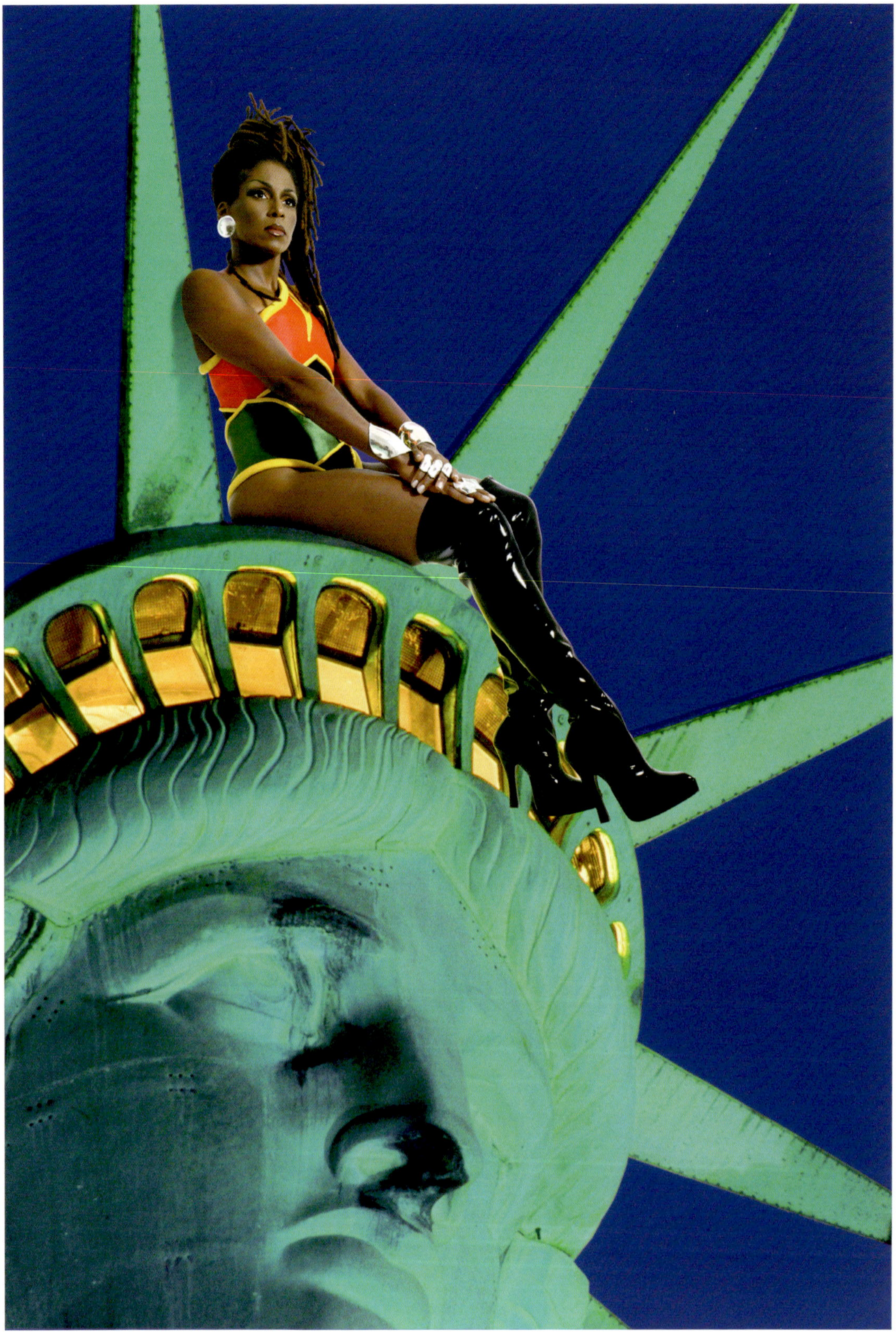

Rajé *came about as a result of two things: having children and being at Toys "R" Us and standing in line trying to fight people to get Power Rangers, and then realizing that, "Whoa . . . there are no black superheroes here." There was only Storm, and Storm is racially ambiguous to say the least.*

The character was born out of my research of William Moulton Marston's Wonder Woman. *I found that there was actually a black Wonder Woman named "Nubia" who appeared on a few comic book covers back in the 1960s. I decided to take artistic license and create* Rajé *as her ancestor—her granddaughter.* **—RENÉE COX**

Renée Cox, *Chillin' with Liberty* (from the Rajé Series), 1998. Cibachrome Print. Courtesy of the artist.

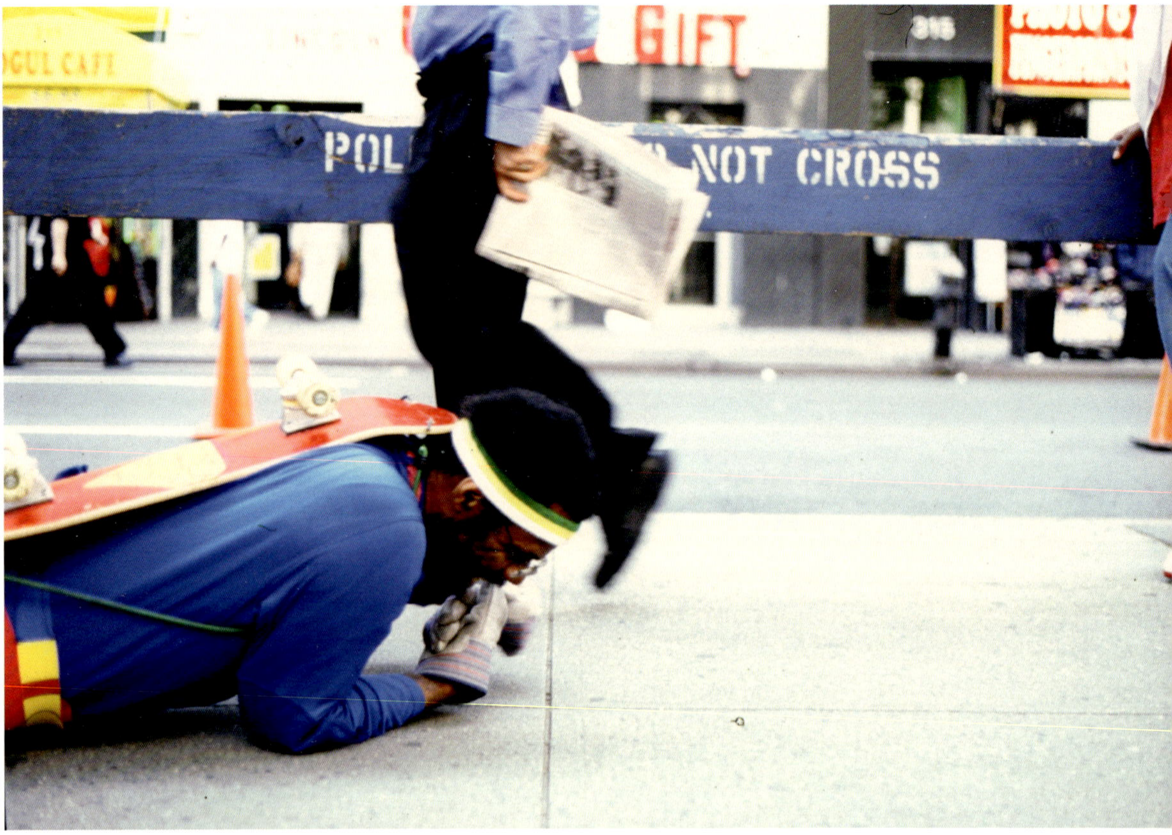

Physically impersonating a 2D superbeing was a rough joke I played on myself, my sweet Aunt Jenny, and well . . . everyone. It was a mean sort of joke. Aunt Jenny married into the family. She wasn't blood. She was ancient. Before Aunt Jenny there was nothing. She loved Superman, the black-and-white TV version. She'd watch him every day. Next to God was the actor George Reeves whose ideal was to do Shakespeare but Superman paid the bills. In our wisdom, we kids, we tried to enlighten Aunt Jenny. Reeves Smeeves!! She'd swat us off with her ignorance. Another way of looking at Aunt Jenny's attachment to a slightly overweight flying white man is love. She loved him. That is why when I saw the misery on the streets of New York City and set my task to embrace it, the most thorough way to do it was to love it.

—POPE.L

neighborhoods to luxury stores to the destitute areas in the Bronx is to navigate the drastically vertical city from a completely powerless horizontal position. As Joanna Fiduccia writes, "Pope.L enacts an 'everyday heroism' of making it in America: namely, strenuously undergoing any number of humiliations to get from the country's gate to its segregated and economically underprivileged boroughs."[17]

Akin to Dulce Pinzón's photograph *Noe Reyes from Puebla works as a delivery person in Brooklyn, New York*, Pope.L makes our eyes aware of people who are often deemed invisible. He reminds us how they may gain visibility in costume. For this reason, Pope.L does not see his work as a form of activism but rather as a place to "change the world," akin to how one might "change the frame on that painting."[18] If the plight of the disadvantaged in this country is an invisibility in terms of justice and a hypervisiblity when charged with a crime, then Pope.L enacts and forces us to contend with the painful conjunction of these issues.

The costumes of Superman, Wonder Woman, and their counterparts set them apart in a world that needed recognizable heroes, a world where heinous crimes were being committed in nations that were considered "civilized." These heroes emerged in the wake of a massive reorganization of the world not seen since the Age of Revolution. At stake were certainly ideals of democratic governance and of the Enlightenment. As the text from *Action Comics* #44 (1942) states, "We are living in an age of superiority, not of force as some European leaders suppose but of intelligence. And it is up to we Americans—you and I—to assert our leadership. We are recognized as the greatest country in the world, and it is up to us to maintain that reputation. Now is the time to make that

Pope.L, *The Great White Way, 22 miles, 5 years, 1 street*, 2001–2006, Performance. Courtesy of the artist and Mitchell-Innes & Nash, New York.

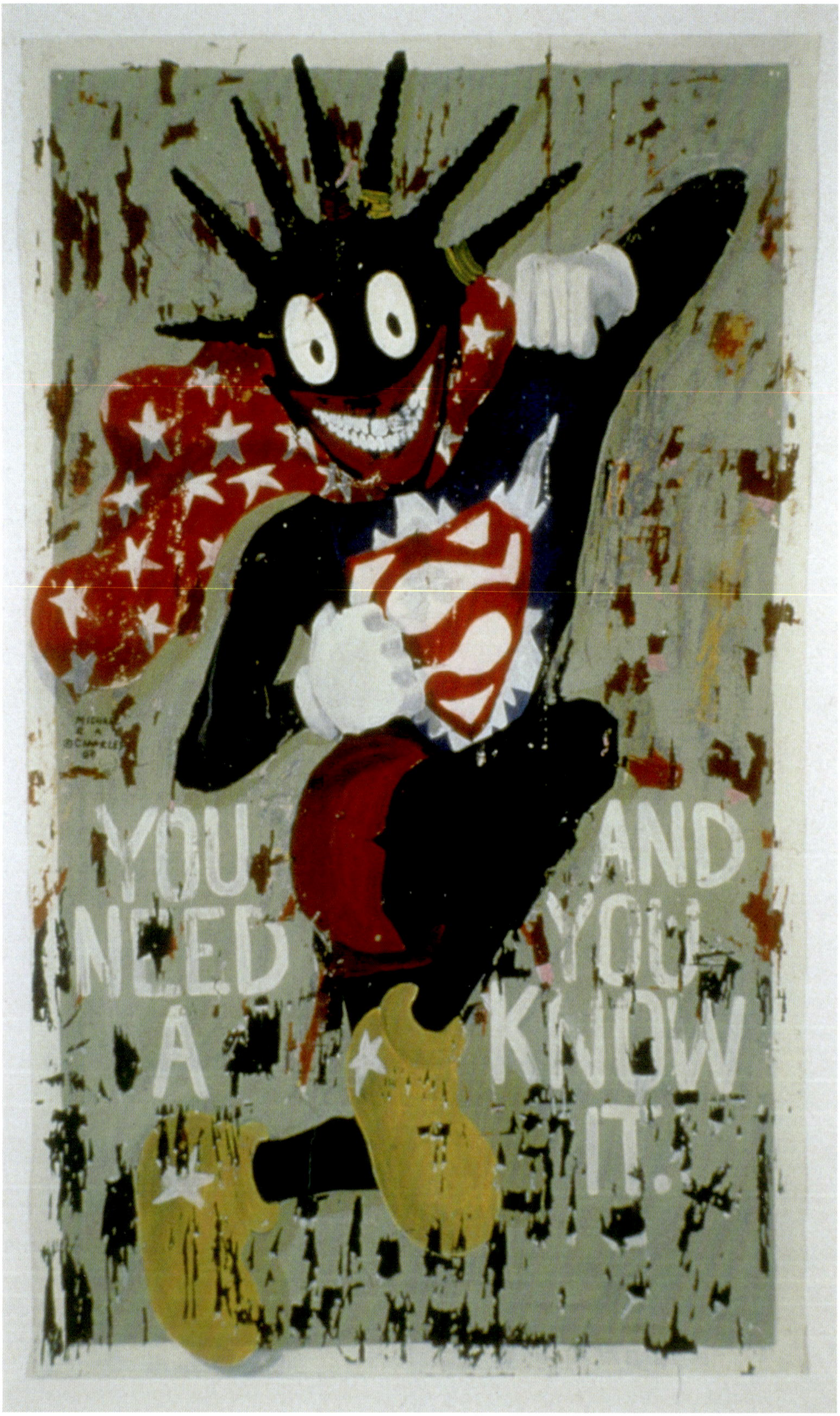
YOU
NEED
A
AND
YOU
KNOW
IT.

As a young boy, the outdoors offered endless adventures. My friends and I blazed uncharted paths around town, built clubhouses and go-carts, rode our bikes to neighboring towns miles away, we even formed a band.

We were curious kids, industrious, inventive, and adventurous. Among our group, in someone's back pocket, there was always a comic book or two. The comic narratives, while equally adventurous, did not captivate me like the images did. Each character charmed me so much, I sought to render them as close to the source images as possible. Funny, I didn't know then that was my introduction to the arts.

—MICHAEL RAY CHARLES

Michael Ray Charles, *You Need a And You Know It (Forever Free)*, 1994. Acrylic latex, oil wash, and copper penny on paper. Barbara Karp Shuster.

O' Superman—

What a childhood hero, someone I could always rely upon, whether it was in comic book form or on TV. There was no racism in Superman, in fact it would never have occurred to me to ask where are the Negroes. It was and is a white man's world.

So it seemed plausible that Superman could, if he were Black, fight the man since he cannot be killed, he has superpowers, and if we're ever to defeat the white man, it will take a hero of super proportions, fearless and fierce.

—PETER WILLIAMS

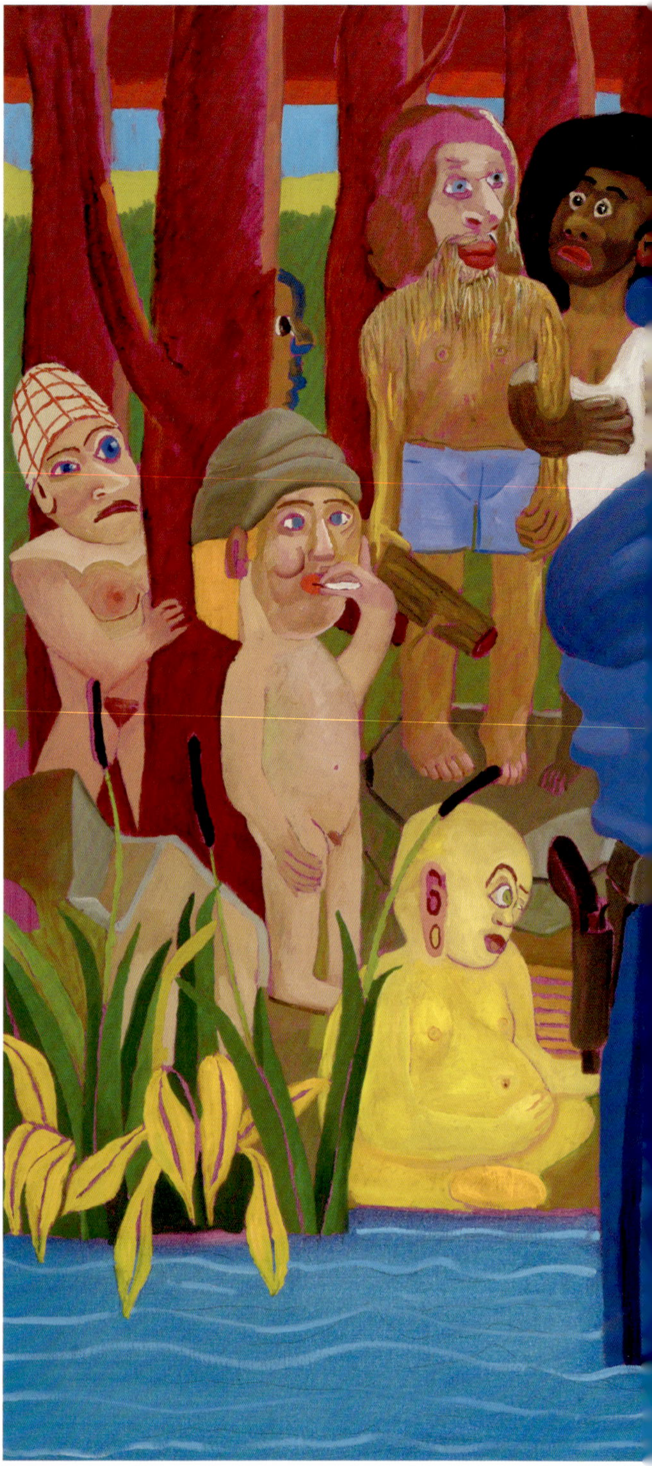

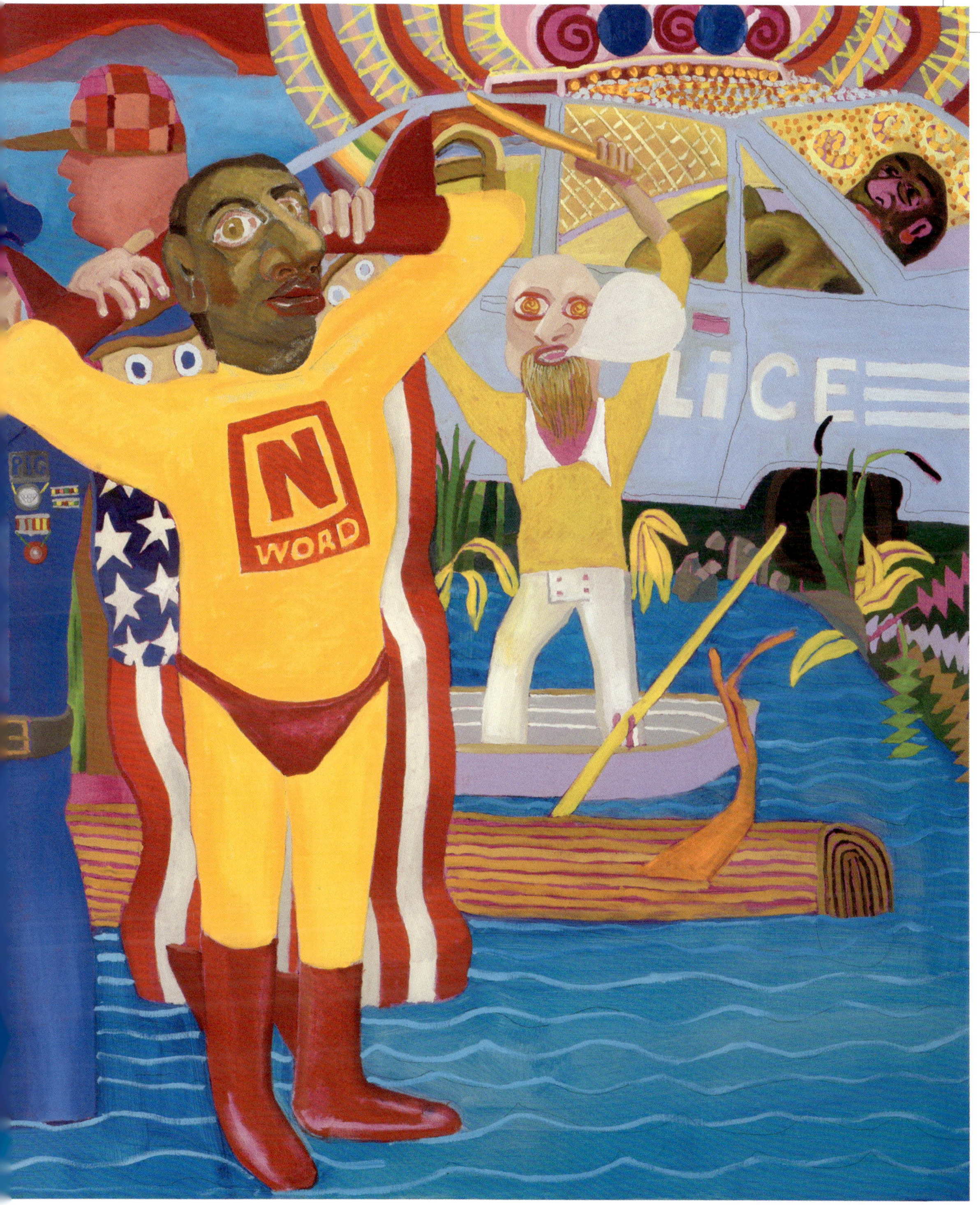

Peter Williams, *Duck Soup, a Comedy*, 2016. Oil on canvas. Courtesy of the artist.

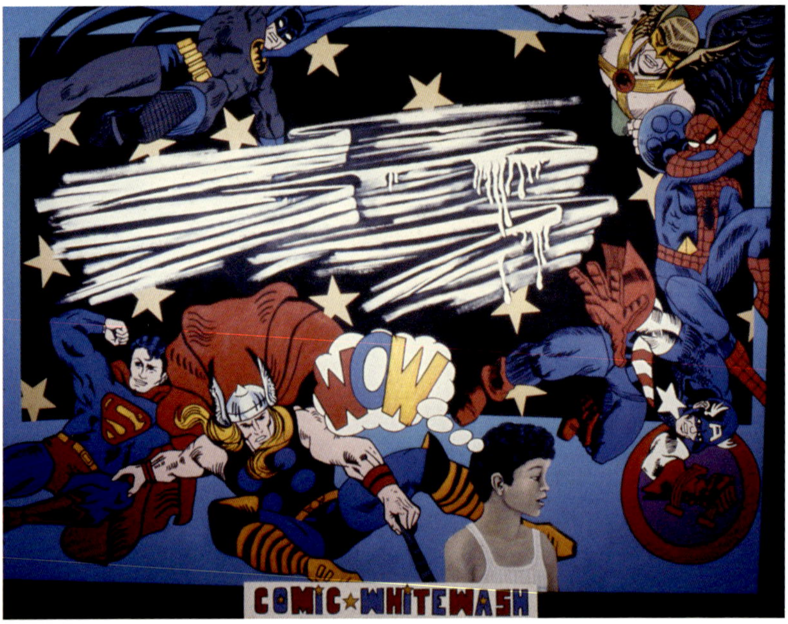

↑ Mel Casas, *Humanscape 70 (Comic Whitewash)*, 1970. Acrylic on canvas. Mel Casas Family Trust.

→ Papo Colo, *Superman 51*, 1977. Photographs of performance. Collection of the artist.

resolution: Be a good citizen."[19] The text goes on to list a series of New Year's resolutions before, in the second to last paragraph, stating, "We are determined more than ever—we are resolved—to make this a happy New Year for the enslaved peoples of the world, to bring peace on earth, good will towards men!"[20] It is a democratic utopianism that rests on the paradox of the superhero, a being superior in strength but advocating the use of intelligence rather than force in an ideal society. Notions of tolerance, for all human beings abound despite the lack of this as reality for so many. It is for this reason that these themes of liberty, equality, and kinship persist in the works of so many artists.

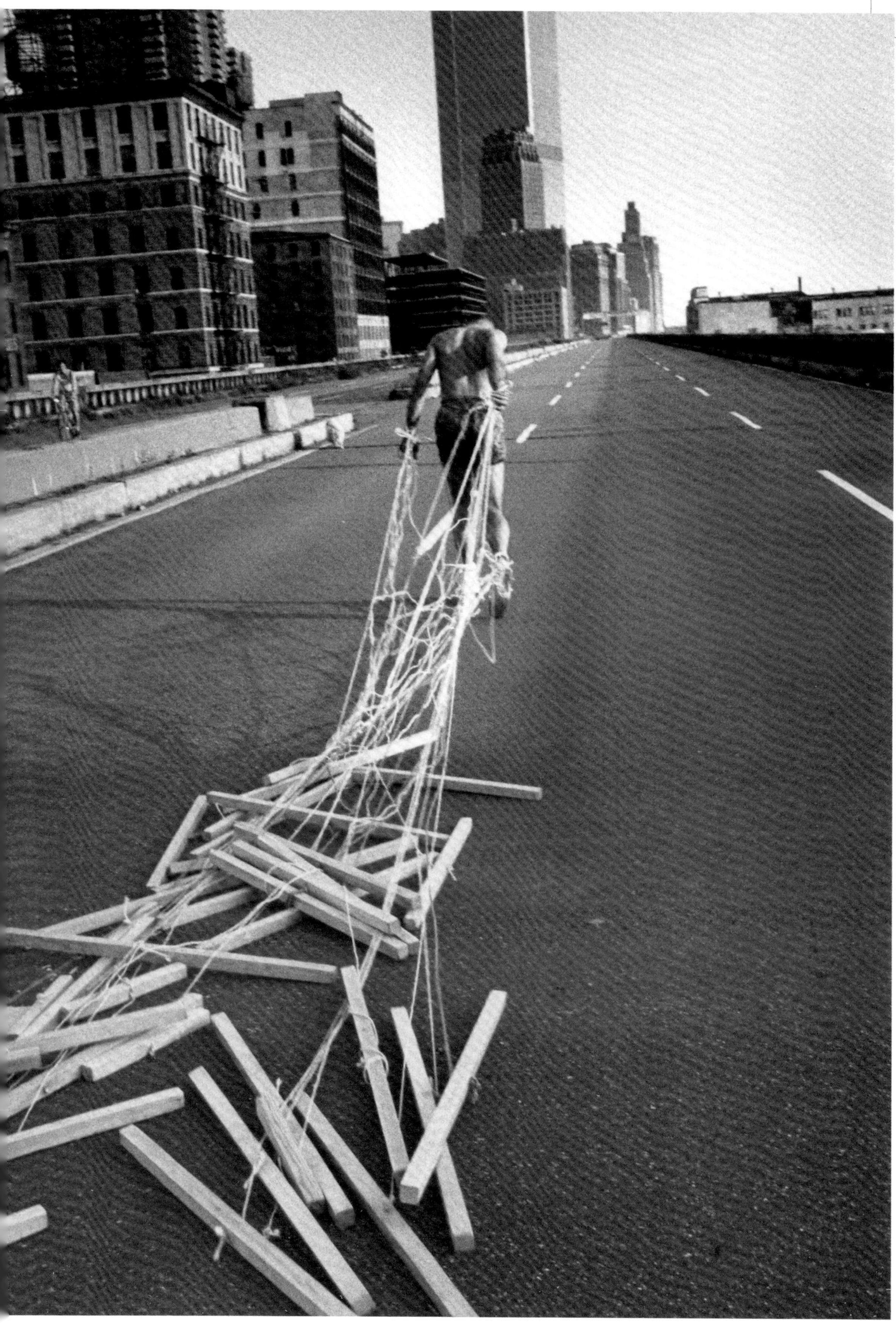

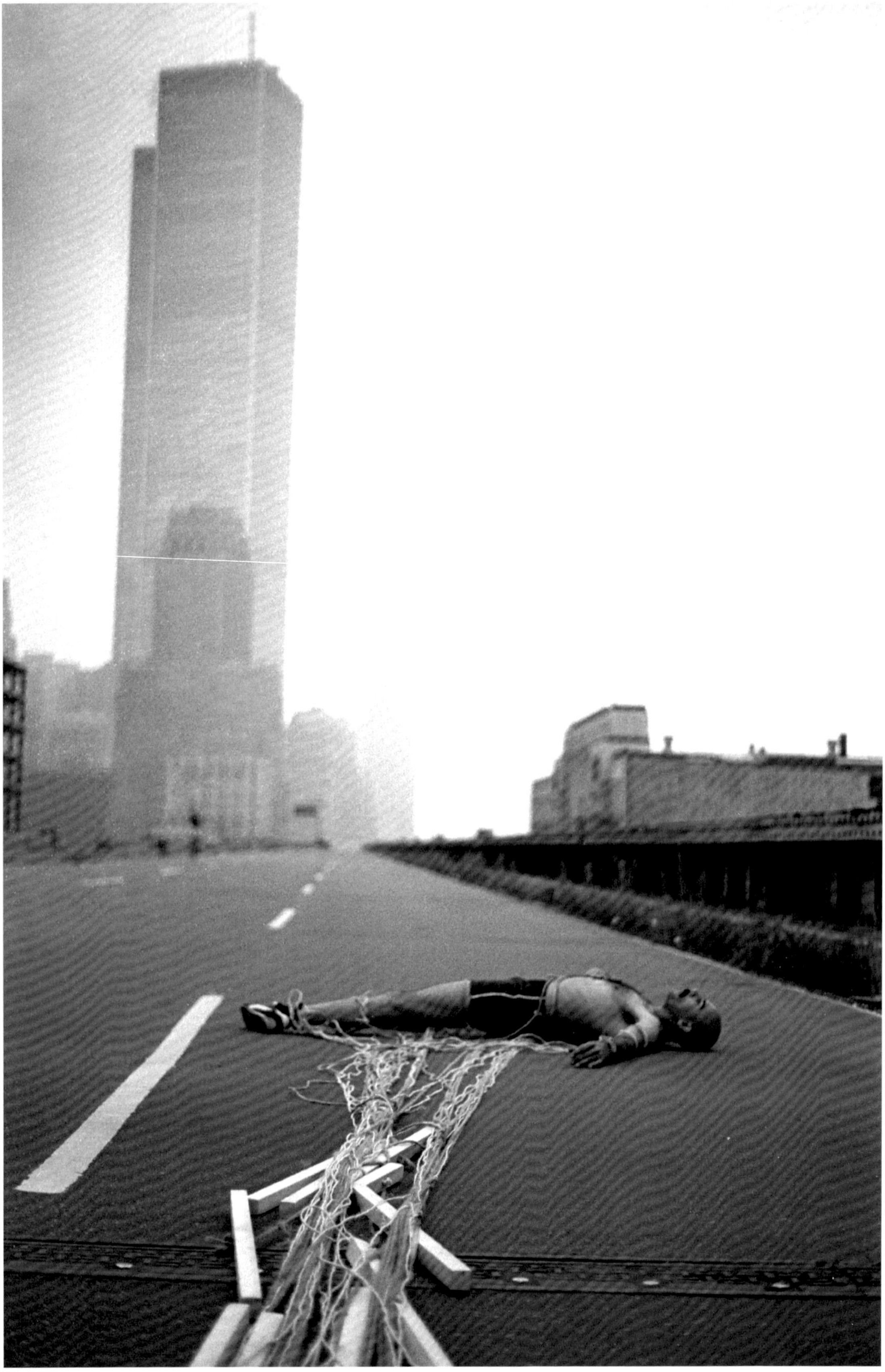

Superman 51 *is about myth interpretation of sacrifice /*
superman / defeat / ideals / local and international politics

Sisyphus, the eternal struggle.

Details of specific politic is up to the public interpretation.

Why 51 sticks 51 state of the American Union?
Why I dragged them?

Because is an act of endurance / human resistance
against any challenge —**PAPO COLO**

Papo Colo, *Superman 51*, 1977. Photographs of performance. Collection of the artist.

ANDRIANNA CAMPBELL

Andrianna Campbell is a doctoral candidate in the Department of Art History at the CUNY Graduate Center, where she specializes in art from the modern and contemporary period. Her doctoral research focuses on Norman Lewis and Abstract Expressionism. Alongside her scholarly research, she is the author of essays and reviews on contemporary art for *Artforum*, *Art in America*, *Frieze* and *Mousse*. In 2016 Campbell was a coeditor of *Shift: A Graduate Journal of Visual and Material Culture* and a special edition of the *International Review of African American Art* dedicated to Norman Lewis. Campbell is a founding editor of the peer-reviewed journal *apricota*. She has taught at Parsons, the New School for Design, and Yale University. She is the recipient of numerous fellowships and awards including the Dean K. Harrison Fellowship, the Preservation of American Modernists Award, the Library Fellowship from the American Philosophical Society, the Andrew W. Mellon Fellowship at the Dia Art Foundation, the Dissertation Writing Fellowship at the New York Public Library, and the CASVA Twelve-Month Chester Dale Fellowship from the National Gallery of Art for 2016–17.

Notes

1 Warhol took the composition and subject matter directly from the comic book *Superman's Girl Friend, Lois Lane* #24, but it was not merely an enlargement of the panel. The colors themselves have a milky finish rather than the washy transparency we associate with comic book reproduction. On top of the paint, Warhol scribbled in crayon using this abstract expressionist gesture found in a limited number of his early paintings and only from 1960 to 1962. For mention of gesture, see Benjamin H. D. Buchloh, "Andy Warhol's One-Dimensional Art: 1956–1966" in *Andy Warhol*, edited by Annette Michelson, October Files 2 (Cambridge: MIT Press, 2001), 9.

2 Chris Gavaler, "The Rise and Fall of Fascist Superpowers" *Journal of Graphic Novels and Comics* 7, no. 1 (2016): 70.

3 Yet already there were contradictions of superbeings serving as judge, jury, and punisher in a democratic society. The attraction to superheroes as defenders of the innocent, as somehow more righteous than our institutions, brought sharp criticism from some cultural detractors.

4 Phillip Pearlstein made superhero paintings in the 1950s. Andy Warhol painted *Superman* in 1961. Roy Lichtenstein famously followed his lead, though Lichtenstein denied seeing *Superman* installed at the department store Bonwit Teller.

5 Buchloh, "One-Dimensional Art," 4.

6 Gavaler expounds on this point, "Superheroes were conceived in response to fascism, achieved massive popularity with the expansion of a fascist-fighting war, and began to wane not at the close of that war but at the earliest signs of victory." Galaver, "Fascist Superpowers," 70.

7 Bradley Bailey, "O Superman: The Many Faces of the Man of Steel" in *ConFiguring America: Iconic Figures, Visuality, and the American Identity*, ed. Klaus Rieser, Michael Fuchs, and Michael Phillips (Bristol: Intellect Books, 2013), 100.

8 This happened through the displacement and massacre of the indigenous populations.

9 Lest we forget, as a child he comes to earth; he is adopted and raised in Kansas.

10 These are akin to the exploits of kings and gods or goddesses and revolutionaries in European examples such as Eugène Delacroix's *Liberty Leading the People* (1830).

11 Christian Metz, "On the Impression of Reality in the Cinema," in *Film Language: A Semiotics of the* Cinema (Chicago: University of Chicago Press, 1974), 3–15.

12 Some of the repetition has been eliminated for clarity, and some of the additional text was removed but not much.

13 Sarah Hill captions their performance online. See Sarah Hill, "They Wonder, Vertigo, Waterloo Center for the Arts, Iowa," Vimeo, accessed July 21, 2018, https://vimeo.com/145797462.

14 Hill.

15 Eve Sedgwick, *Epistemology of the Closet* (Berkeley: University of California Press, 1990), 4.

16 Introduced in 1966, Black Panther was the first African American superhero followed by Luke Cage in 1972.

17 Joanna Fiduccia, "Lacks Worth Having: William Pope.L and Land Art," *Shift Journal of Visual and Material Culture*, no. 8 (Fall 2015): 13.

18 Pope.L, interview by Ross Simonini , *Interview Magazine*, January 20, 2013, https://www.interviewmagazine.com/art/william-popel

19 Jerry Siegel, *Action Comics* #44, New York: DC Comics, 1942.

20 Siegel.

INDEX

MEN OF STEEL, WOMEN OF WONDER

ISSUE

03

GLIMPSING HUMANITY

ALEJO BENEDETTI

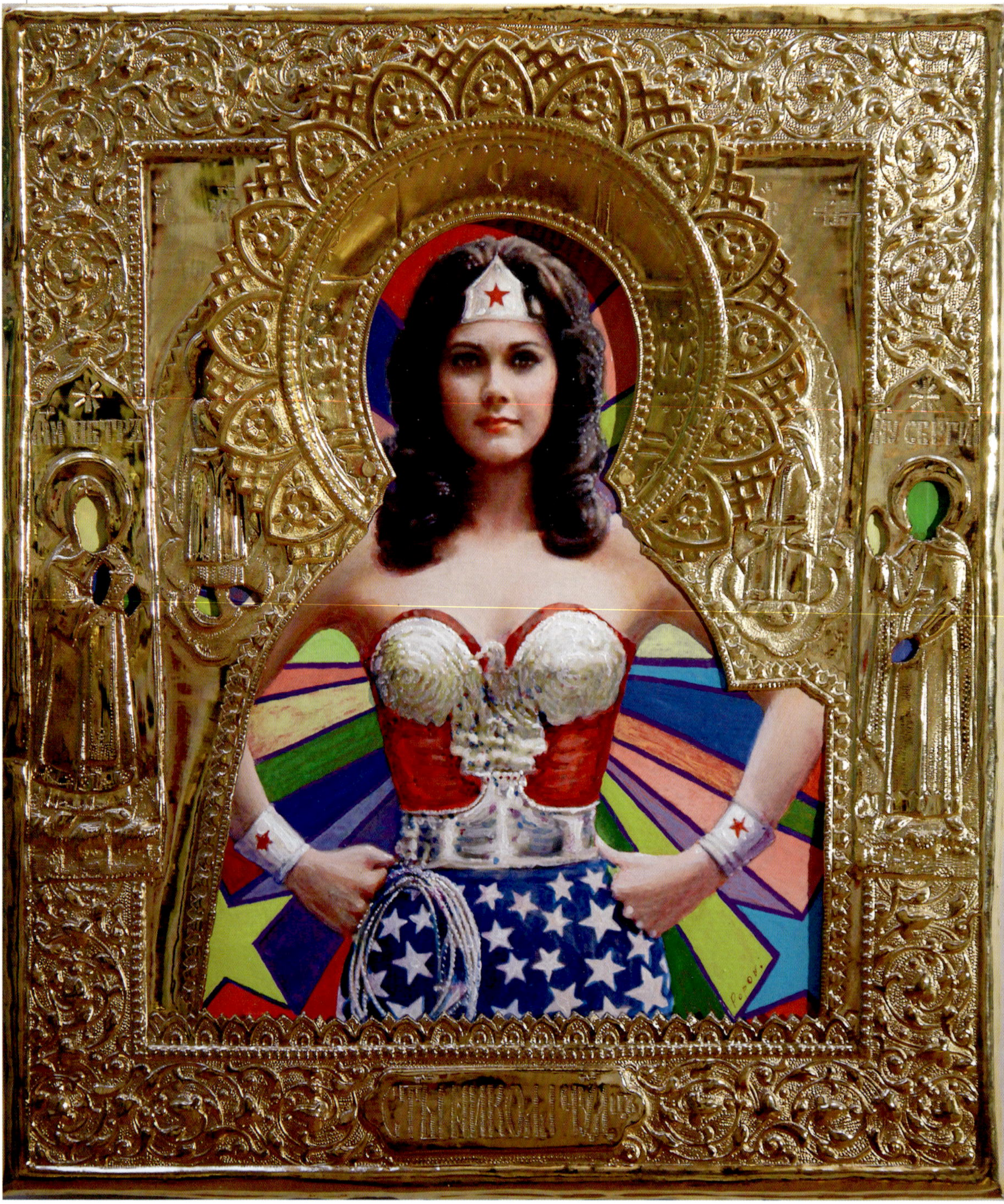

When They Bleed

Our Vulnerable American Gods

ALEJO BENEDETTI

We know them as modern-day gods. The caped, spandexed, and dazzling defenders of American ideals. Of the entire pantheon of superheroes, few are as immediately recognizable as Superman and Wonder Woman. In the art world, numerous artists draw attention to America's deification of these characters—everything from the gilt-framed Christian icons of Valentin Popov, the recasting of Superman as Satan in Jim Shaw's allusions to William Blake's illustrations of *Paradise Lost*, or Mary Beth Edelson's massive painting presenting Wonder Woman as a goddess of second-wave feminism. In American culture these titans are ever present. They adorn clothing, advertisements, cinemas, and toy stores. Not unlike religious idols of the past, parents give action figures to children as beacons of goodness—to be admired, cared for, and used as models for behavior. However, these are also ageless collectibles whose value and worth expand as they remain sealed and unblemished. This is a point Simon Monk drives home in his paintings of heroes sealed in bags, reiterating that society connects worth with the illusion of unmarred perfection.

But between the godlike abilities, the eternal youth, and the unflappable moral compasses, there are some who would argue that Superman and Wonder Woman are too perfect. Indeed, even the author and superfan Glen Weldon described Superman as "every handsome, athletic, trust-fund kid who roars his convertible into the high school parking lot as the sweater around his neck flutters in the breeze."[1] The idea here being that, at some point, Superman is so privileged by his abilities that he extends beyond the point of relatability. While Weldon says this tongue in cheek, the point is well taken. Superman is an alien that draws power from the sun, Wonder Woman is an Amazon princess

Valentin Popov, *St. Wonder Woman*, 2009. Oil on wood block with eighteenth-century 24 karat gold-plated oclad. Courtesy of the artist and Modernism Inc., San Francisco.

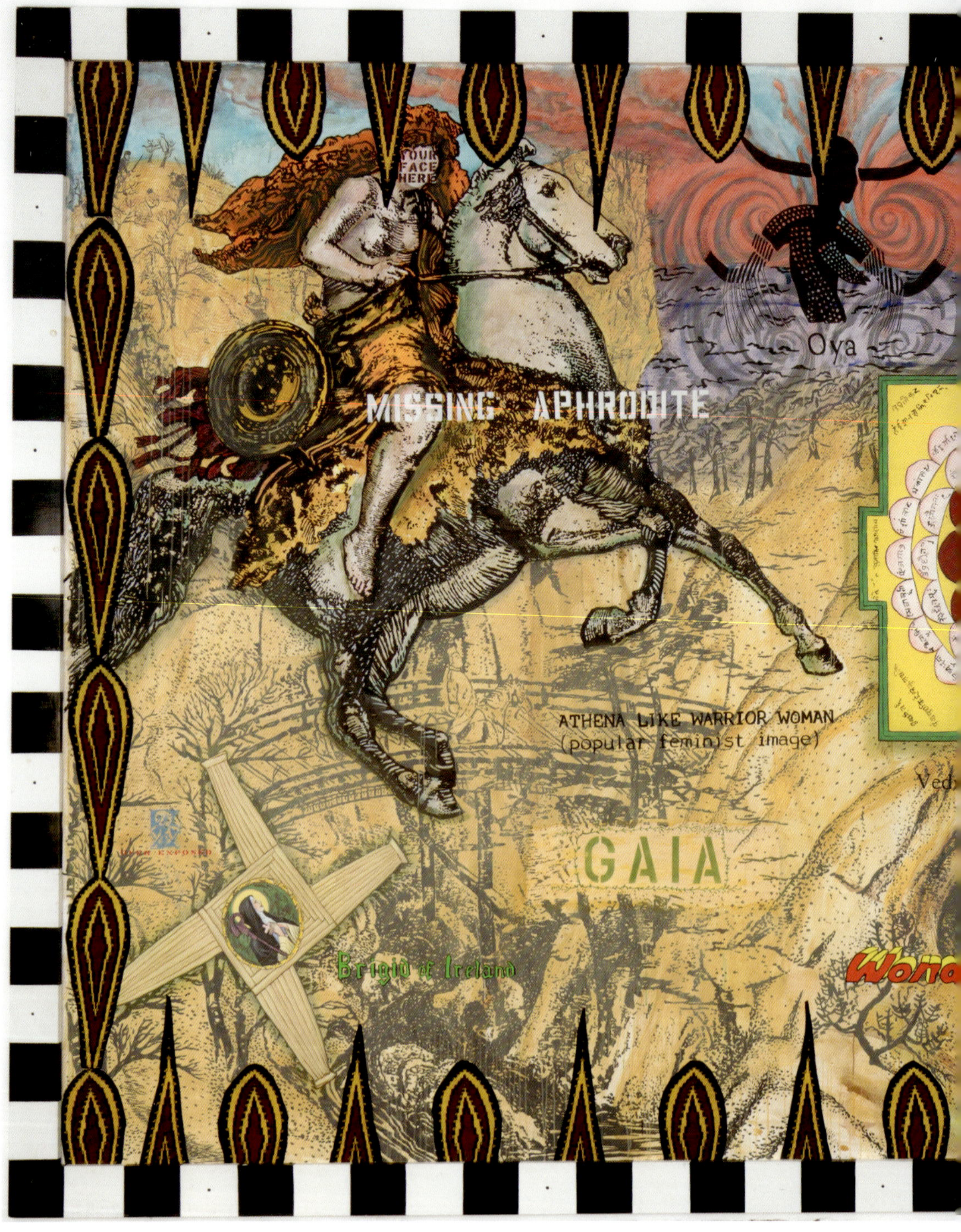

Mary Beth Edelson, *In Exile*, 1989. Acrylic, fabric, and collage on canvas. The artist and David Lewis Gallery.

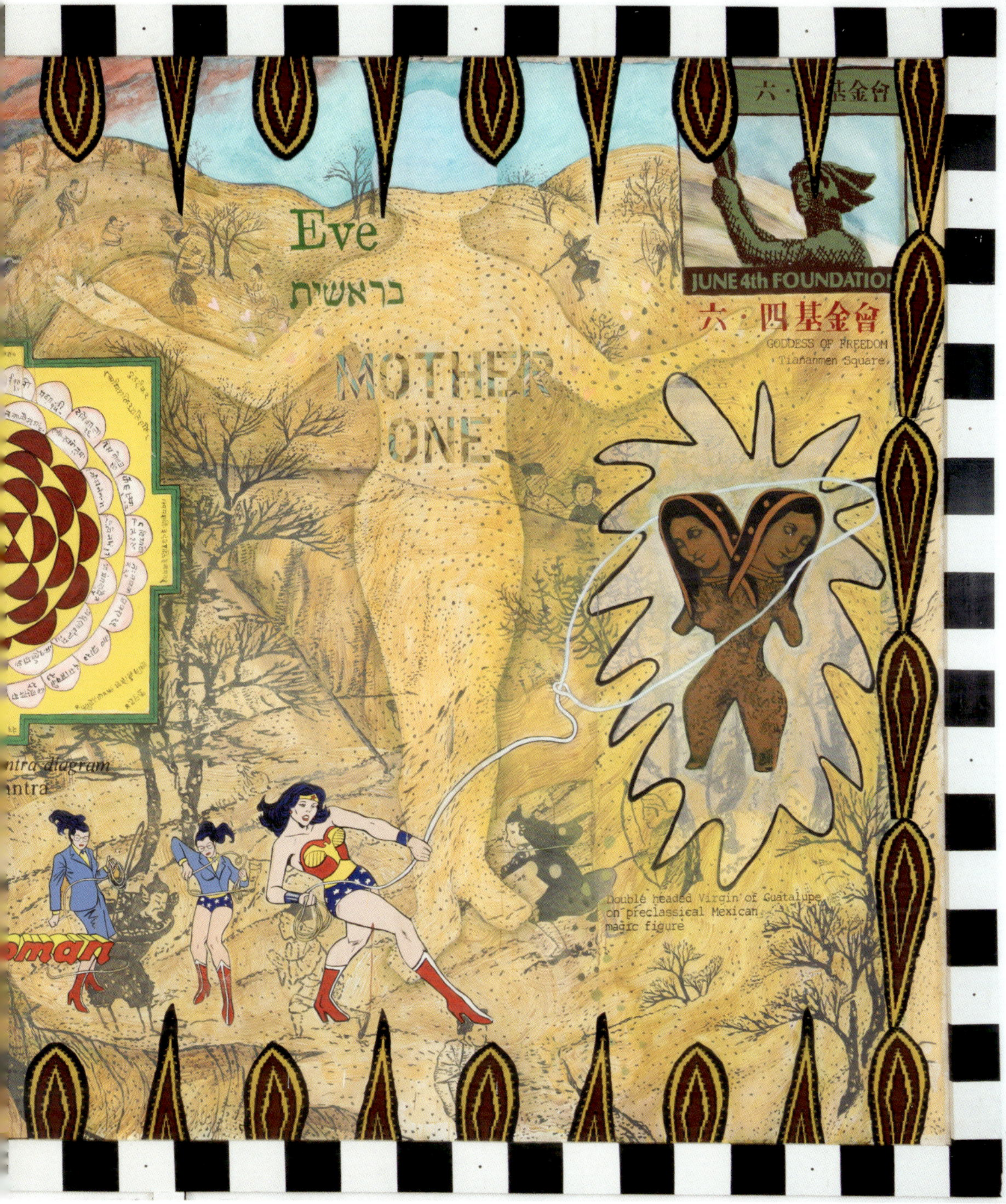
Eve
בראשית
MOTHER
ONE
JUNE 4th FOUNDATION
六・四基金會
GODDESS OF FREEDOM
Tiananmen Square
Double headed Virgin of Guatalupe
on preclassical Mexican
magic figure

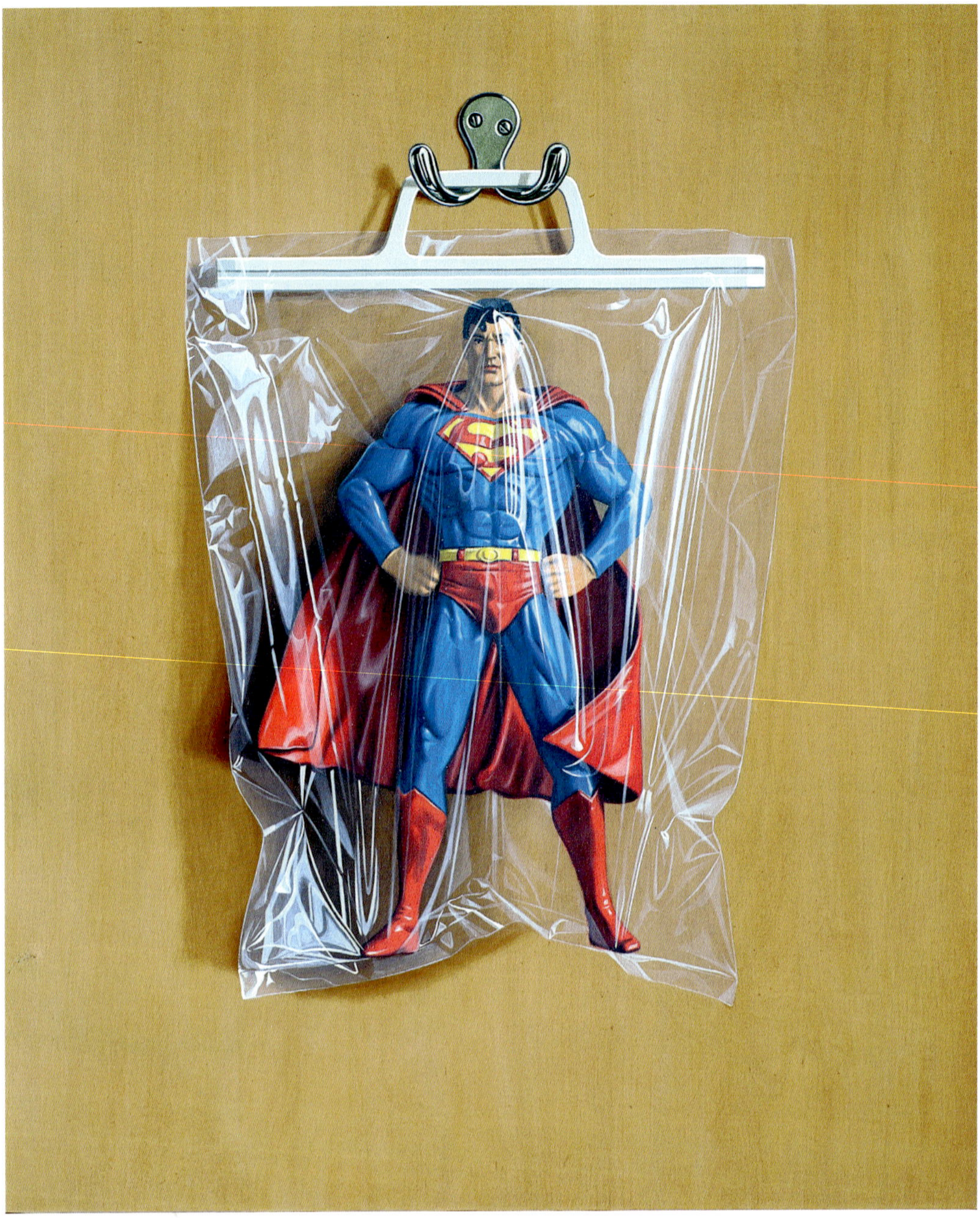

Simon Monk, *Superman II*, 2013. Oil and alkyd on wood. Private collection.

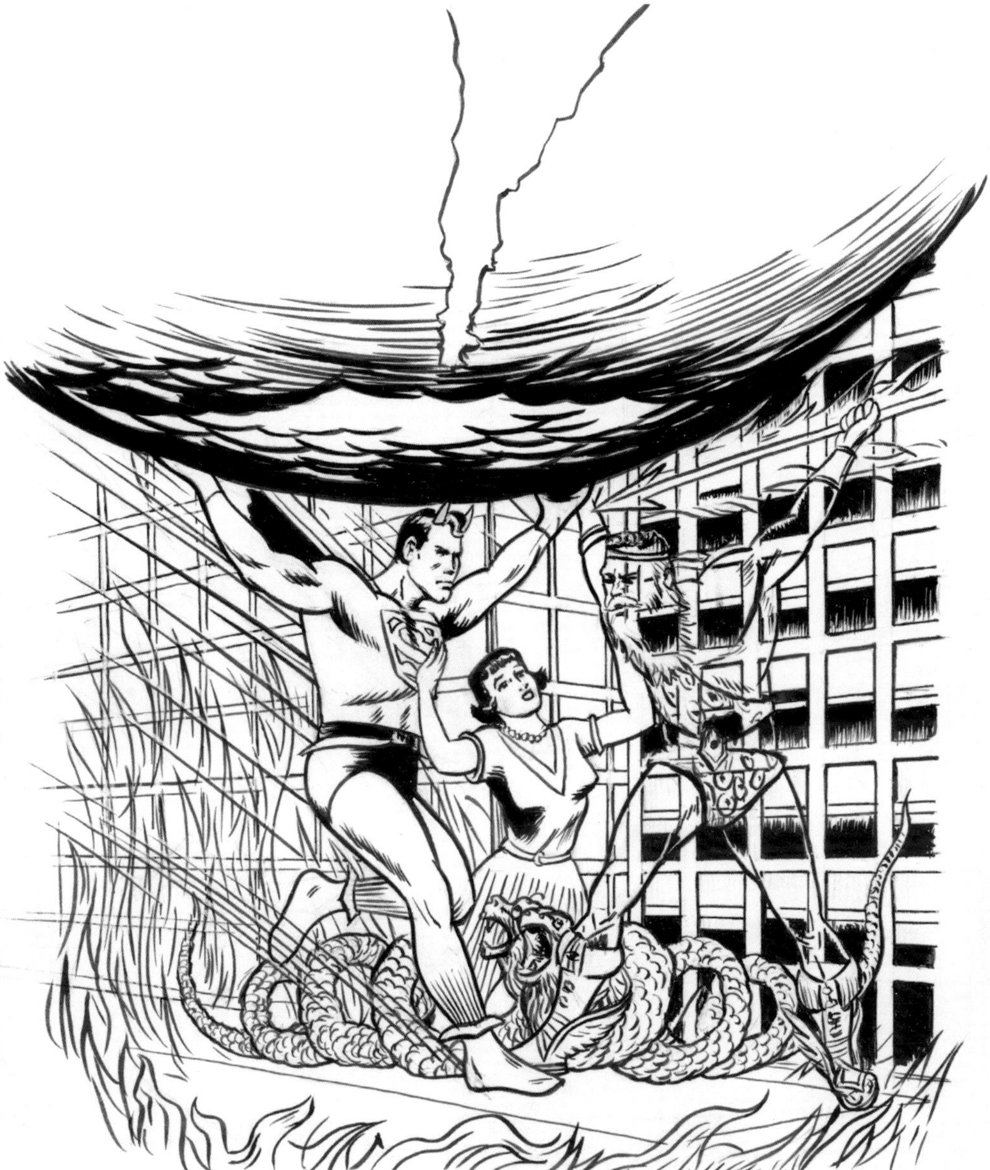

Jim Shaw, *Blake/Boring*, 2010. Ink on paper. Courtesy the artist + Simon Lee Gallery, London + Hong Kong.

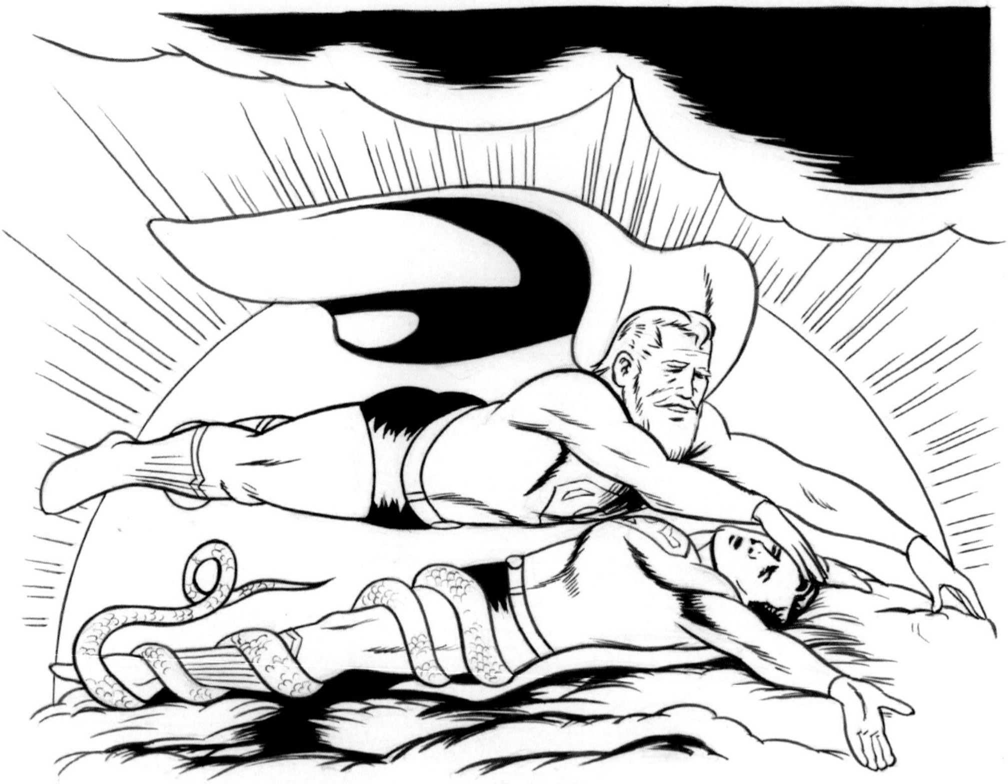

and (depending on the origin story you prefer), a Goddess in her own right.[2] Unlike the entirely human (if filthy rich) Batman, the Man of Steel and the Goddess of Truth are by their very origins unrelated to any of the humans they swear to protect.[3]

However, unrelatable characters do not remain continuously in print for eighty years and consistently break records at the box office. These characters resonate with generations of audiences because, against all odds, people find relatable traits in both of them. For the scholar Mark D. White, this point of connection is a result of the need for superheroes to make judgements. He states that no amount of super strength or flight can help resolve an ethical dilemma, which in effect leaves them without an advantage on ordinary people.[4] And while a situation like that certainly makes those characters appear more relatable, I would argue that judgement is simply one part of a larger idea enabling connection. While doubtless many theories exist for why that is, mine is rather simple: people relate to their vulnerability.

Jim Shaw, *Blake/Boring*, 2010. Lent by Keith Fox and Tom Keyes.

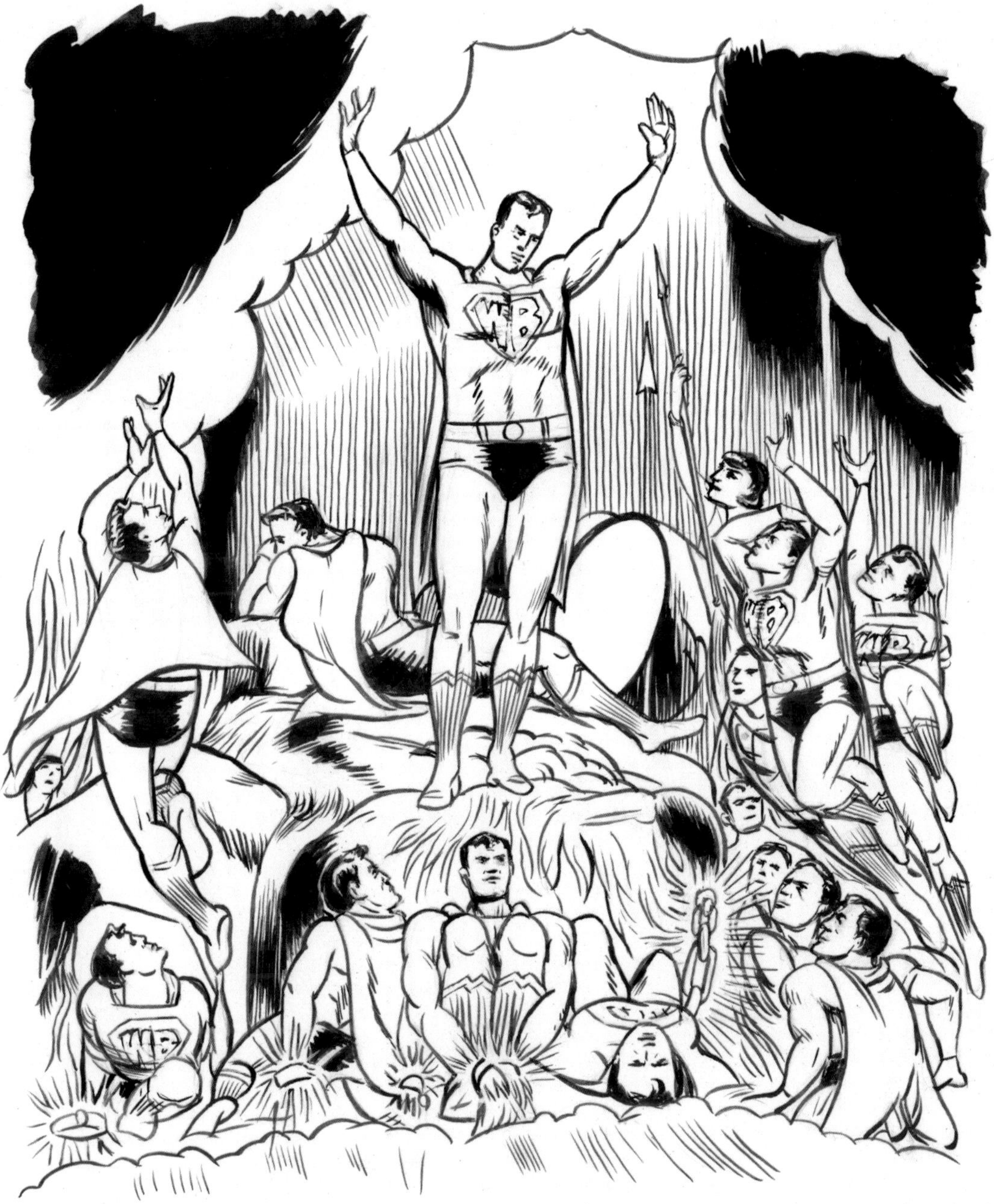

Jim Shaw, *Blake/Boring*, 2010. Lent by Keith Fox and Tom Keyes.

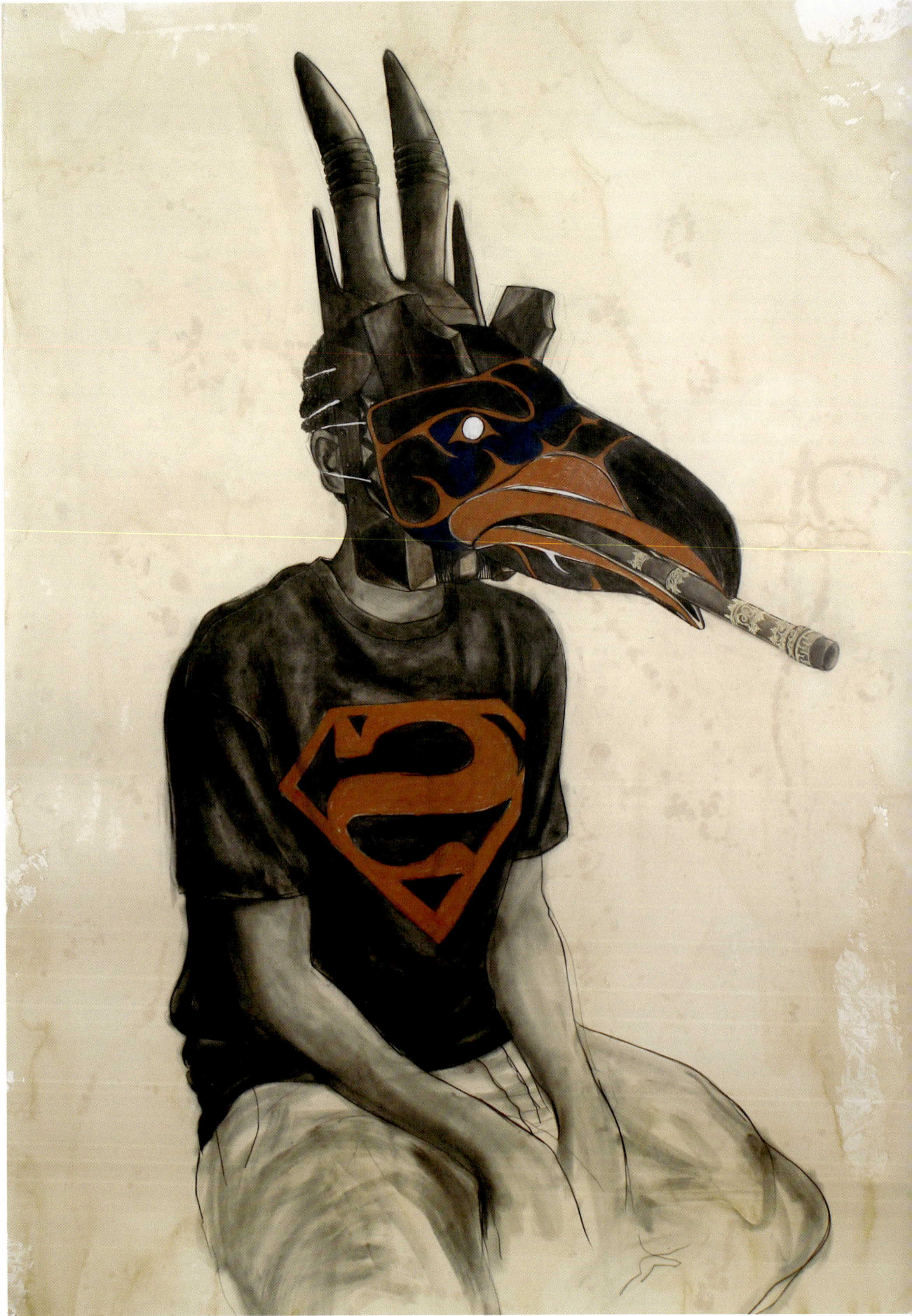

Comic books, with their serialized format and tales of heroism and morality, in many ways embody our contemporary relationship to mythology. Setting the worlds of monsters and mutants into comics, a platform for children but frequently accessed by adults, allows a fitting distance for a population largely agnostic to the notions of magic and the extraordinary. As my art practice is rooted in a childhood consuming and copying comics, I find that Superman holds a central role in this universe. He is both a liberating and problematic character with an origin story entrenched in alienation and longing while also reifying ideas of White Patriarchal Supremacy. This makes Superman an ideal pole in which to critically navigate perceptions of Race and Identity.

—ROBERT PRUITT

Robert Pruitt,
Heliocentrist, 2013.
Conte, gold leaf, coffee.
#menelik Woolcock
Collection: Zewditu
Menelik, Aron Woolcock,
Daniel Woolcock,
Adrian Woolcock.

In the comics and movies alone Superman and Wonder Woman lose battles, die (only to be resurrected), and lose their powers—whether by kryptonite, Superman's own volition, or—for the short period from 1968 to 1972—when DC made Wonder Woman a white-jumpsuit-wearing powerless detective. All of that is just within the DC Comics canon. Even the publisher is aware of the effects of repeatedly humanizing these characters.

Therefore, it should come as little surprise that artists from outside the world of comics—the focus of this exhibition—would naturally attach themselves to this approach of flexing vulnerability in order to connect with viewers. Research in the field of social psychology reveals that humans perceive people that show vulnerability to be more attractive because they are seen as more honest, real, and relatable.[5] Wonder Woman's and Superman's personas are built on truth and justice, so it stands to reason that any additional actions taken to improve the perception of these attributes directly helps their respective brands. To this end, a flawed Wonder Woman means a more likeable and attractive heroine. A Superman bravely confronting his inadequacies in front of in-comic and real-world readers alike helps endear him to his audiences.

Superman and Wonder Woman are not the only godlike figures to make mistakes and show vulnerabilities—in other words, to be humanized. It has happened for millennia across cultures. In Aztec mythology, the rain god Tlaloc was so heartbroken after another god stole his wife that he forgot to water the earth, bringing on the end of the third age. In Ancient Greece, the demigod and hero of the Iliad, Achilles, sacked cities and defeated great foes but is best remembered for a weak heel. In Christianity, the fact that Christ was human and died on the cross is the

Simon Monk, *Bargain Box 3—Box of Superheroes*, 2015. Charcoal on paper. Courtesy of Alida Anderson Art Projects, Washington, DC.

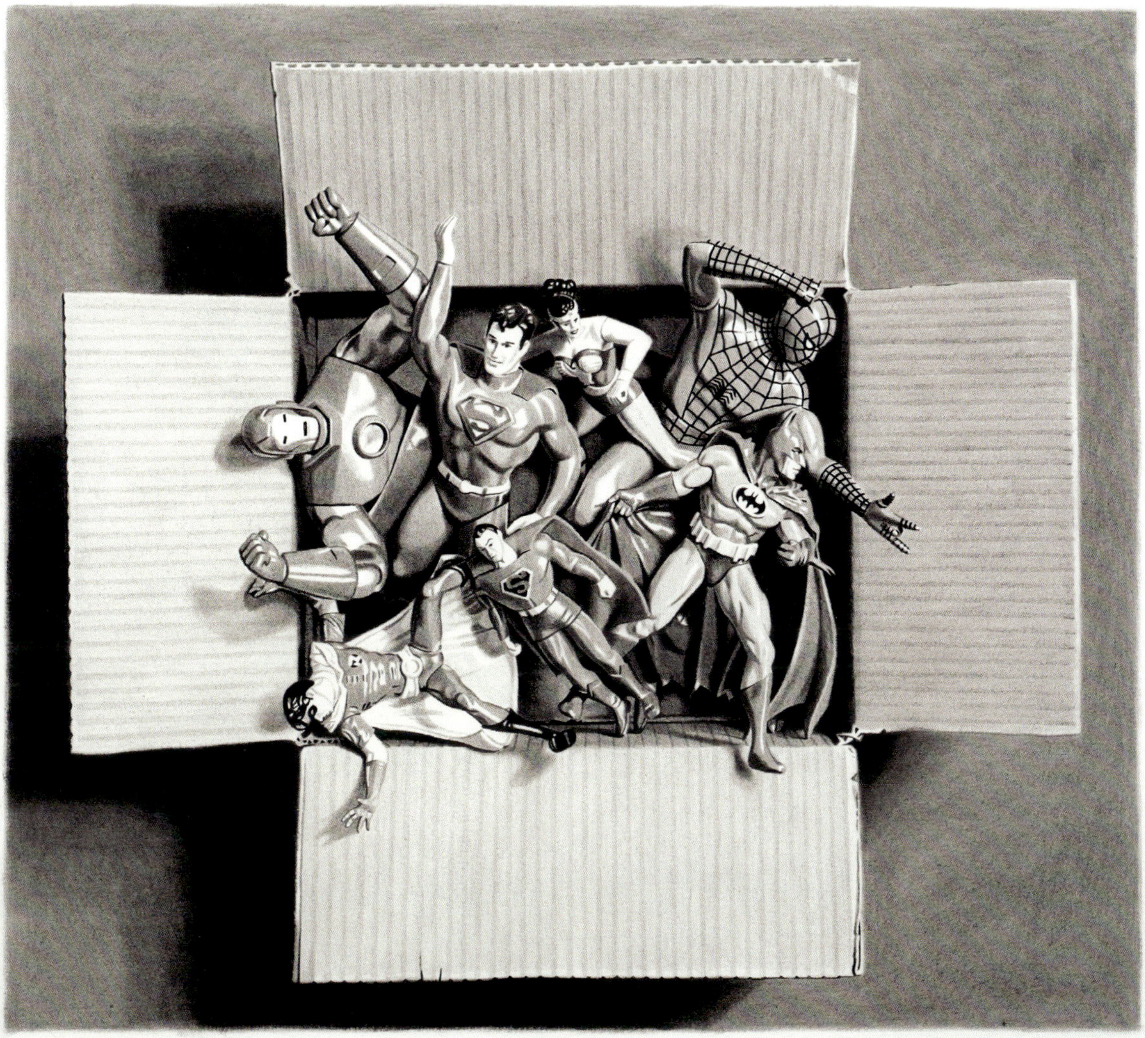

I first discovered American comics in 1973 at the age of six and they immediately exerted a powerful hold over my imagination. Superheroes were vastly important to me throughout my childhood and continue to be significant. A classic superhero trope involves the victory of the hero against seemingly insurmountable odds. As often as not the hero's superpowers alone are insufficient to achieve victory but their innate human characteristics such as determination, hope, trust, and empathy are the factors that allow them to finally succeed. Anybody struggling to survive as an artist will recognize the essential truth of this narrative structure.

—SIMON MONK

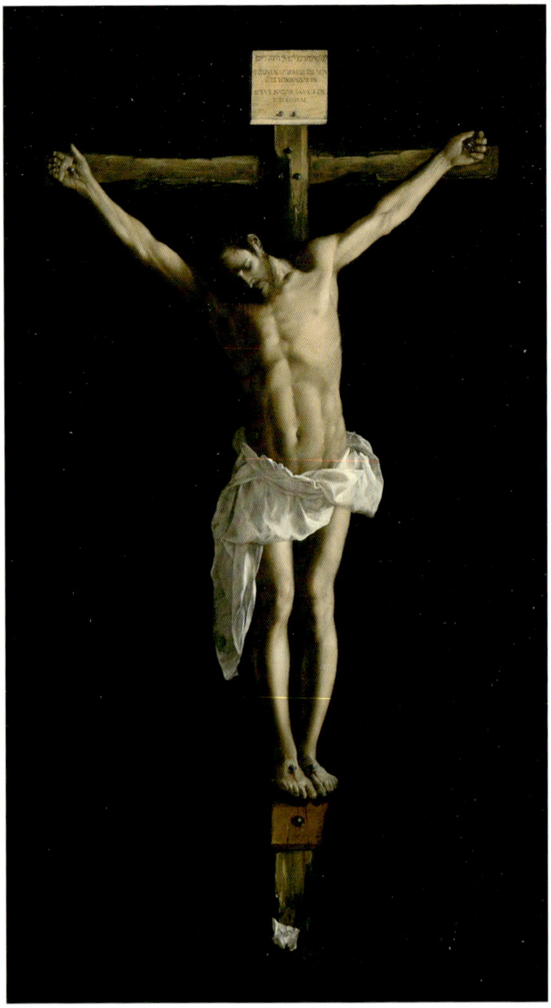

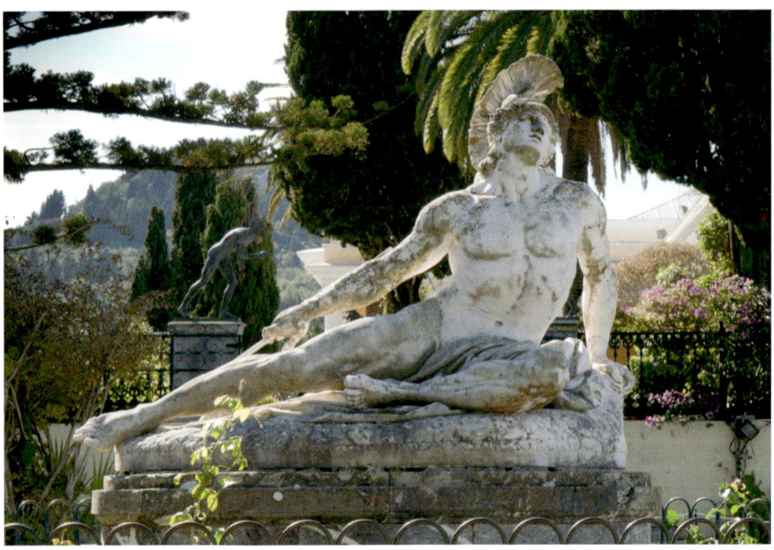

↑ Francisco de Zurburán, *The Crucifixion*, 1627. Oil on canvas. The Art Institute of Chicago.

→ Ernst Herter, *Dying Achilles*, 1885. Stone sculpture. Museo Archilleio in Corfu, Greece.

very source of all human redemption. All of these figures have weaknesses, and for centuries artists have exploited those vulnerabilities in their works. In Ernst Herter's 1885 statue of a dying Achilles, the demigod winces from pain as he grips the arrow through his heel. In Francisco de Zurburán's *Crucifixion* from 1627, Christ's face is pallid and gaunt, and his expression is one of exhaustion and suffering. These representations are far cries from the impenetrable visages of all-powerful beings but these signs of humanity are intentionally employed here by the artists to create points of entry and connection for viewers.

This same approach holds true among the so-called Zeus and Hera of American mythology, Superman and Wonder Woman. Humanizing these national deities can be read as a continuation of a longstanding tradition, and artists often do this in one of two ways: either by intentionally inverting or removing existing abilities or by highlighting a shortcoming already in place. In so doing, these artists employ these characters' vulnerabilities as platforms upon which to discuss a broader swath of issues. What is sometimes lost is a consideration of both the nuanced popular culture references of the heroes alongside discussions more directly related to art world concerns. In a conversation ahead of this exhibition, the artist Robert Pruitt stated, "I wish more people would talk about my work the way they talk about comics," meaning with an eye toward the narrative and backstory of each of the characters and references within each work.[6] The rest of this essay attempts to do just that while also grounding these discussions squarely within an art world context.

In the case of Jason Bard Yarmosky's painting *Wintered Fields*, it is difficult to even consider the content of the work without first addressing the

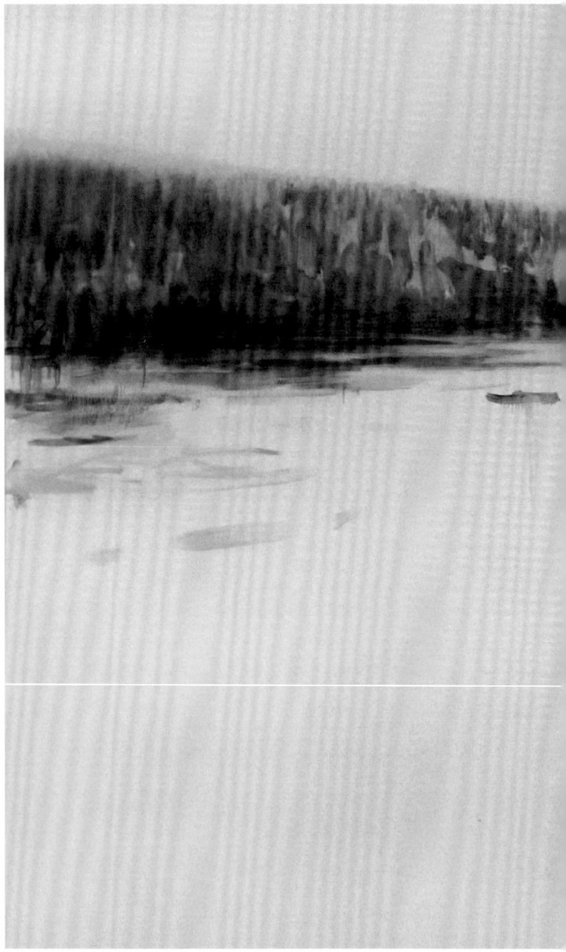

Jason Bard Yarmosky, *Wintered Fields*, 2016. Oil on canvas. Courtesy of the artist.

utterly striking technical skill. Rendered in grayscale, these are textbook accurate proportions and elegantly painted features that help realize the aging female figure to jaw-dropping perfection. For most viewers, painting this realistically is about as attainable a goal as suiting up in a star-spangled outfit and blocking bullets with metal cuffs. To this end, Yarmosky's work is rather isolating, perhaps in a way that is not so separate from the perceived perfection imbued into a character like Wonder Woman. And yet viewers are still able to connect with this painting. Indeed, for some, Yarmosky's incredible abilities are what draw them to the work in the first place, allowing them to then delve into the subject matter.

Standing slightly hunched and peering directly out toward the viewer, the elderly woman in the center panel emerges from a dreamlike, loosely painted winter scene in the background. Sporting the iconic starred briefs and W-emblazoned top, she is easily identified as a

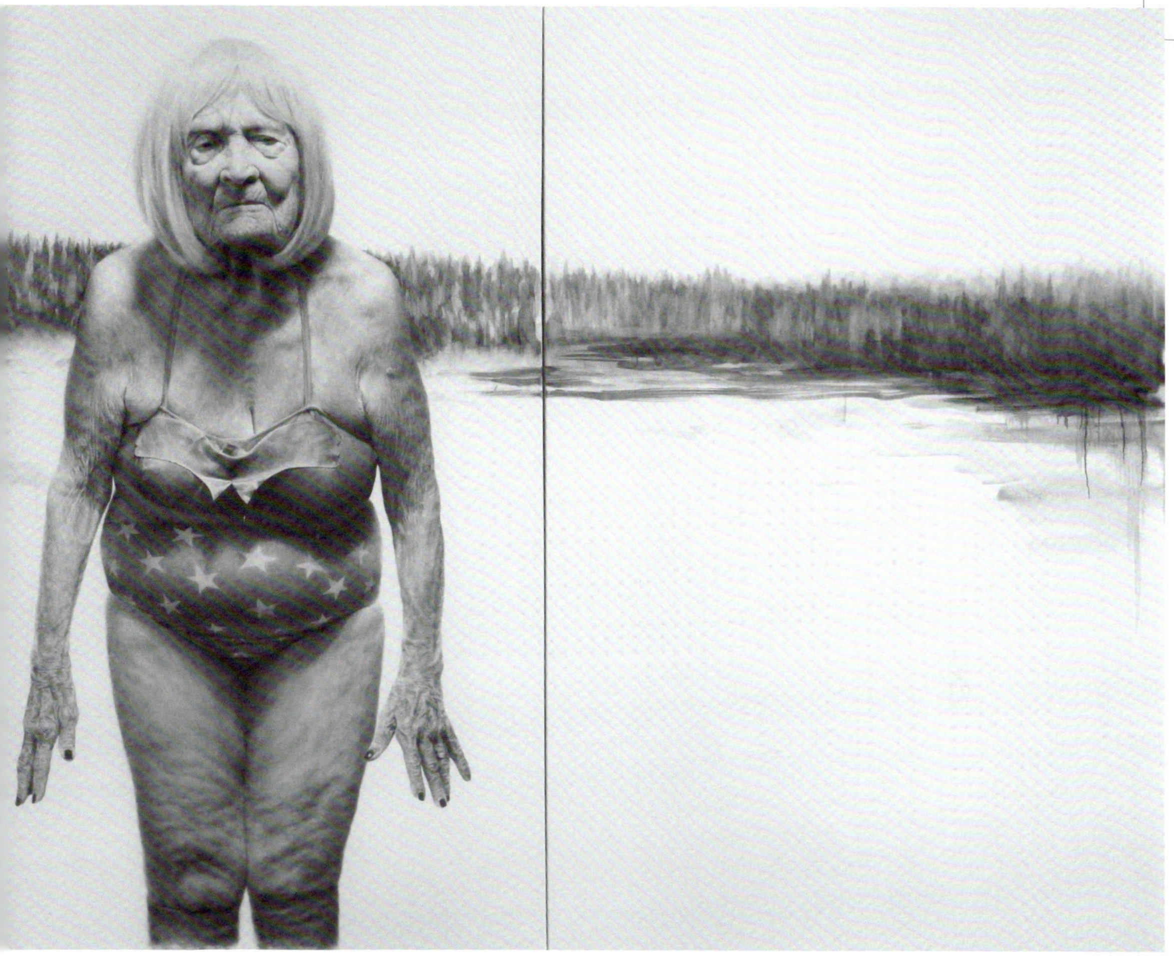

Since the beginning of time we continue to seek comfort in a life we have little control over. Our culture loves superheroes, godlike figures that we tend to put on pedestals. We celebrate these iconic symbols impervious to harm. What we often overlook is another important dimension to their character—their vulnerability, a quality that makes us truly human. My grandmother was a wonder woman to me. Her heroic battle with Alzheimer's Disease left her vulnerable. In my work Wintered Fields, *I wanted to contrast her age and predicament with this symbolic costume to show both the heroism and vulnerability of the human condition.* —**JASON BARD YARMOSKY**

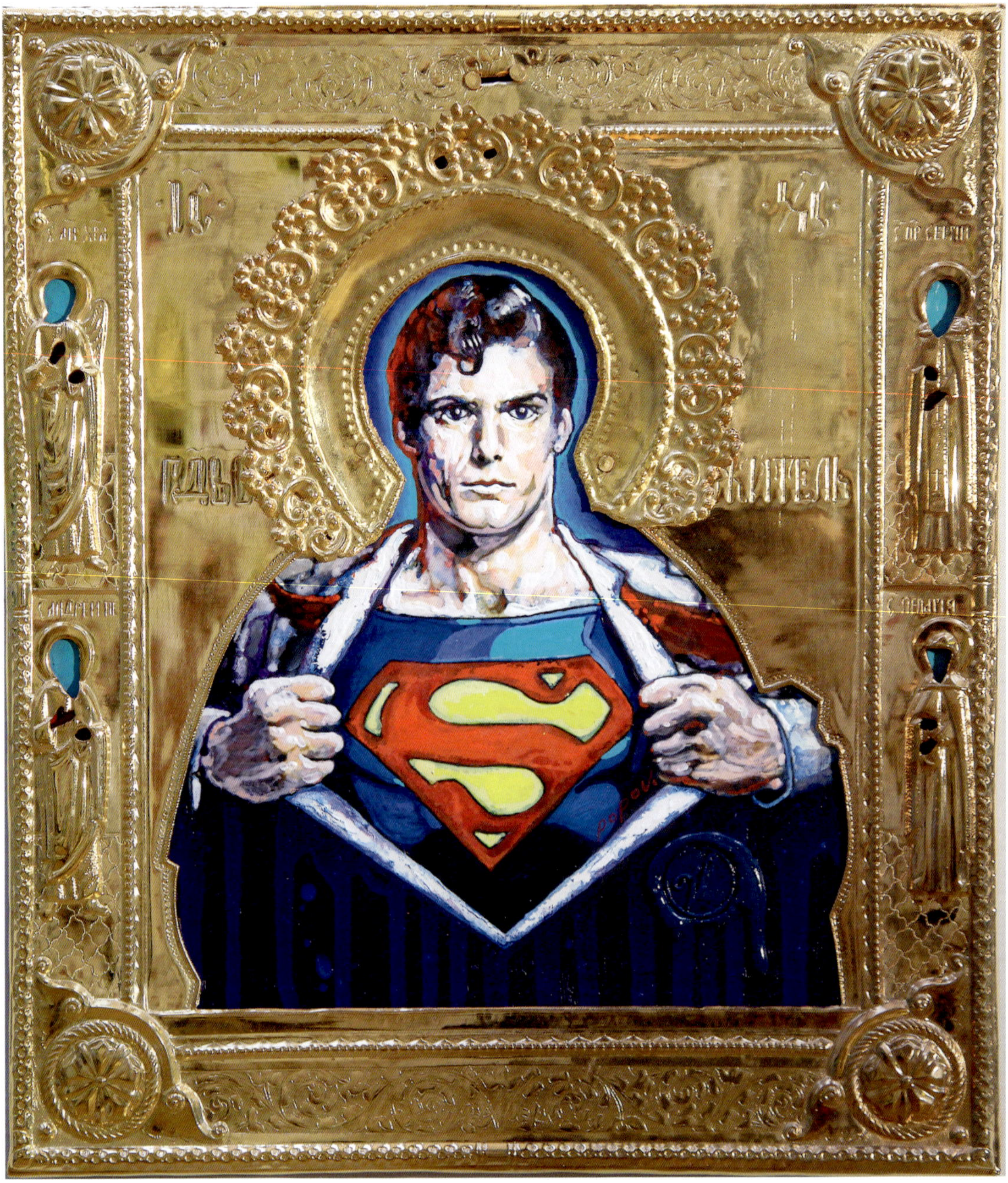

Since launching my St. Batman *project in 1994, I have continued to explore the theme of the superhero in contemporary consciousness. Exemplars of a modern mythology, Superman, Wonder Woman, and their superpowered siblings serve as guardians and saviors of humanity, replacing the gods and heroes of classical antiquity and performing an almost religious function. They also serve as poetic expressions of humanity's frailties, vulnerabilities, aspirations and ideals and act as universal metaphors for the conflation of high- and low-brow imagery, the fusion of pedigreed and popular elements permeating the current cultural terrain.* **—VALENTIN POPOV**

Valentin Popov, *St. Superman*, 2009. Oil on wood block with eighteenth-century 24 karat gold-plated oclad. Courtesy of the artist and Modernism Inc., San Francisco.

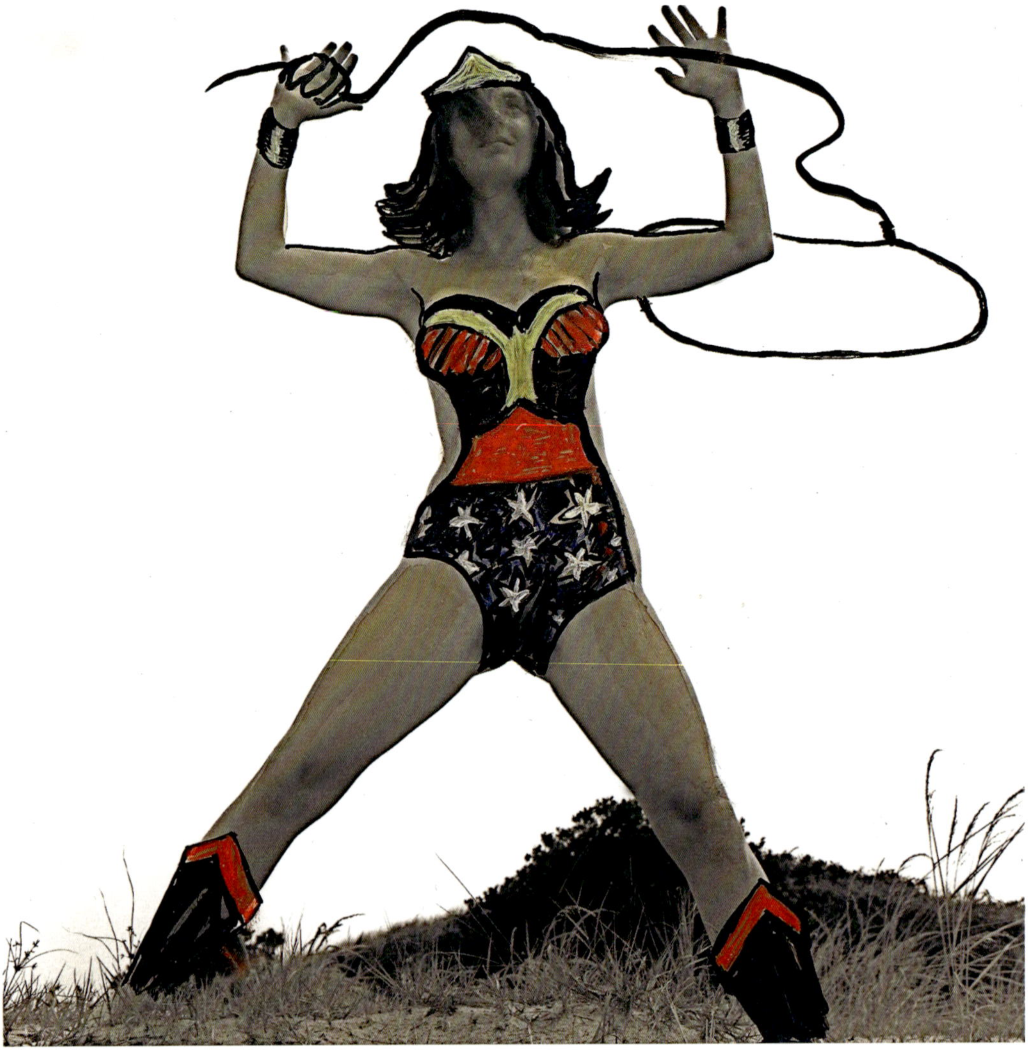

Mary Beth Edelson, *To the Rescue*, 1973. Oil and ink on silver gelatin print. Collection of Amy Gold and Brett Gorvy.

reference to Wonder Woman. But this is a far stretch from the youthful and confident heroine typically depicted. This is a direct inversion of the very qualities that often define the Amazon Princess. Yarmosky's painting prompts viewers to reassess how society values appearance and the able-bodied, creating space for other attributes to be considered.

Wintered Fields is one work from a series featuring Yarmosky's grandmother who lived with Alzheimer's for multiple years. According to the artist, on one hand the work "captures the emotion of not being in control, lost even."[7] This is represented by the vast murky expanse in the background and the pensive expression on his grandmother's face as she "[confronts] the viewer with psychological vulnerability."[8] However, by featuring this costume, the work also underscores Yarmosky's admiration for his grandmother as a kind of wonder woman in her own right. Her bravery during her battle with Alzheimer's is in a way akin to the bravery expressed weekly in Wonder Woman comics. To this end, it draws a real-world and human connection to the otherwise unattainably superheroic bravery championed by the heroine.

Bravery is certainly an important attribute associated with these characters, but power is perhaps the most immediate way society understands these heroes. One need only see the aspiring body builder sporting a Superman shirt at the gym to understand the shorthand for strength. And because a character like Superman so readily elicits conversations around this theme, he became a perfect subject for the artist Laylah Ali. Power has been the ongoing focus of her work: the amount some people have over others, the lack held by certain groups, and how visual cues communicate the possession of power to society.

For Ali and American culture at large, part of Superman's strength as a heroic figure comes from his iconic look. Since his inception, everything from his belt and underwear worn on the outside to his bulging pectorals functioned to immediately communicate his physical might.[9] Therefore it creates a moment of pause when Ali presents a work like *Untitled* in which three caped and booted figures look otherwise radically unlike the known hero. In Ali's work the figures are frail, the iconic square jawline is rounded and masked, their skin is green, and the expressions on their faces are ones of surprise, unease, or perhaps even terror. Gone are the muscles, and apparently, gone is the ever-important power of flight as arms and legs flail in the air.

In an article discussing images of bodies in free fall, the scholar

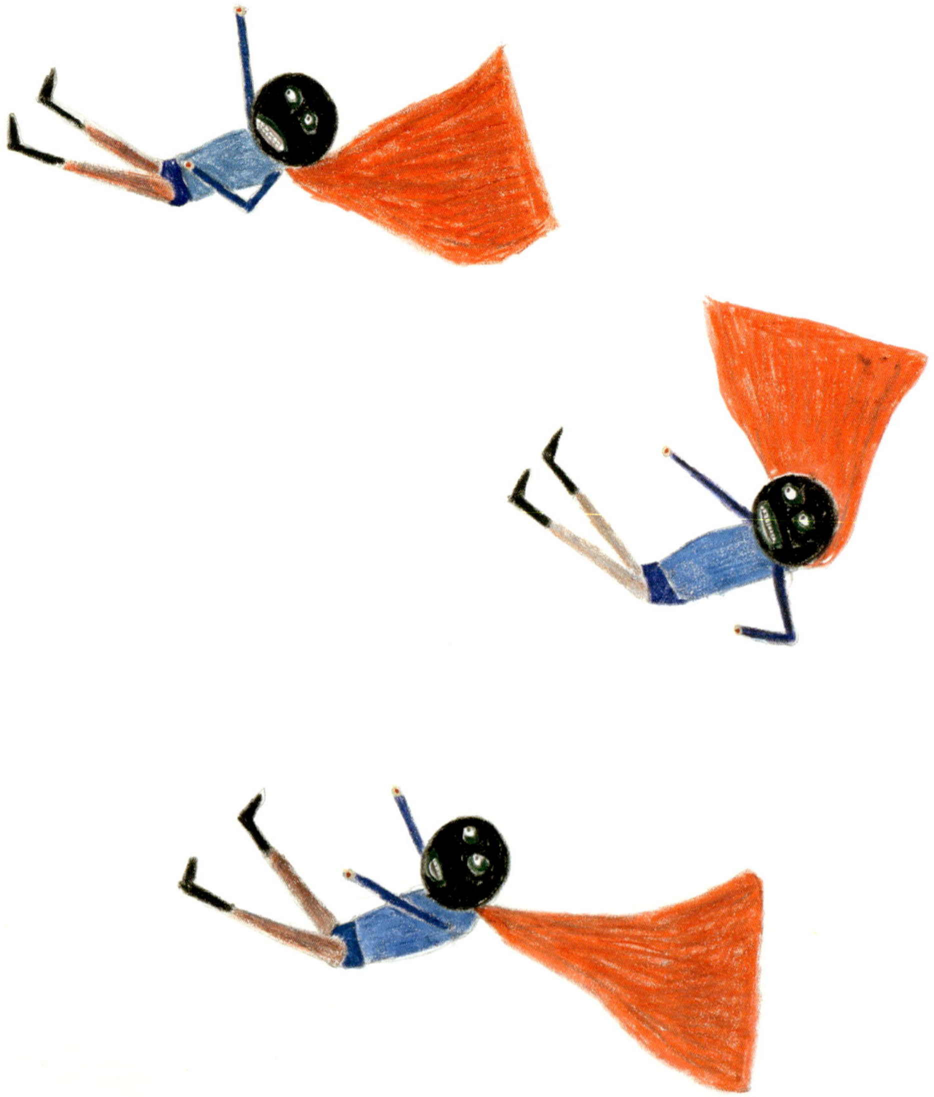

↑ Laylah Ali, *Untitled*, 2005. Colored pencil and graphite on paper. Collection Walker Art Center, Minneapolis, Miriam and Erwin Kelen Acquisition Fund for Drawings, 2005.

→ Laylah Ali, *Untitled*, 2005. Colored pencil and graphite on paper. Collection Walker Art Center, Minneapolis, Miriam and Erwin Kelen Acquisition Fund for Drawings, 2005.

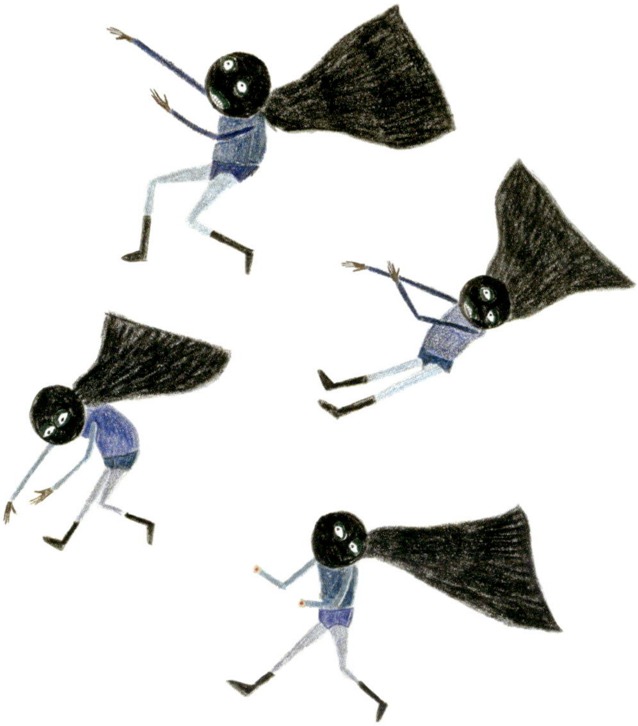

First, it's about the cape. It's a mark in the sky. Sometimes it looks like a question mark.

Second, it's about defying. They can't fly for long—or even at all. They are pulled aside and are prevented from entering the sky by Sky Patrol.

Third, they won't die. It's remarkable how adept they are at refusing death.

Despair is harder to avoid. They curl up on the floor sometimes, knees to chin and weep until they can't breathe.

But then—they are up. Dry-mouthed and dazed, seeking water. **—LAYLAH ALI**

Andrea D. Fitzpatrick argued that falling figures make viewers acutely aware of the vulnerability of the human body.[10] This stems from what she calls "the awareness of mutual vulnerability" and the immediate rush of empathy emerging from a realization of one's own mortality.[11] In regard to Ali's work, while no viewer can fly like Superman, by suddenly removing flight from these characters, she provides a point of entry, empathy, and a platform for consideration of an uneven power dynamic.

Her falling heroes in this work come from her *Greenheads* series, whose figures are described as "homogenous, androgynous, dark-skinned characters."[12] Ali's greenheads are intentionally not a specific race but instead are meant to simply be read as people of color. Using the tropes of Superman as a point of access, she removes attributes associated with his power like muscles or flight. This draws attention to societal imbalances preventing many minorities opportunities to progress, represented here quite literally by preventing people of color the ability to soar.

These superhuman abilities emphasize the ultimate power of these two characters. While the accomplishments of their feats are predicated on their abilities to complete physical actions, they are also the foundation of perhaps their most humanizing attributes. While people often say "it's lonely at the top" when underscoring the sense of loneliness felt by a person in power, this sense of isolation is only further deepened when one adds superhuman abilities into the mix.

For Superman and Wonder Woman, their only true equals are their fellow members of the Justice League—and with all of them doing their own crime fighting—each spends most of their time independently.[13] With so much power at their disposal, these characters constantly bear the weight of responsibility for earth's well-being on their shoulders.

Llyn Foulkes, *Where did I go wrong?*, 1991. Oil and mixed media on board. Collection of Alan Hergott and Curt Shepard.

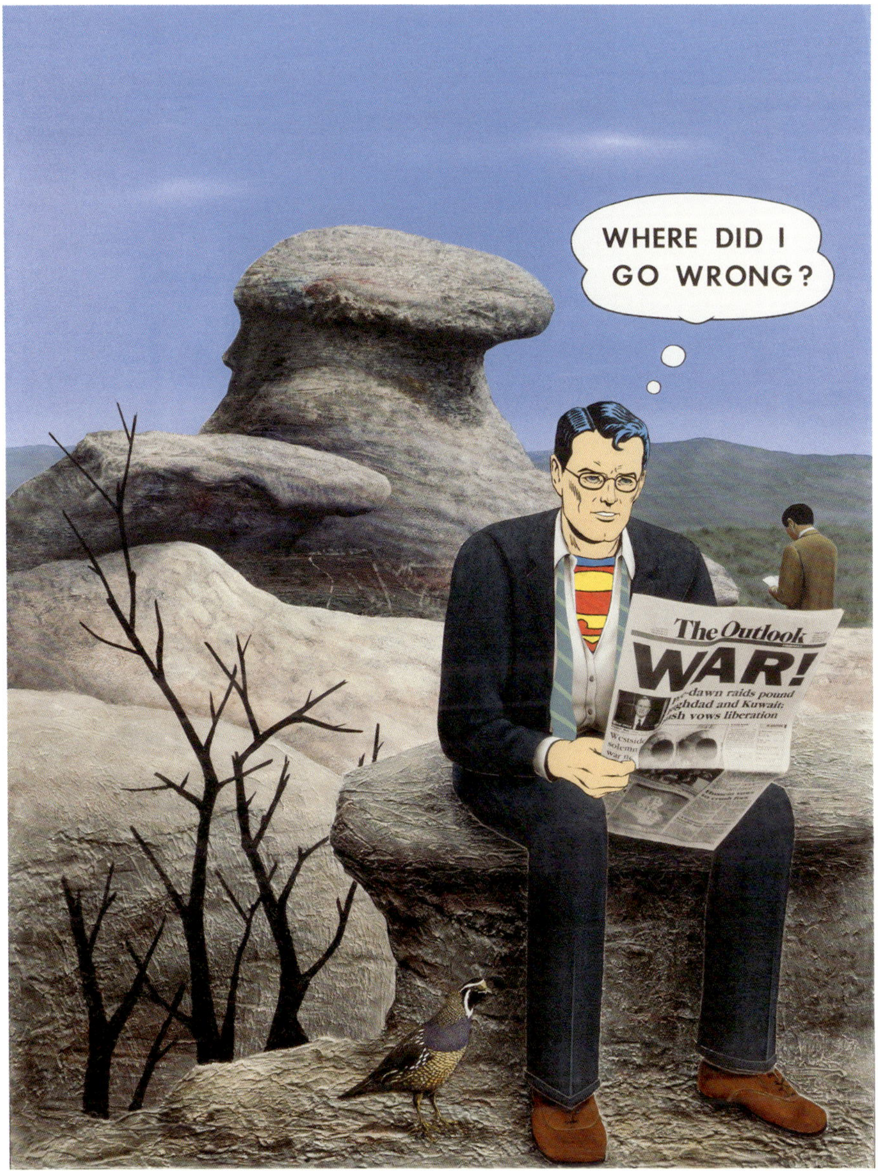

This painting was done as a response to the ever-expanding reach of capitalism. With George Bush Sr. as President of the United States and Dan Quayle as Vice President, here represented by a live quail and dead bush at the feet of Clark Kent, our nation found itself in the Gulf War. Superman had always represented America; a super nation. In this painting Superman finds himself superseded by big money and greed. Tucked into the landscape, a Japanese man is wondering if there is anything left to purchase, representing the bubble that had peaked in 1988 and recently burst.

—LLYN FOULKES

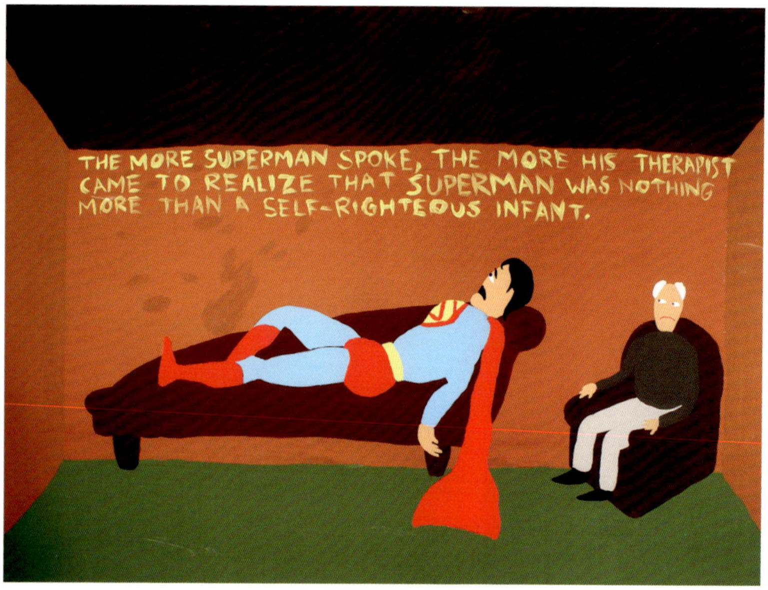

When something goes wrong they carry the guilt of that oversight, a point Llyn Foulkes notes in his work *Where Did I Go Wrong?* When faced with the day-to-day psychological turmoil of their jobs, their enormous abilities make them difficult to console, as is the case with Jayson Musson's painting *Superman's Therapist* in which even his therapist is unable to sympathize with the Man of Steel. Superman is so isolated from the world that his frozen tundra secret lair is even named the Fortress of Solitude. Of all the myriad artists contending with Superman in their work, likely none dealt with isolation and loss more than Mike Kelley. His expansive *Kandors* series ran for the final twelve years of the artist's life in one state or another. While perhaps the most strikingly beautiful works belong to the later years of the series, during which time *Kandor 17* was made, it is one of the earlier works that is the focus of this essay: *Superman Recites Selections from 'The Bell Jar' and Other Works by Sylvia Plath.*

Jayson Musson, *Superman's Therapist*, 2009. Tempera on paper. Destroyed.

Filmed on a decidedly lo-fi 8 mm camera, the square-chinned actor portraying Superman looks the part even while uniformed in what appears to be a drugstore supersuit. The entire aesthetic of the work is humble and imperfect. Unlike the beautifully cast resin cities and massive custom-blown bell jars that comprise the later *Kandors*, the

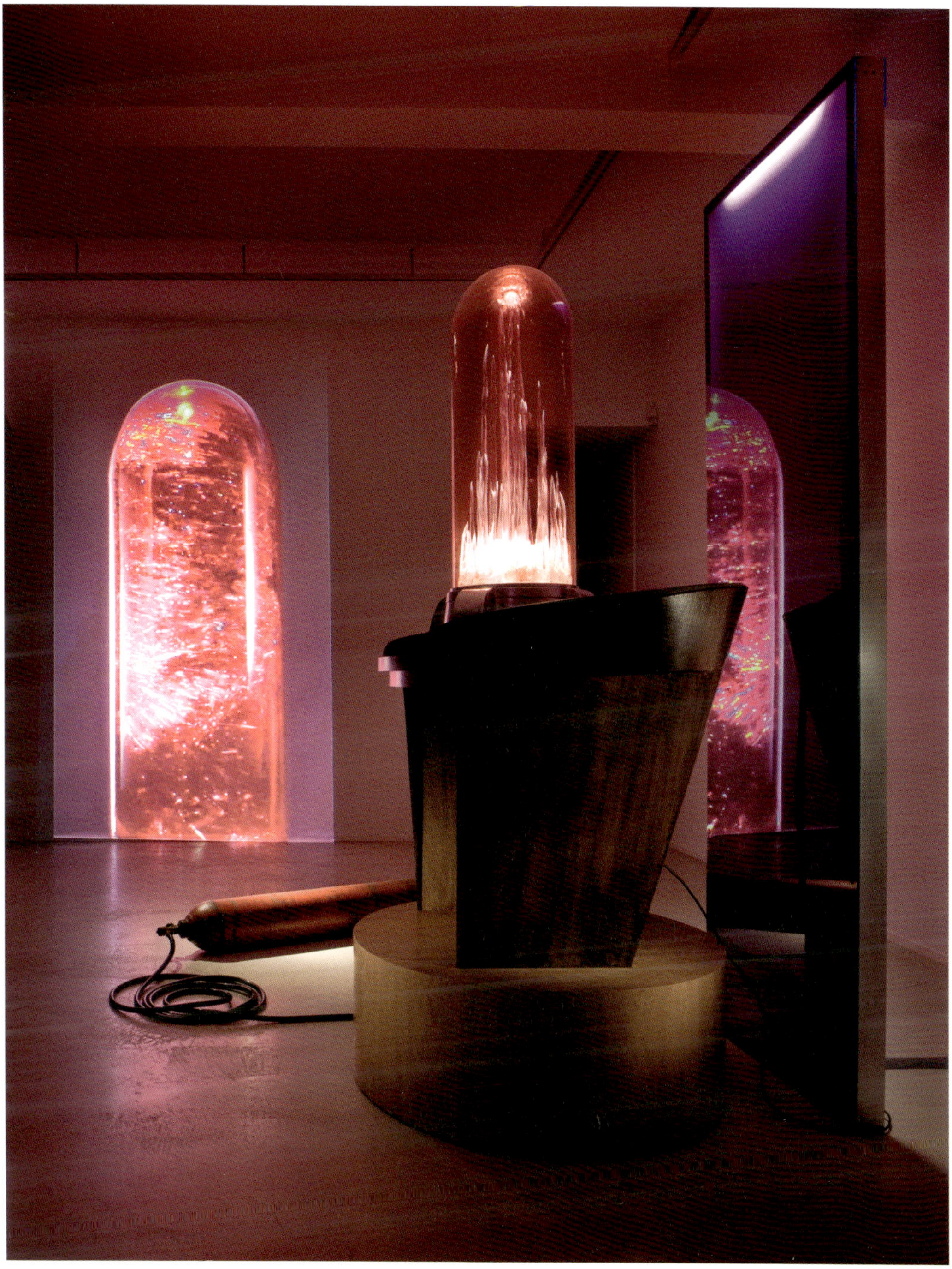

Mike Kelley, *Kandor 17*, 2007 (edition of 2). Mixed media with video, sound. Mike Kelley Foundation.

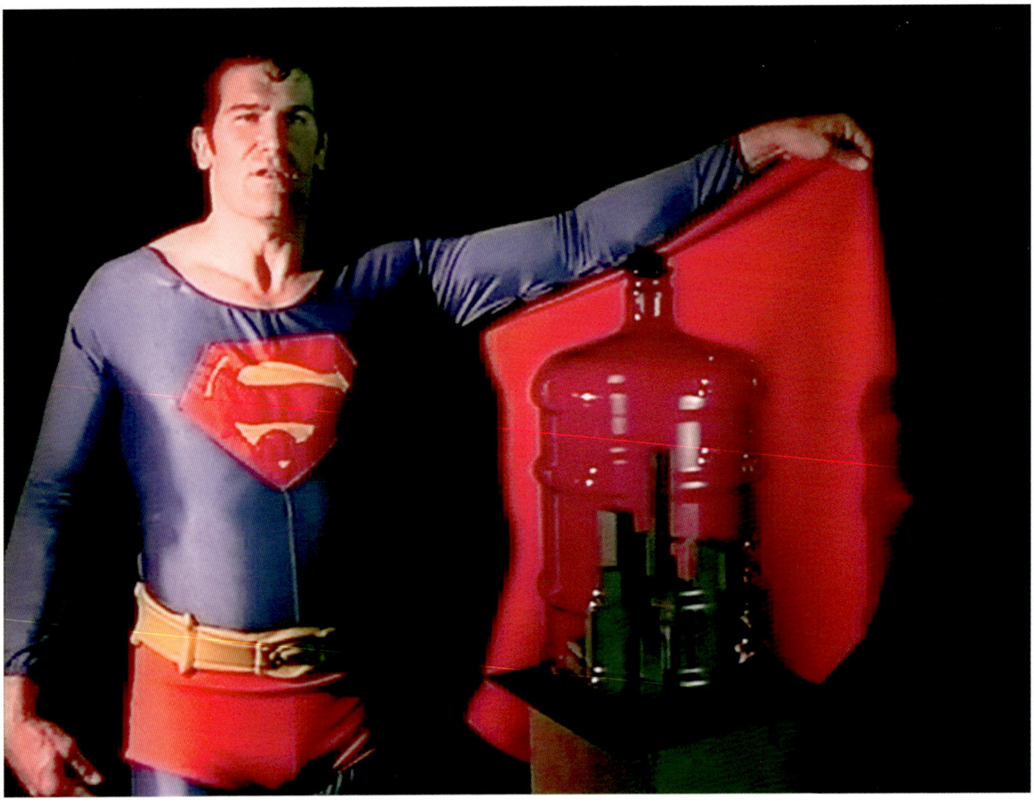

↑ Mike Kelley, *Superman Recites Selections from 'The Bell Jar' and Other Works by Sylvia Plath,* 1999. Video. Mike Kelley Foundation.

→ Raymond Pettibon, *No Title (Do you see . . .),* 2015. Ink and acrylic on paper. Courtesy the artist and David Zwirner.

bottle city in the film appears to be a water jug, similar to those used in an office water cooler. In the comics, Kandor was a bizarre thirty-year-long story arc in which the capital city of Superman's home planet was shrunken down along with its inhabitants and kept in a bell jar in Superman's Fortress of Solitude. The ultimate destruction of the city and the marooning of the inhabitants in a different dimension while under Superman's care means that Kandor is now understood as a symbol of Superman's failure and continued isolation on earth.[14] In fitting anguish, the video by Kelley positions Superman gazing longingly at the bottle city reciting all of the passages from Sylvia Plath's book that use the imagery of a bell jar.

Superman appears in a dark void that Kelley described as "evocative of Superman's own psychic 'Fortress of Solitude,' " which reminds viewers just how alone the hero must feel.[15] Plath's book deals with invented identities, depression, societal expectations placed upon the

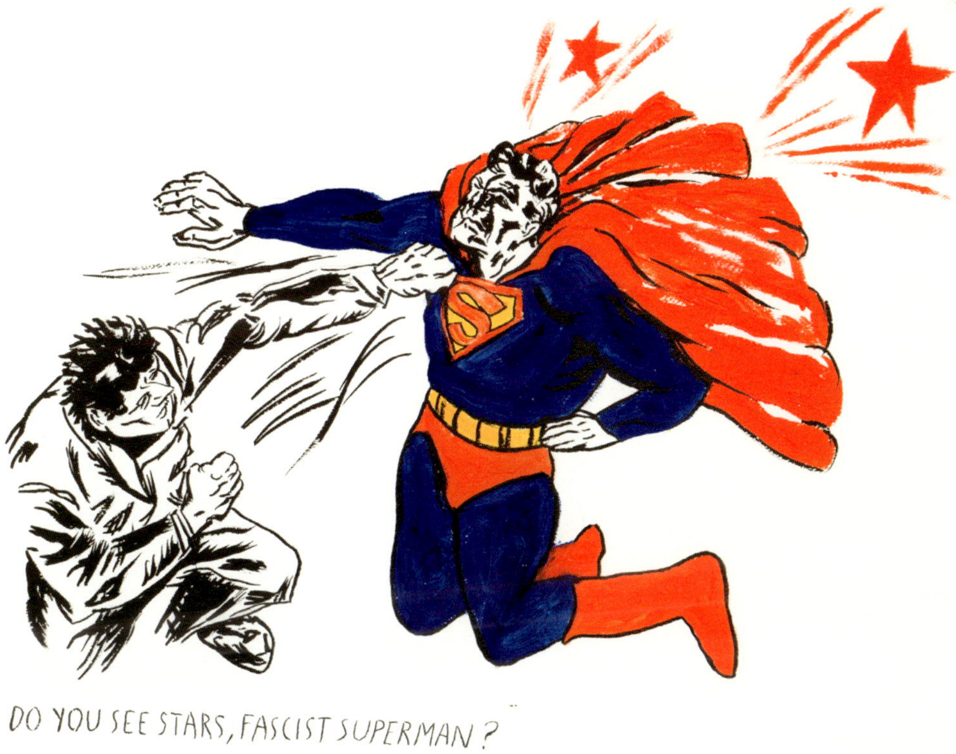

I've never read a superhero comic to the end nor watched a superhero film. Missed out on a lot of box office. Comics fandom puzzles me as much as video games. However, I owe a debt to comics, which is apparent for all to see in my own work—the lingua franca style of golden age comics and certain cultural archetypes, namely Superman and Batman. I have affection and admiration for Superman's Siegel and Shuster, who created the character at fifteen years old but were renamed by the superpowers-at-be brutally thenceforward. Not a happy ending. And for Bob Kane (with great help from other hands), creator of Batman. I have my own Superman/Batman script extant but gathering dust. Someday it may be realised on planet Earth or Krypton.

—RAYMOND PETTIBON

protagonist, and the recurring symbol of the bell jar indicating both her own entrapment and society's unwillingness to change. Reading aloud, Superman bellows phrases like, "I tried to picture my world, and the people in it through a distorted lens, a bell jar" before a campy transition leads to Superman shrieking in pain as he continues to recite the passage. Though written by Plath as a vulnerable response to the pressures of a decidedly unheroic humanity, when recited here by Superman the performance seems oddly fitting. Unlike the previous examples by Yarmosky and Ali, there is no removal of ability in this artistic rendering of the hero. Instead Kelley simply presses down on the existing isolation of ultimate power and pairs the pop icon with a well-known literary component. The result is a cerebral juxtaposition in which Kelley does not force humanity onto the Man of Steel but rather invites consideration of that which already exists within the hero.

The artworks discussed throughout this essay peel back the veil of perfection frequently draped over Superman and Wonder Woman. When the artists expose weaknesses in these characters, they bring them down to a human level, reiterating the appropriateness of this section's title, *Glimpsing Humanity*. In those moments of fear or loss, the characters reveal their vulnerabilities, providing a narrow opening for viewers to slip in and relate to an otherwise omnipotent god.

But these chinks in the armor are not confined to works solely in the *Glimpsing Humanity* section. Viewers see super heroic imperfections when Renée Cox calls out Wonder Woman for lacking a diverse scope of innocents worthy of saving, when Margaret Harrison replaces Superman's genitals to call attention to patriarchal power structures, or when Mel Casas pointedly calls out heroes like Superman for

Laurie Anderson, Documention Performing *O Superman*, 1982.

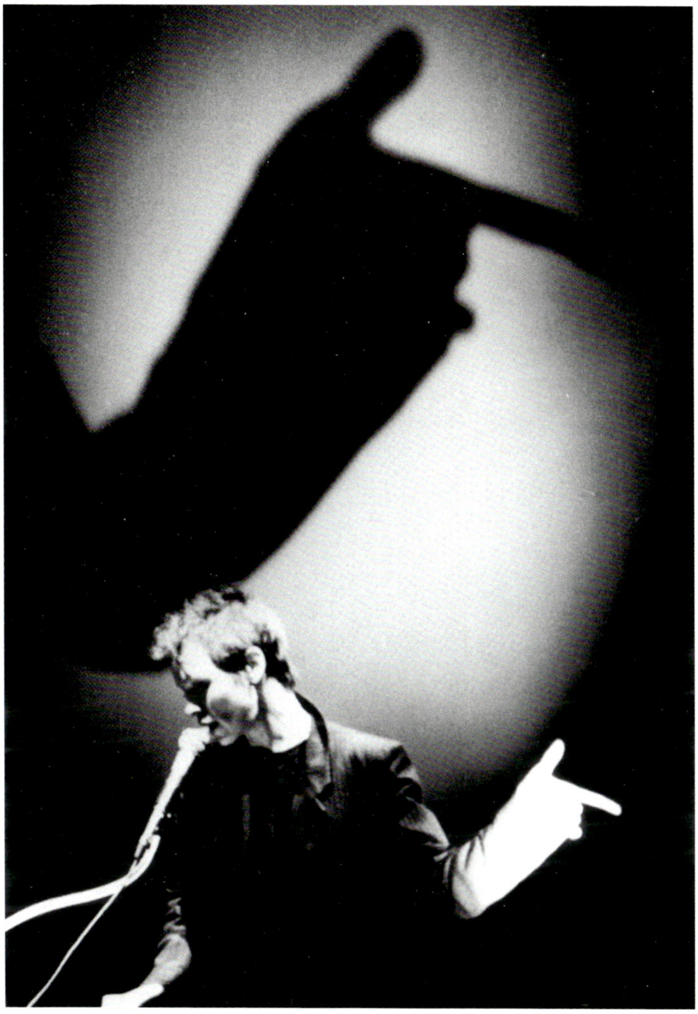

I based my song "O Superman" on a song by Jules Massenet from the 1885 opera Le Cid. *Here are his lyrics and then mine.*

> *"O Sovereign, o Judge, o Father, always hidden yet always present,*
>
> *I worshipped You in time of success, and bless You in these dark days.*
>
> *I go where Your law commands, free of all human regret."*
>
> *"O Superman. O judge. O Mom and Dad.*
>
> *Hi. I'm not home right now. But if you want to leave a message,*
> *just start talking at the sound of the tone.*
>
> *Hello? This is your Mother. Are you there? Are you coming home?*
>
> *Hello? Is anybody home?"*

—LAURIE ANDERSON

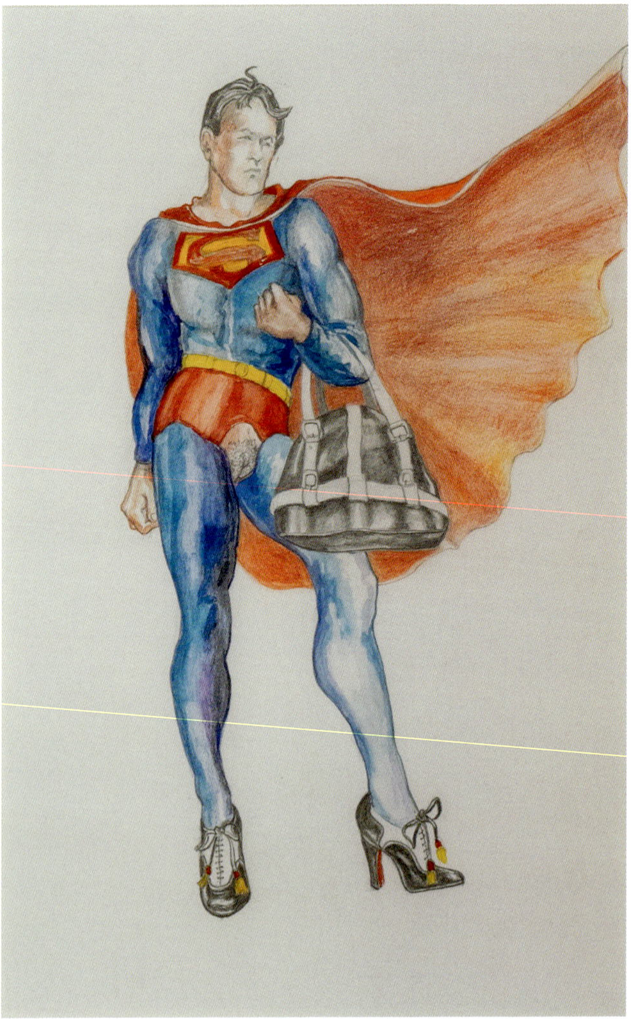

Margaret Harrison, *The Healthier Choice*, 2007. Watercolor and drawing materials. Courtesy of the artist and Ronald Feldman Gallery, New York.

perpetuating a white savior narrative. When artists expose these shortcomings in these beloved heroes it sometimes seems like a personal attack. But what it actually does is remind viewers that these characters are imperfect. And to that end, the critiques of them become points of connection for audiences. They become ways to bring America's gods down to earth. And for those who might fear that these actions will damage their idols, I offer this reminder: these are superheroes—they can take it. And indeed their long histories of acting as the watchers of society have proven that when they are used as platforms to discuss societal issues, they always come out unscathed, more relevant, and ultimately more powerful because of it.

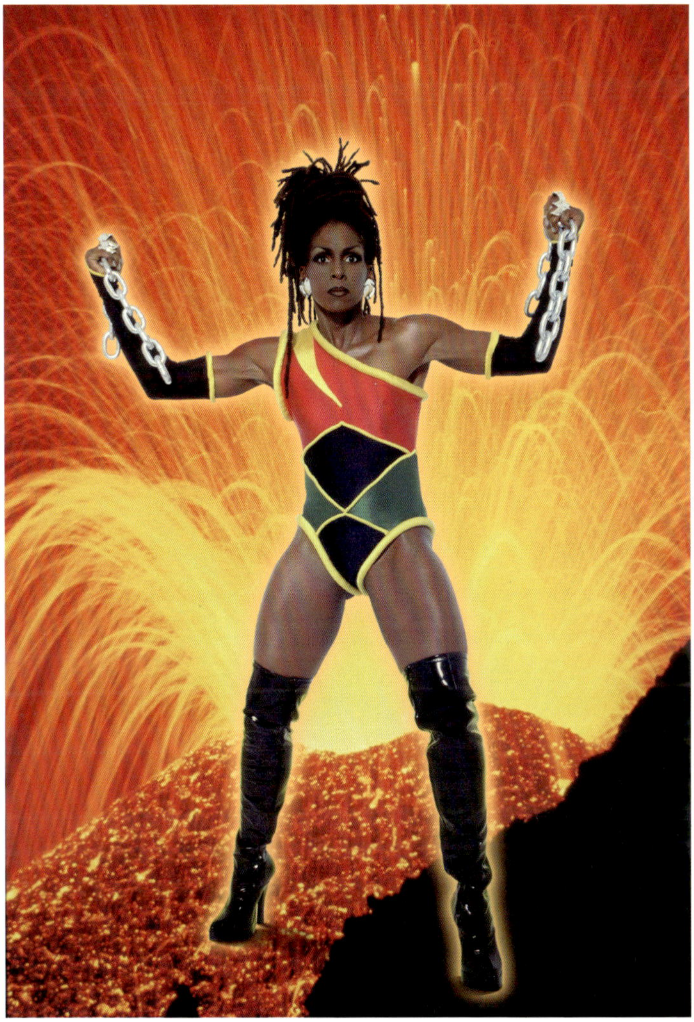

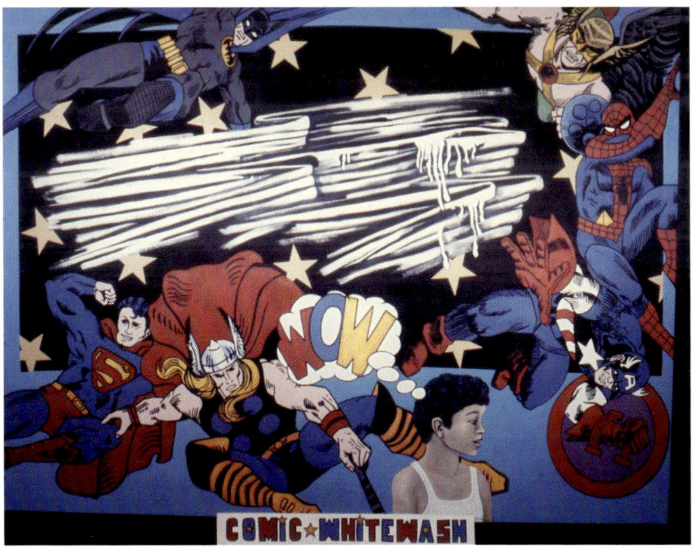

↑ Renée Cox, *Eruption* (from the Rajé Series), 1998. Cibachrome print. Courtesy of the artist.

← Mel Casas, *Humanscape 70 (Comic Whitewash)*, 1970. Acrylic on canvas. Mel Casas Family Trust.

ALEJO BENEDETTI

Alejo Benedetti is an assistant curator at Crystal Bridges Museum of American Art. Since joining the museum in 2015, Benedetti has organized and led a number of temporary exhibitions, including *Black Unity; Animal Meet Human; How Do You Figure?*; and *Men of Steel, Women of Wonder*. In 2016 he acted as the venue curator for *The Art of American Dance*, an exhibition that traveled to Crystal Bridges from the Detroit Institute of Art. Benedetti contributed to the 2018 exhibition catalog *The Beyond: Georgia O'Keeffe and Contemporary Art*. Benedetti lives in Northwest Arkansas with his wife, two dogs, and a steadily growing comic book collection.

Notes

1 Glen Weldon, *Superman: The Unauthorized Biography* (Hoboken, NJ: John Wiley & Sons, 2013), 1.

2 Depending on which origin story one adheres to, she was either formed out of clay and granted life by the Gods or is in fact the daughter of Zeus himself.

3 The philosopher Leonard Finkelman refers to this as being biologically inhuman but for all intents and purposes, being "morally human." Leonard Finkelman, "What A Kryptonian Can Teach Us About Humanity," in *Superman and Philosophy*, ed. Mark D. White, (Hoboken, NJ: Wiley-Blackwell), 171–73.

4 Mark D. White "Moral Judgment: The Power that Makes Superman Human," in *Superman and Philosophy*, ed. Mark D. White, (Hoboken, NJ: Wiley-Blackwell), 5.

5 Vanessa Van Edwards, "Why Showing Vulnerability the First Time You Meet Someone Is a Genius Idea," *Medium*, April 25, 2017, https://medium.com/thrive-global/why-showing-vulnerability-the-first-time-you-meet-someone-is-a-genius-idea-cf4db4a4967.

6 Robert Pruitt, in discussion with the author, November 29, 2017.

7 Jason Bard Yarmosky, email message to author, February 1, 2018.

8 Yarmosky.

9 Grant Morrison, *Supergods: What Masked Vigilantes, Miraculous Mutants, and a Sun God from Smallville Can Teach Us about Being Human* (New York: Spiegel & Grau, 2012), 14.

10 Andrea D. Fitzpatrick, "The Movement of Vulnerability: Images of Falling and September 11." *Art Journal* 66, no. 4 (2007): 85.

11 Fitzpatrick, 87.

12 "Laylah Ali's Greenheads Are More than They Seem (VIDEO, PHOTOS)" *Huffington Post*, January 16, 2012, https://www.huffingtonpost.com/2012/01/13/laylah-alis-powerful-comi_n_1205629.html.

13 The Justice League is a team of superheroes within the DC Comics universe that band together to protect against evildoers. Membership in this varies over the years but features heroes like Superman, Wonder Woman, Aquaman, Batman, The Flash, Cyborg, and Green Lantern, among many others.

14 For a much longer explanation of this story arc, see Otto O. Binder et al., *Superman: The Bottle City of Kandor* (New York: DC Comics, 2007).

15 Mike Kelley, quoted in "Superman Recites Selections from 'The Bell Jar' and Other Works by Sylvia Plath," Electronic Arts Intermix, June, 1 2018, *https://www.eai.org/titles/superman-recites-selections-from-the-bell-jar-and-other-works-by-sylvia-plath.*

MEN OF STEEL, WOMEN OF WONDER

ISSUE 02

ORIGIN STORIES

ERIKA DOSS

MEN OF STEEL, WOMEN OF WONDER

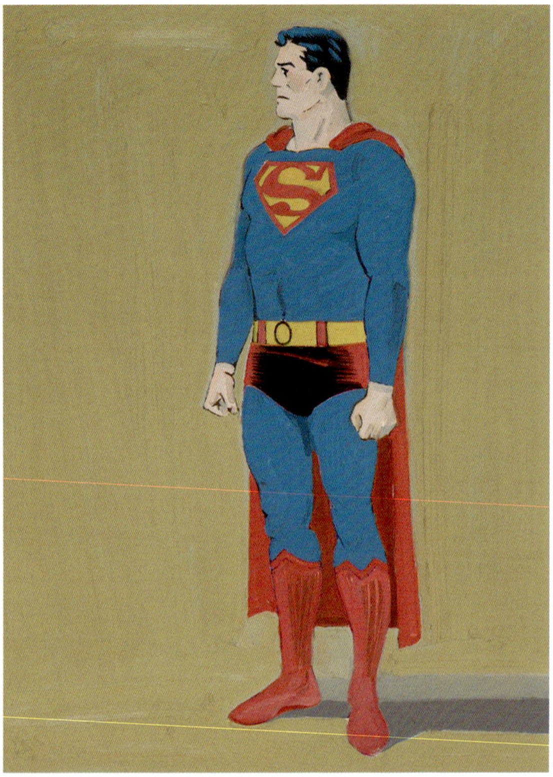

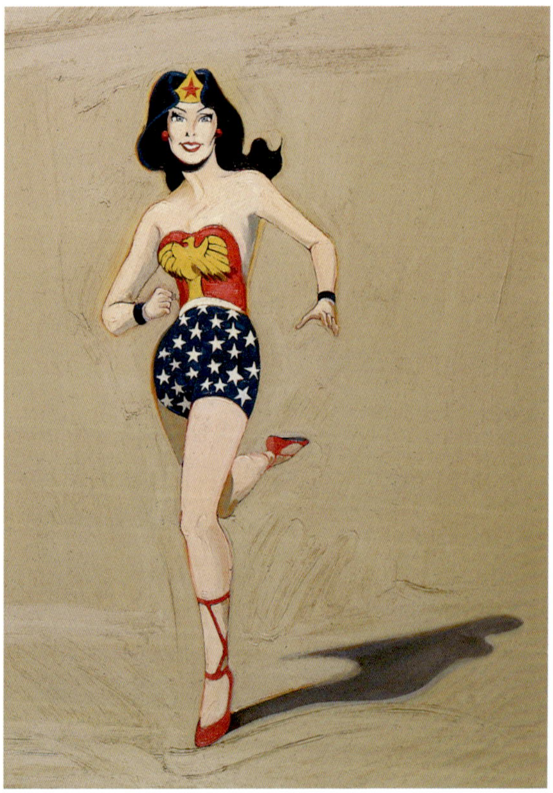

Manly Workers and Pin-up Girls

Sources for Comic Book Superheroes in 1930s American Visual Culture

ERIKA DOSS

The breadth of artistic license in the exhibition *Men of Steel, Women of Wonder* reveals both the visual perseverance and continual reinvention of comic book superheroes since they first appeared eighty years ago. Mel Ramos's Pop art canvases *Superman* and *Wonder Woman*, painted in 1962, were conceived by the artist as "a celebration of comic book heroes, in a heraldic way, the way Gainsborough would do a portrait."[1] Fahamu Pecou's self-portrait *Nunna My Heros: After Barkley Hendricks' 'Icon for My Man Superman,' 1969* (2011), by contrast, interrogates assumptions of all-white superheroes by showing a black man ripping open his shirt to reveal a Superman costume underneath. Scrawling the words "ain't nuthin but a sandwich" at the top of his painting's red, white, and blue frame further drives Pecou's astute critique. And Jacky Tsai's *Golden Fortune Tree* (2017), a fusion of traditional Chinese lacquer carving and cartoon style graphics in Dayglo colors, depicts Superman, Wonder Woman, and Batman banding together with classical Chinese characters to fight evil forces of rampant industrialization and environmental destruction (symbolized by pictures of Donald Trump, bulldozers, and assorted villains). Tsai, born in Shanghai and based in London, relates, "My first memory of American superheroes was watching the classic *Superman* movies with Christopher Reeve when I was a kid. He had superhuman strength, could travel a thousand miles in a flash and can see through everything, and I thought to myself, 'This is the American Monkey King!'"[2] Artists have been repeatedly drawn to the identity, adventures, and popularity of comic book superheroes since the genre debuted in the late 1930s.

Mel Ramos, *Superman*, 1962. Oil on canvas. Fine Arts Museums of San Francisco. Museum purchase. Dr. Leland A and Gladys K. Barber Fund and American Art Trust Fund.

Mel Ramos, *Wonder Woman*, 1962. Oil on canvas. Rochelle and Darren Leininger Family Collection.

Their popularity shows no sign of abating: in 2018, two of Hollywood's most profitable pictures were *Black Panther*, based on the comic

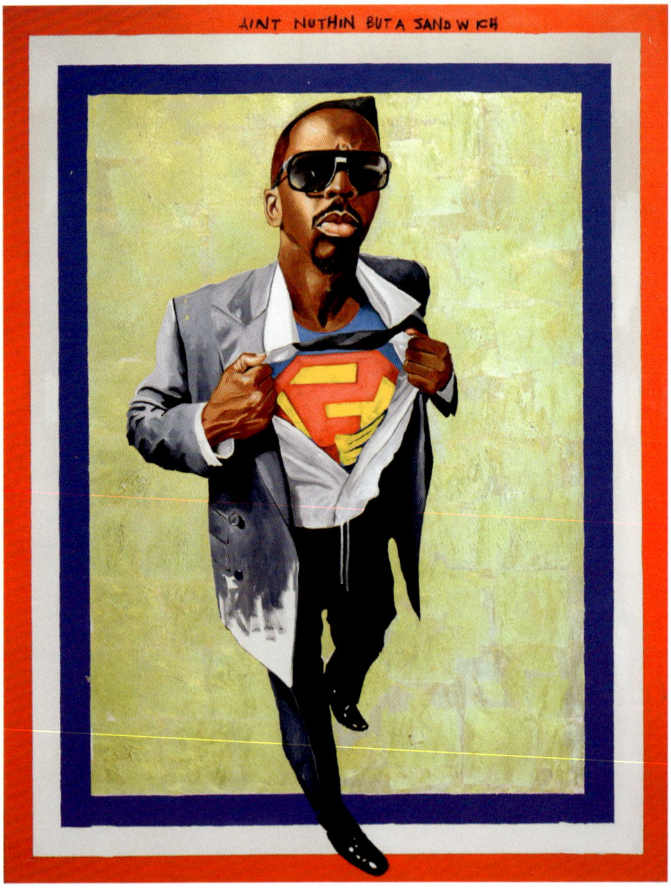

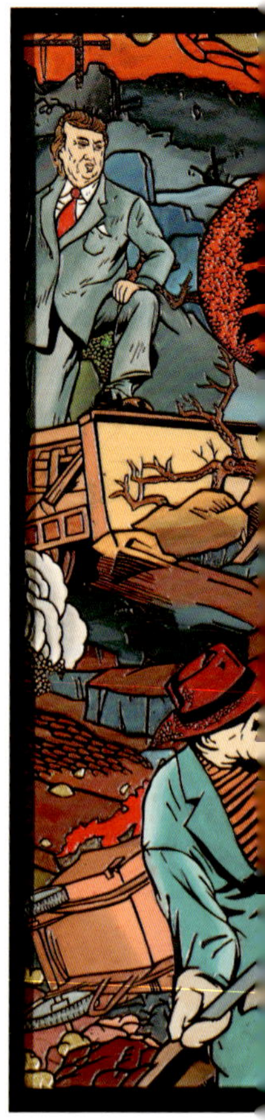

Fahamu Pecou, *Nunna My Heros: After Barkley Hendricks' 'Icon for My Man Superman,' 1969*, 2011. Acrylic, gold leaf, and oil stick on canvas. Nasher Museum of Art at Duke University. Gift of Marjorie and Michael Levine.

book superhero of the same name, and *Avengers: Infinity War*, an action-packed spectacle of superheroes including Iron Man, Thor, and the Hulk battling for the survival of the planet (and mostly losing, a dark ending guaranteeing a redemptive sequel). Both blockbusters were the products of the Marvel Cinematic Universe, an American media franchise of movies, TV shows, and theme park attractions (Disney acquired Marvel in 2009) that feature the fictional characters originally drawn for Marvel Comics, from Captain America (introduced in 1941) and Spider-Man (1962) to Black Panther (1966) and the Guardians of the Galaxy (1969). In 2017, many of America's top grossing movies—*Justice League*, *Guardians of the Galaxy Vol. 2*, *Thor: Ragnarok*, and *Wonder Woman*—were adapted from comic book characters originally created by Marvel or by its main competitor DC Comics, whose superhero pantheon includes the iconic trinity of Superman (introduced in 1938), Batman (1939) and

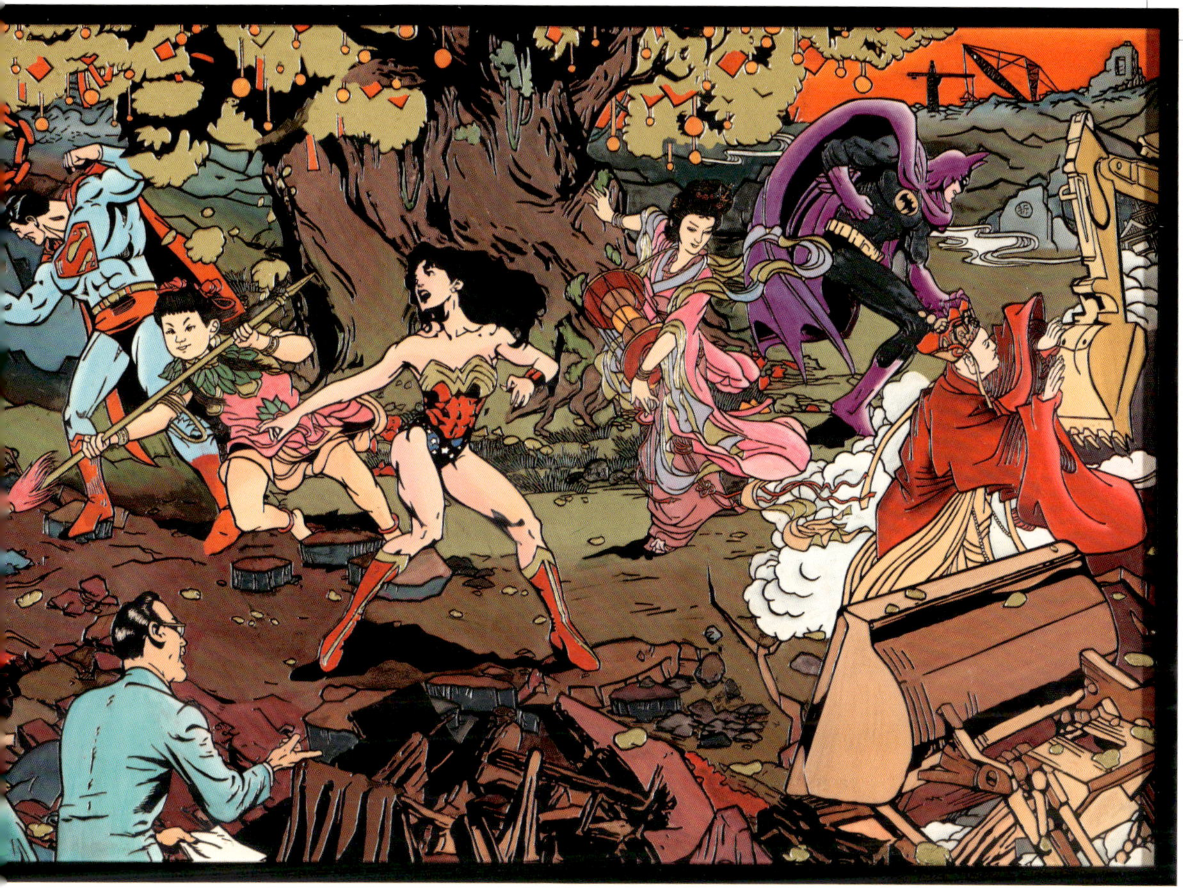

Wonder Woman (1941). In 2016, millions of American moviegoers similarly flocked to *Batman v. Superman: Dawn of Justice*, *Captain America: Civil War*, *Deadpool*, *Doctor Strange*, and *X-Men Apocalypse*.[3] Comic book movies featuring hard-bodied superheroes dishing out vigilante justice dominate today's box office, and more are on the way.

Often mistakenly identified as the escapist fare of teenagers, adults drive their ticket sales. Broadly speaking, mainstream movies—like other kinds of popular culture—reflect the values and feelings of their mass audiences, illuminating collective understandings of social relationships, gender roles, racial views, political cultures, legal processes, national identity, and more.[4] Today, as incendiary political discord, gun violence, racist and sexist denigration, and episodes of terrorism test American ideals of exceptionalism, democracy, equality, and invulnerability, the huge success of comic book-based movies suggests that

Jacky Tsai, *Golden Fortune Tree*, 2017. Lacquer carving on wood panel. Courtesy of the artist.

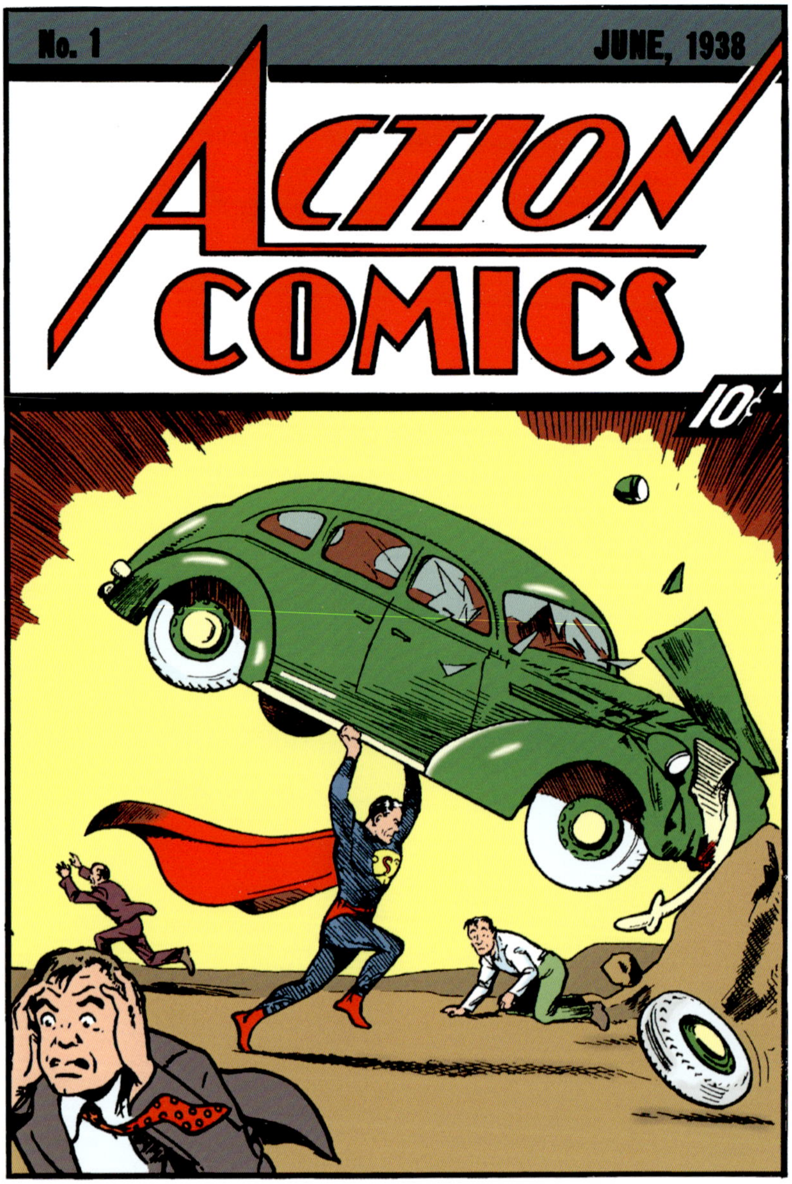

Joe Shuster, cover of *Action Comics* #1, June 1938. © DC Comics.

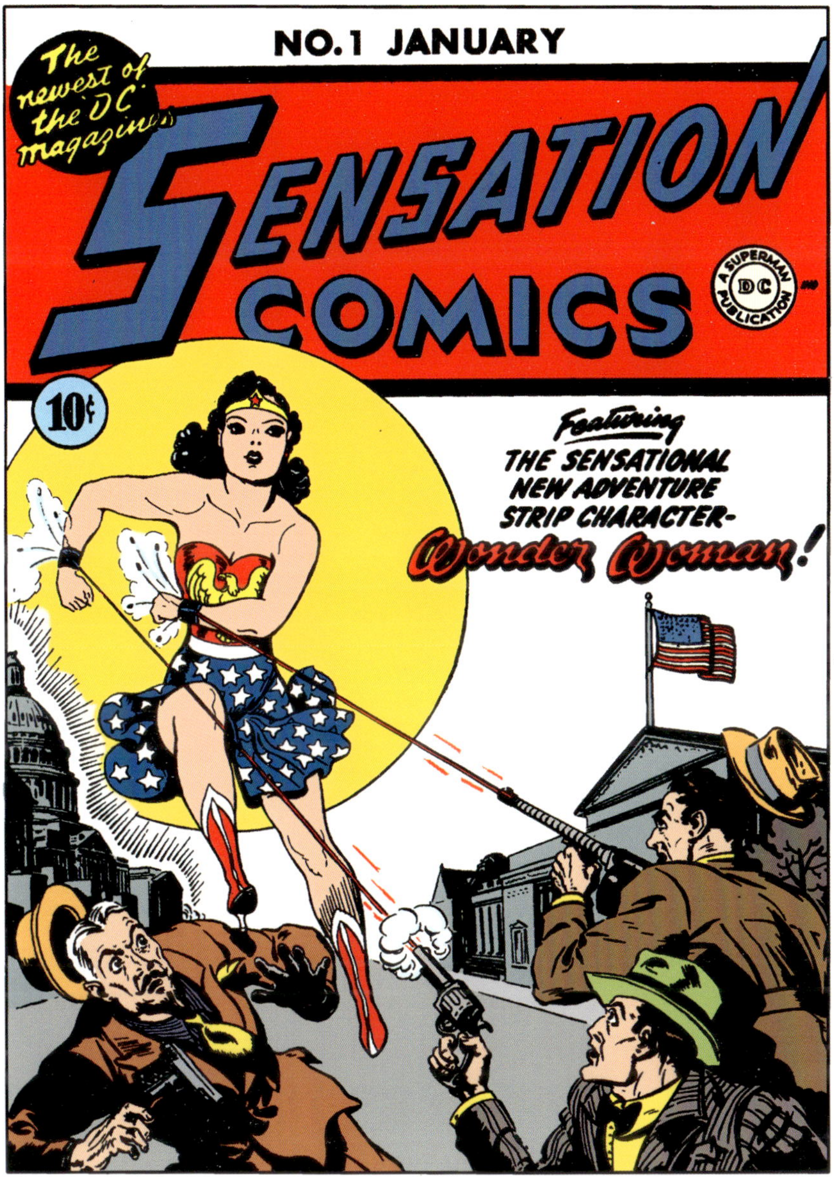

Harry G. Peter, cover of *Sensation Comics* #1, January 1942. © DC Comics.

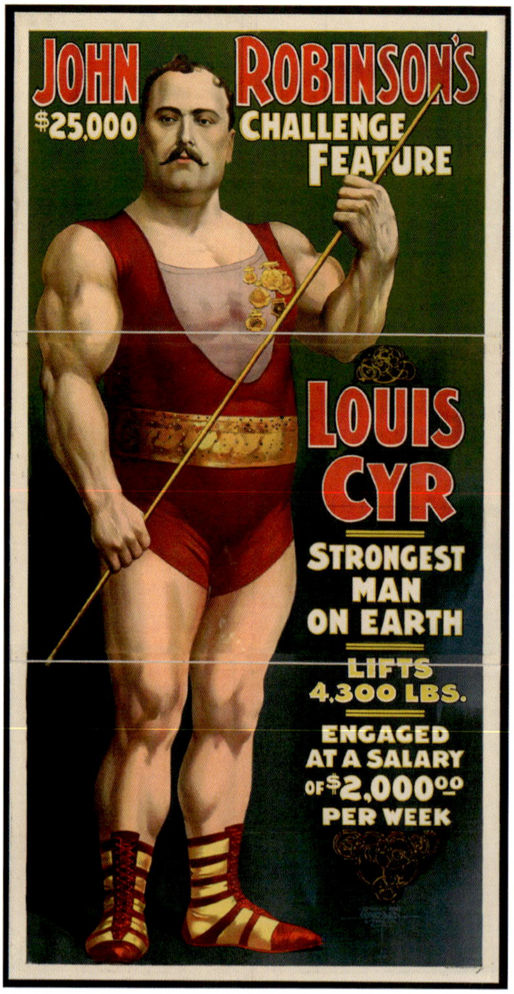

Courier Lithography Company, *John Robinson's $25,000 Challenge Feature – Louis Cyr, strongest man on earth, lifts 4300 lbs.*, 1898. Chromolithograph. *Prints and Photographs Division, Library of Congress, Washington, DC.*

filmgoers place their faith in costumed superheroes to "fix" things and make the nation great again.

To be sure, the current popularity of these movies is strongly driven by their franchising and special effects (especially CGI, or computer generated imagery).[5] Likewise, their A-list casts and directors, and occasionally witty dialogue, also appeal. But as Seth Frantzman observes, "the US has increasingly come to believe in magical solutions" to its multiple problems, especially those bestowed by godlike beings in skintight suits who possess special powers and miraculous weapons: Superman's superhuman strength, for example, and Wonder Woman's "Lasso of Truth."[6] As Marvel character Nick Fury relates in *The Avengers* (2012), "The idea was to bring together a group of remarkable people, see if they could become something more. See if they could work together when we needed them to, to fight the battles that we never

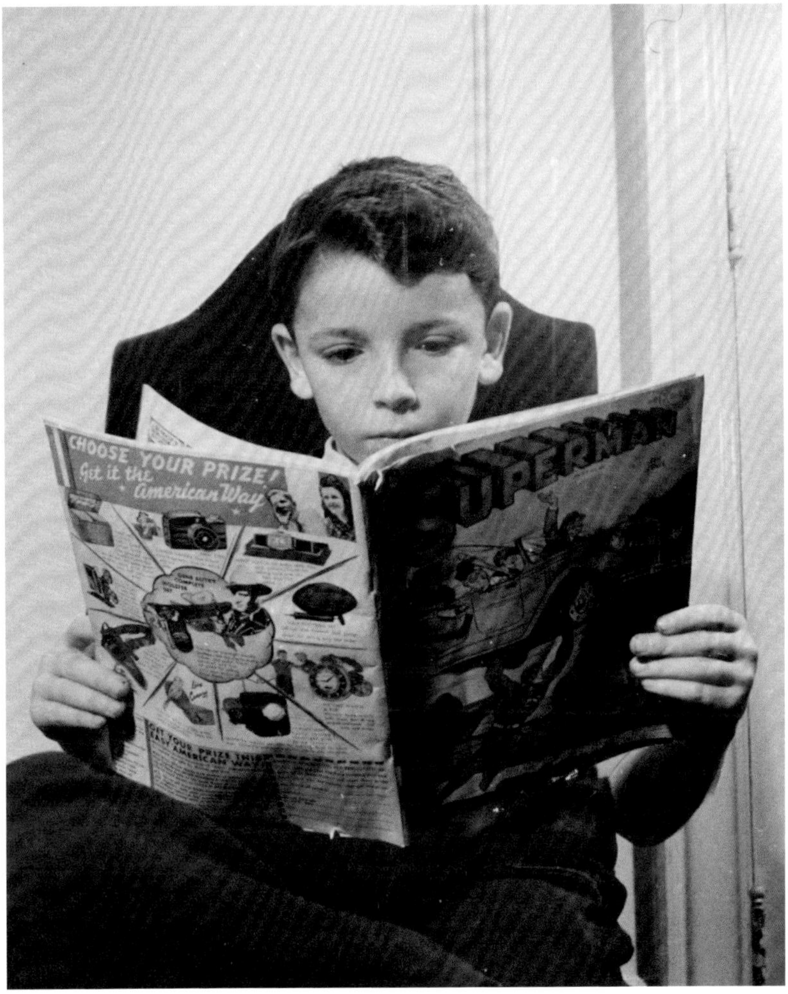

Mary Collins, *New York, N.Y. Children's Colony, a school for refugee children administered by a Viennese. German refugee child, a devotee of Superman*, 1942. Photograph. Library of Congress.

could."[7] The "idea" that ordinary or unremarkable Americans are seemingly incapable and uninterested in solving the nation's problems, and that "something more" is required, is telling. In today's movie-made America, superheroes, not citizens, are called on to "fight the battles," and accomplishing these deeds with violence, vigilantism, and supernatural effects, rather than diplomacy and the rule of law, is applauded.

Various writers trace America's contemporary veneration for comic book icons and magical thinking to the attacks of September 11, 2001; as Annika Hagley remarks, "Superhero movies have been one of the most successful mediators of post-9/11 American political culture."[8] The sources of such veneration date earlier, to the Great Depression. The iconic trinity of costumed superheroes invented at DC Comics from 1938 to 1941 were inspired by the dire social and political circumstances of the era. Their physical dimensions, expertise, and exploits were

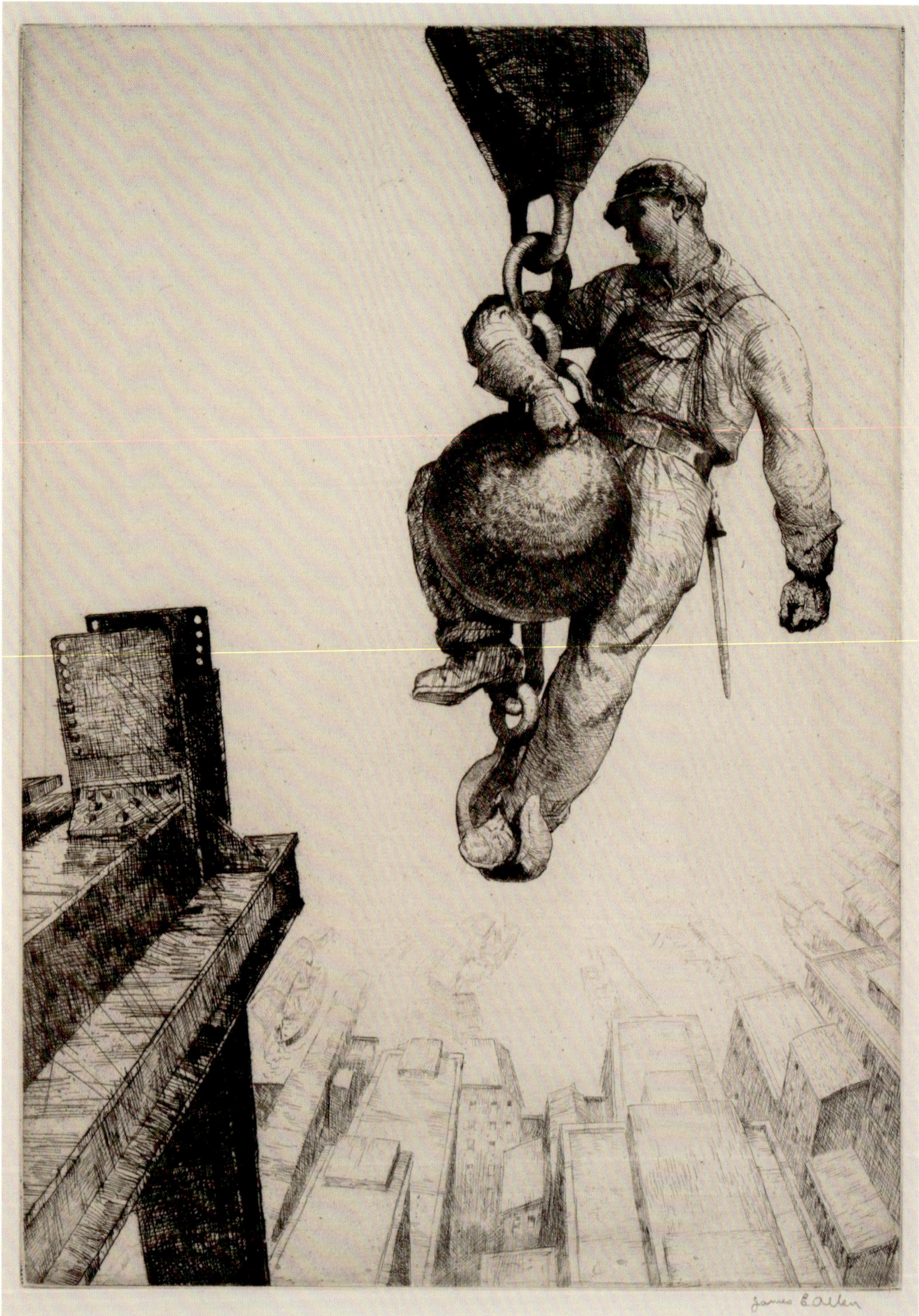

James Edward B. Allen, *The Skyman*, 1932. Etching. Crystal Bridges Museum of American Art, Bentonville, Arkansas, 2012.37.

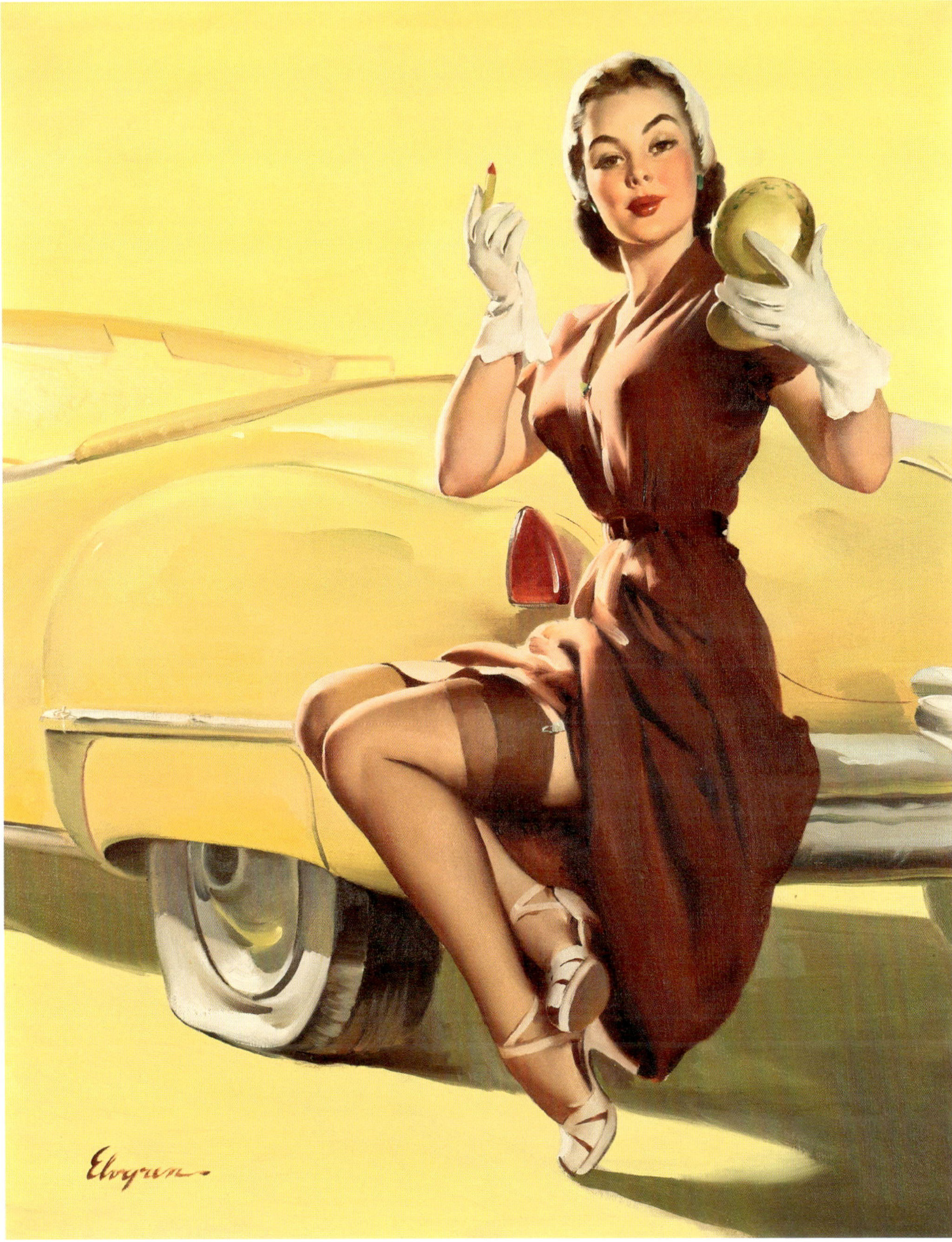

Gil Elvgren, *Jill Needs Jack*, 1950. Oil on canvas. Courtesy of Louis K. and Susan P. Meisel.

informed by a highly symbolic visual culture of working-class Americans that corresponded with New Deal values and by sexualized images of women in pin-up calendars and interwar pulp fiction.

Following the collapse of the stock market in the fall of 1929, American factories shuttered and urban and industrial construction plummeted. By 1932 the nation's steel mills operated at only 12 percent of capacity; by 1933 nearly half of US banks had failed, and the jobless rate had risen to 25 percent. Work is central to American understandings of self and national identity, to self-worth and social standing; work, Daniel T. Rodgers argues, is "the core of the moral life" of the nation.[9] Recognizing the threat that millions of unemployed workers posed to American patterns of corporate capitalism and governance, the New Deal programs organized under President Franklin Delano Roosevelt, who took office in March 1933, focused especially on job creation. New Dealers viewed employment as the single most important factor in reviving the US economy, restoring American dignity, and dodging the radical alternatives proposed by both left- and right-wing social and political movements. Newly formed government agencies like the WPA (Works Progress Administration) hired millions of Americans on public projects ranging from road building to mural painting. More than twelve thousand artists found work on New Deal projects during the Great Depression, producing an estimated 3,350 murals, 18,000 sculptures, 108,000 easel paintings, and hundreds of thousands of prints, posters, and photographs.[10] The federal government became the major patron of American art.

New Deal artists had considerable freedom in terms of style and media: Stuart Davis and William S. Schwartz produced abstract

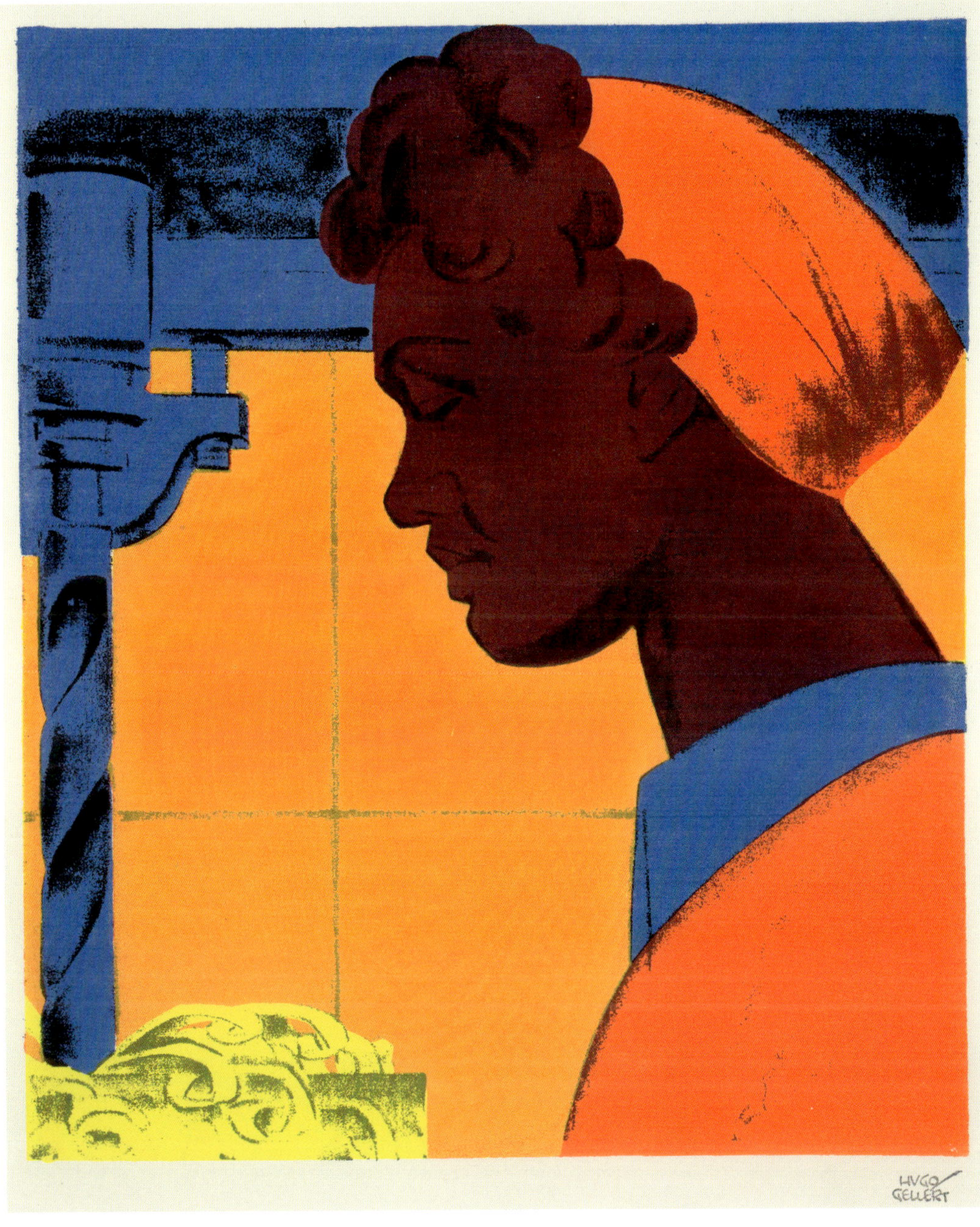

Hugo Gellert, *Free Man's Duties I*, 1943. Screen print. Crystal Bridges Museum of American Art, Bentonville, Arkansas, 2012.124.

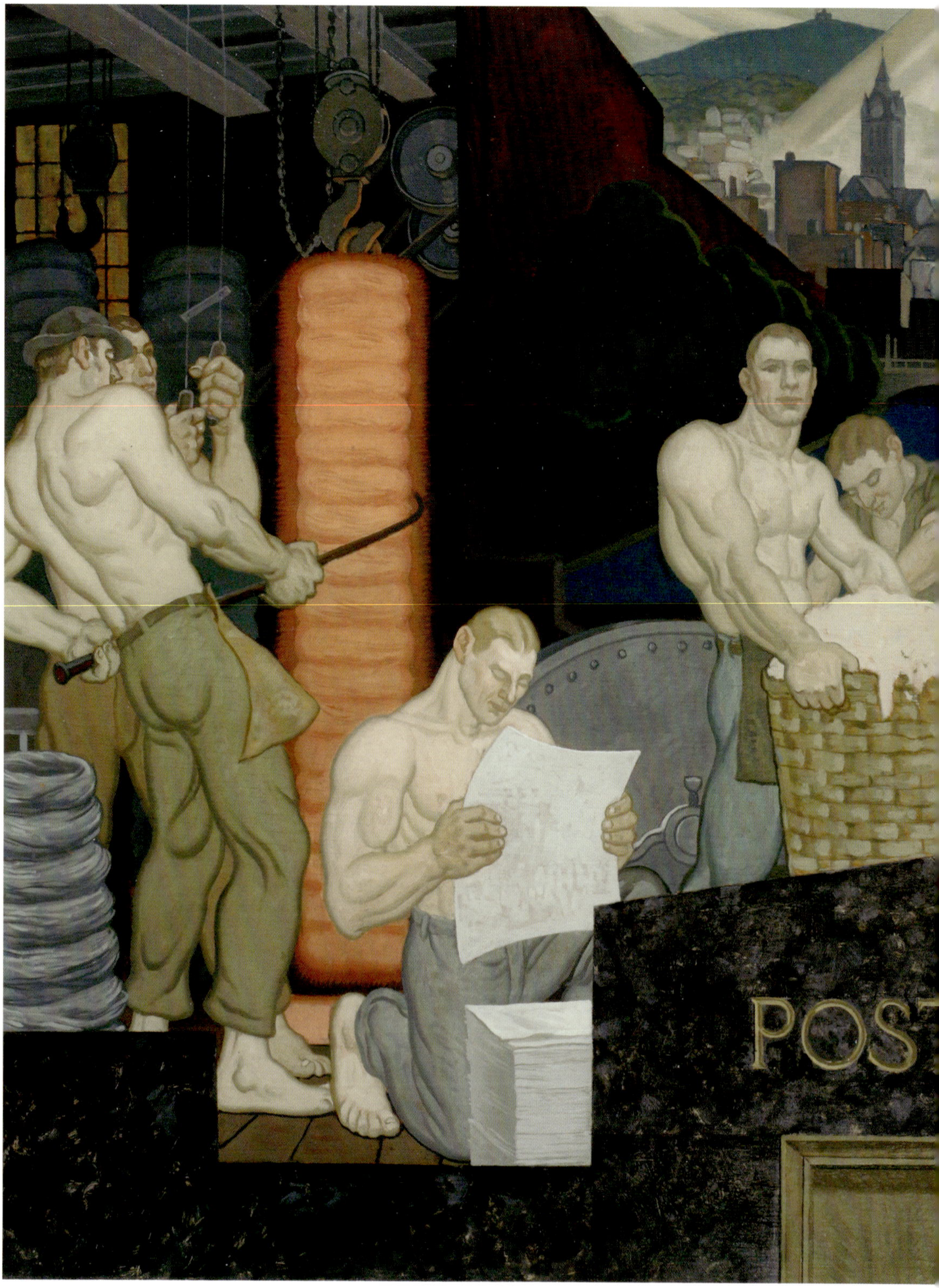

Aiden Lassell Ripley, *Industries of Holyoke*, 1935. Oil on plywood panel.
The Westmoreland Museum of American Art, Bequest of Richard M. Scaife, 2015.88.

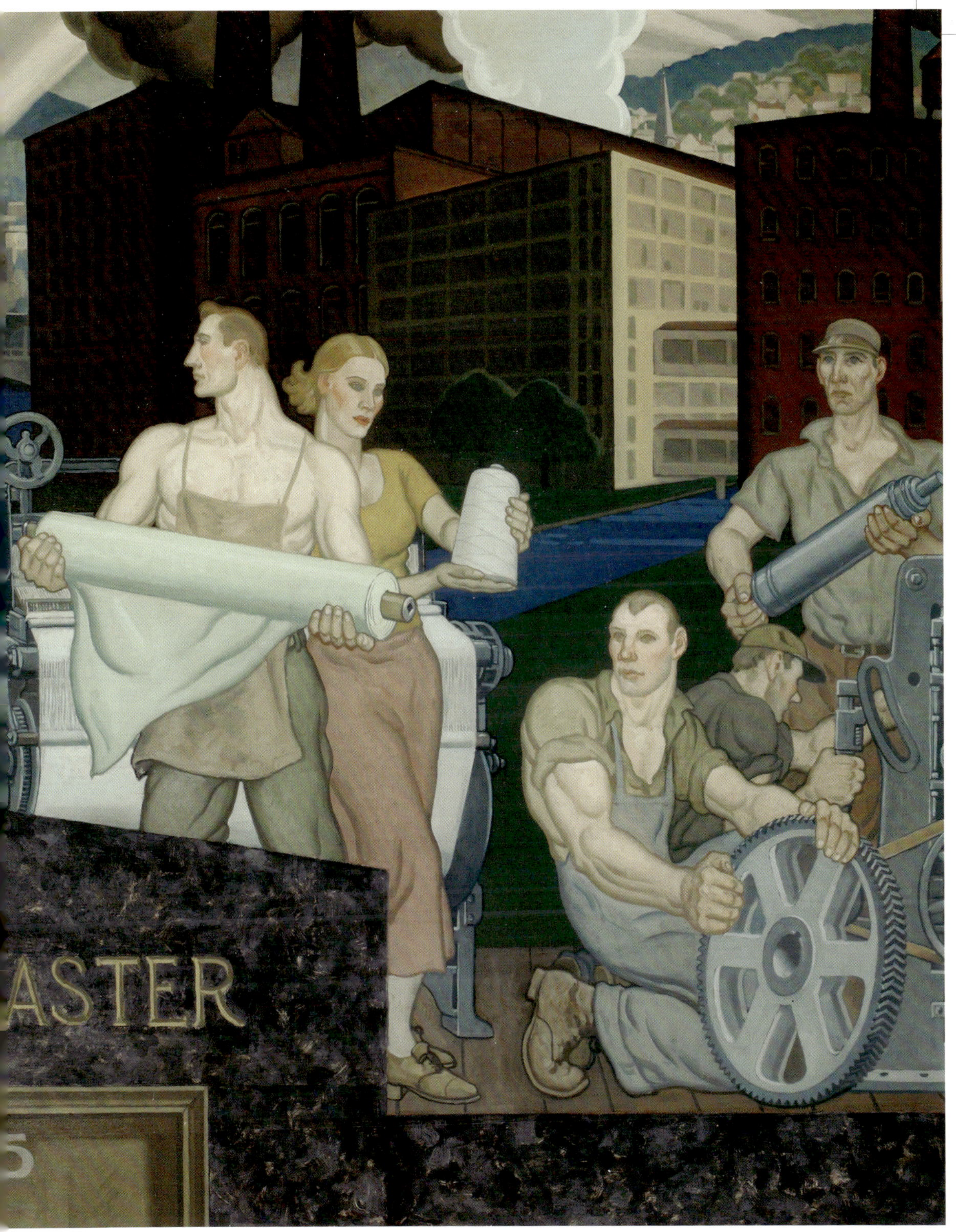
ASTER

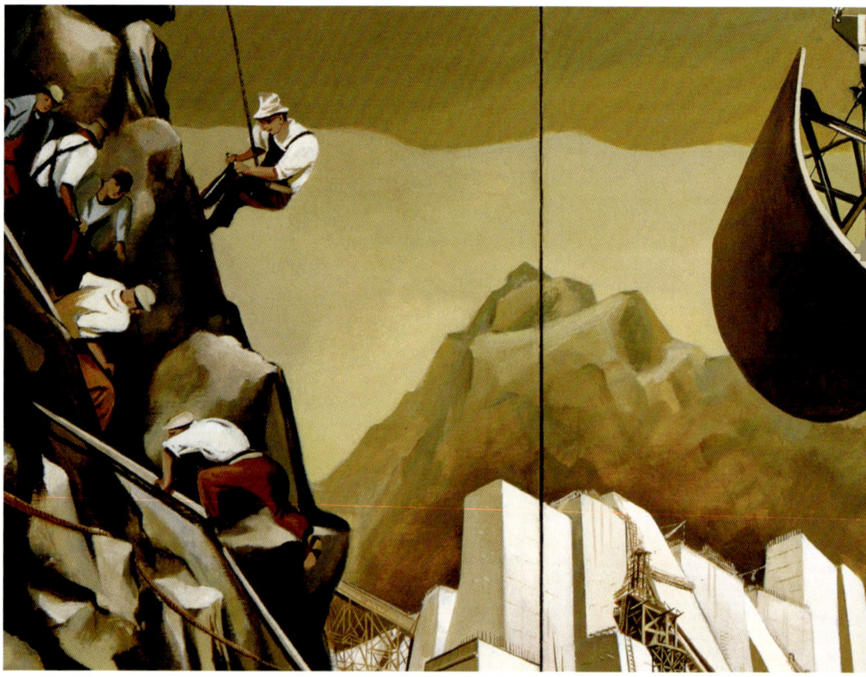

paintings, Ben Shahn designed Social Realist murals, and Elizabeth Olds, Harry Sternberg, and Dox Thrash made experimental prints. Still, a significant body of New Deal art, made by artists from vastly different backgrounds, shared an iconography of labor that celebrated work and workers.[11]

Boston artist Aiden Lassell Ripley, for example, who trained as an illustrator and was best known for sporting scenes and wildlife subjects, including an award-winning Federal Duck Stamp in 1942, painted *Industries of Holyoke* in 1935. A proposal for a New Deal post office mural, Ripley's scene posed nine manly workers—five of them bare chested, all of them beefy and broad shouldered with rippling muscles and Herculean biceps—as symbolic bodies attached to various jobs. (The single woman depicted in his sketch holds aloft a large spool of industrial machine thread like a precious trophy.) By contrast, William Gropper's 1938 mural study *Construction of the Dam*, based on his sketches of two hydroelectric power plants built in the 1930s, the Boulder (later Hoover) and Grand Coulee dams, was more attentive to the actual terms of labor—physical and intellectual—required in industry. A leftist whose editorial cartoons were regularly featured in the Communist Party newspaper *The Daily Worker* and whose first solo show (in 1936 at New

William Gropper, Construction of the Dam (study for mural, the Department of the Interior, Washington, DC), 1938. Oil on canvas. Smithsonian American Art Museum, Transfer from the US Department of the Interior, National Park Service.

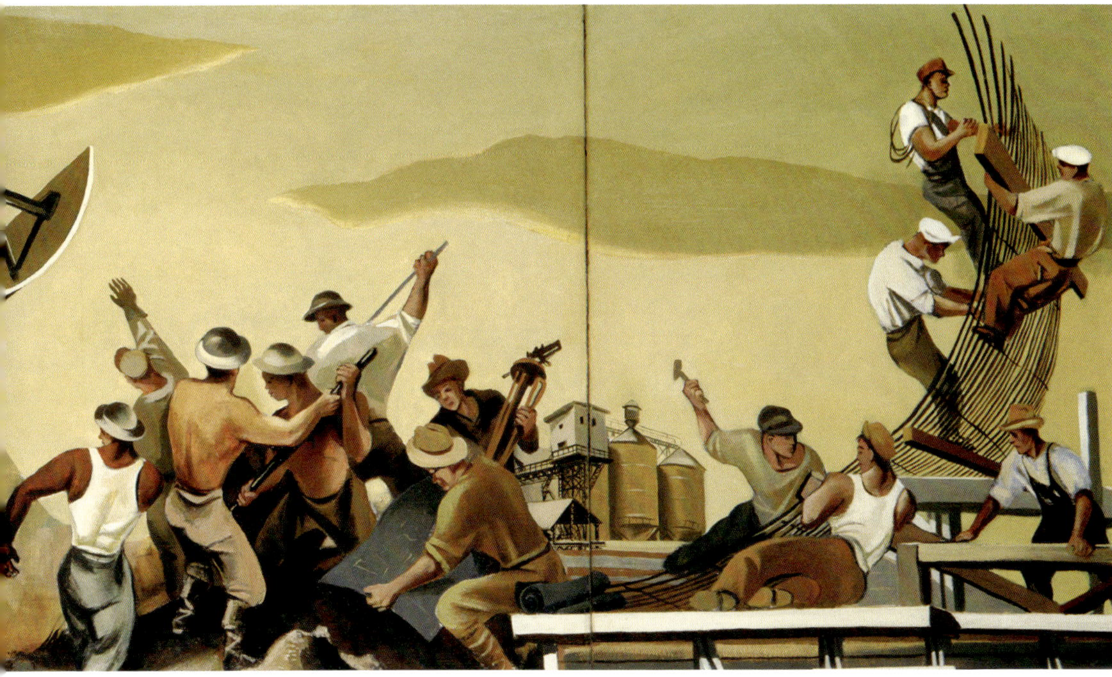

York's ACA Galleries) consisted of paintings of sweatshop workers, farm workers, steel workers, migrant workers, and other workers in multiple trades and industries, Gropper was commissioned to design a mural for the new Department of the Interior Building in Washington.[12] His study pays tribute to the skills of working men—hammering cables, adjusting braces, examining blueprints—and their mastery over nature. He also emphasized the dangers they encountered in these massive construction projects: the "high scalers" depicted on the left of his picture, some of them former circus acrobats, many of them Native American, had the perilous job of climbing canyon walls and drilling holes for dynamite. Gropper's inclusion of an integrated work force, however, seen in his portrayal of black and white workers in the center of the mural, was aspirational: discriminatory hiring practices on these Depression-era dam projects prohibited mixed race crews.[13]

The New Deal's "recovery rhetoric," writes Laura Hapke, "linked national vitality to the revitalized body."[14] Ironically, when the nation seemed most inert, upbeat images of brawny and dynamic workers gained heightened visibility, as if these symbols of manly might and movement might propel America out of the Great Depression and into a better tomorrow. Tyrone Comfort's painting of a tough,

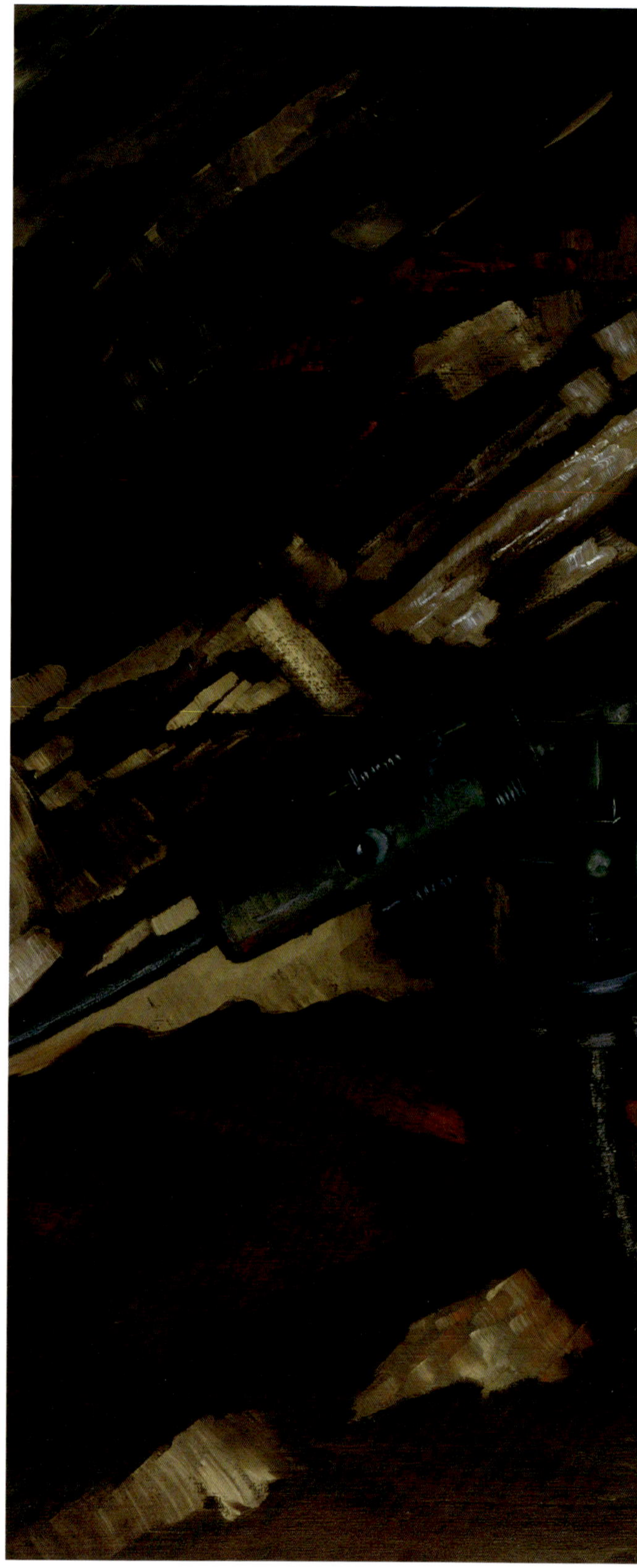

Tyrone Comfort, *Gold Is Where You Find It*, 1934. Oil on canvas. Smithsonian American Art Museum, Transfer from the US Department of the Interior, National Park Service.

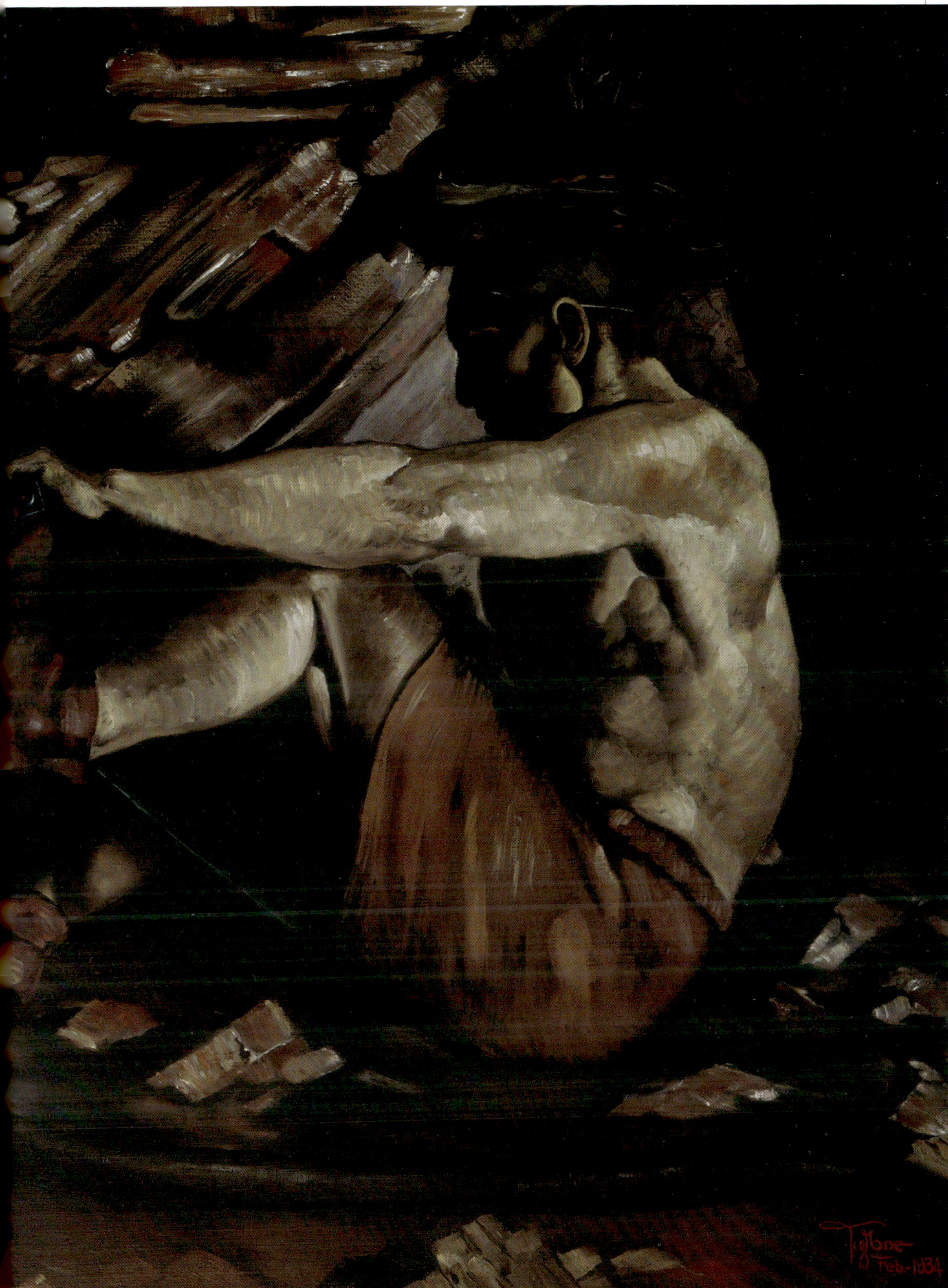

strong-bodied prospector bracing his foot against a pneumatic drill deep inside a California gold mine was among several work-themed canvases that FDR and Eleanor Roosevelt chose to hang in the White House in the 1930s.[15] Harry Sternberg's brightly colored serigraph of a lone riveter working high above the streets of Manhattan similarly celebrated the skill and independence of America's working class men. Sternberg's "stress on the worker's disciplined concentration" suggests that "determination and physical endurance . . . constituted the real essence of labor heroism."[16] Yet his focus on the riveter's body—his face is almost entirely obscured—and especially on his lower torso, renders him an anonymous physical icon of a well-bodied American economy.

Trade unions became increasingly aggressive in the 1930s: expanding membership, organizing successful strikes, and putting pressure on Congress to enact prolabor legislation. Little of the New Deal's iconography of labor, however, featured real-life subjects like labor-management conflict, deskilling, collective bargaining, and employer prerogatives regarding product design, prices, and profits.[17] As seen in two prints from 1940, Herschel Levit's *Take it Away* and Samuel Margolies's *Men of Steel*, American workers were more often pictured as autonomous individuals rather than collective members of mass-production factories and labor unions, and the hierarchical facts of corporate management and control were typically occluded.

These and other images of manly workers deflected Depression era anxieties about unemployment and undercut worries about the roles and responsibilities of masculine breadwinners. The focus on men was deliberate. The economic downturn of the 1930s wreaked havoc on the ideal of gender equality launched by the success of women's suffrage.

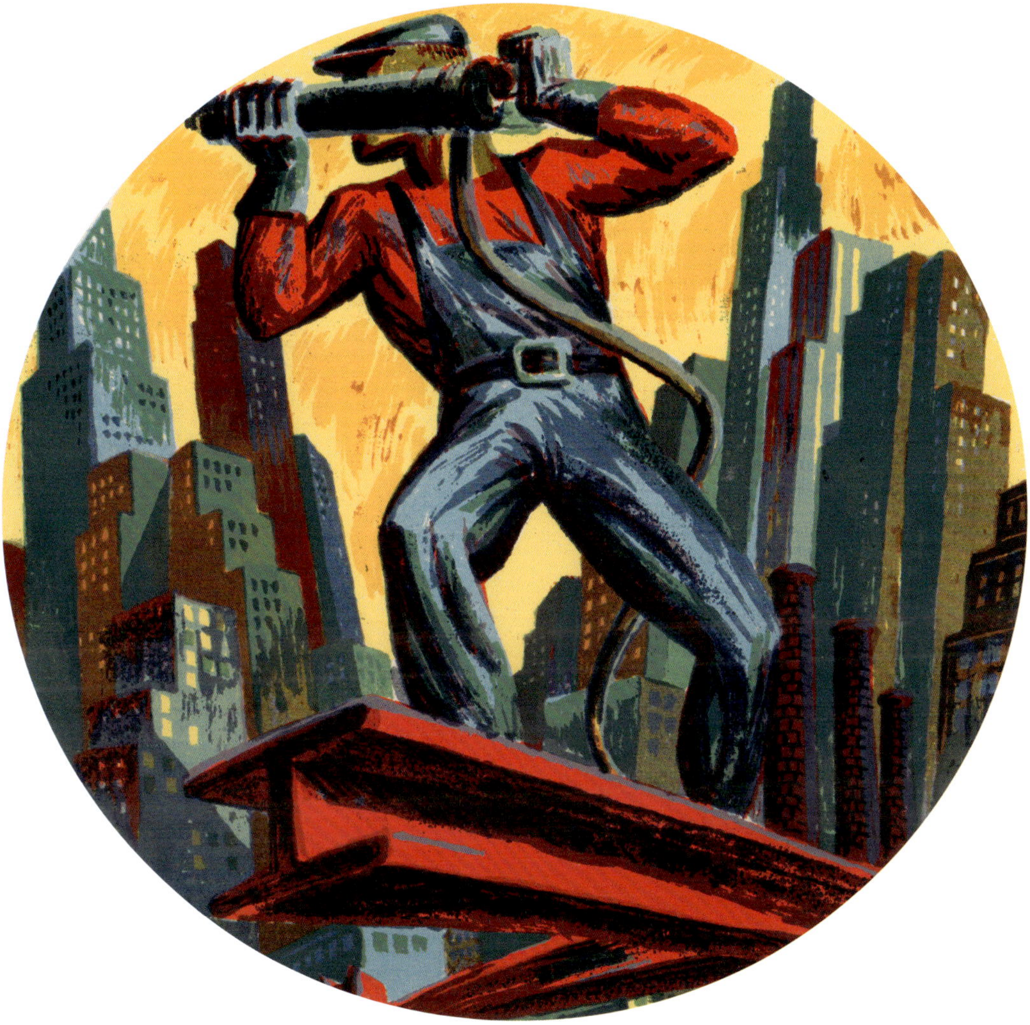

Although married women were the sole wage earners in one third of US families, they (and other women) were repeatedly exhorted to be "self-sacrificing" and to give up jobs to unemployed men. "Simply fire the women, who shouldn't be working anyway, and hire the men," journalist Norman Cousins advised in *Current History*. "Presto! No unemployment. No relief rolls. No depression."[18] If some New Deal art showed men and women laboring together in a trope Barbara Melosh terms the "comradely ideal," images of "manly" work dominated.[19] Women were habitually represented in 1930s visual culture in eroticized terms, as sexualized bodies and scantily clad calendar girls: consider the musical numbers orchestrated by Busby Berkeley in Hollywood movies

Harry Sternberg, *Riveter*, 1935. Color screen print. Crystal Bridges Museum of American Art, Bentonville, Arkansas. 2012.406.

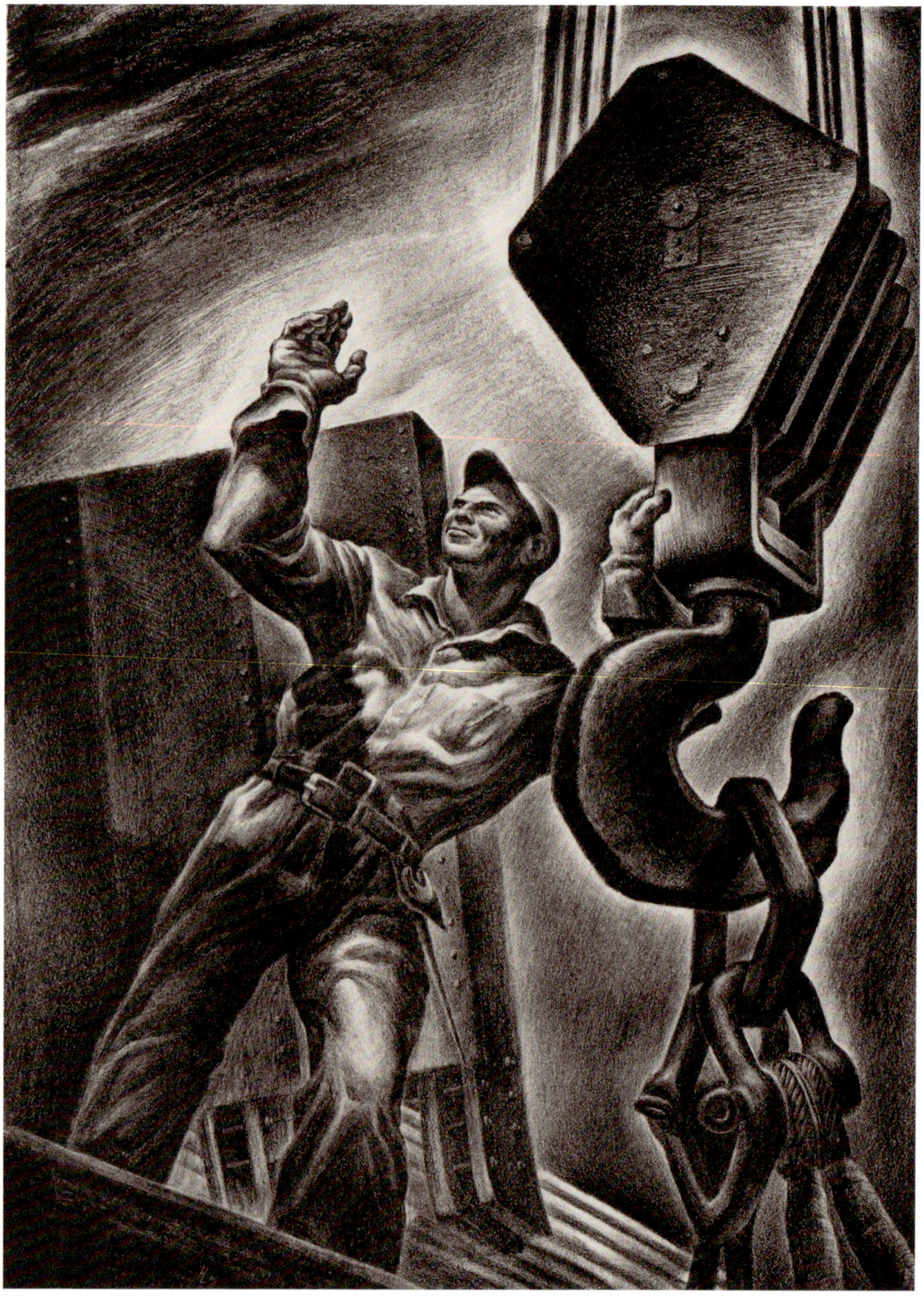

Herschel Levit, *Take it Away*, 1940. Lithograph. Crystal Bridges Museum of American Art, Bentonville, Arkansas, 2012.255.

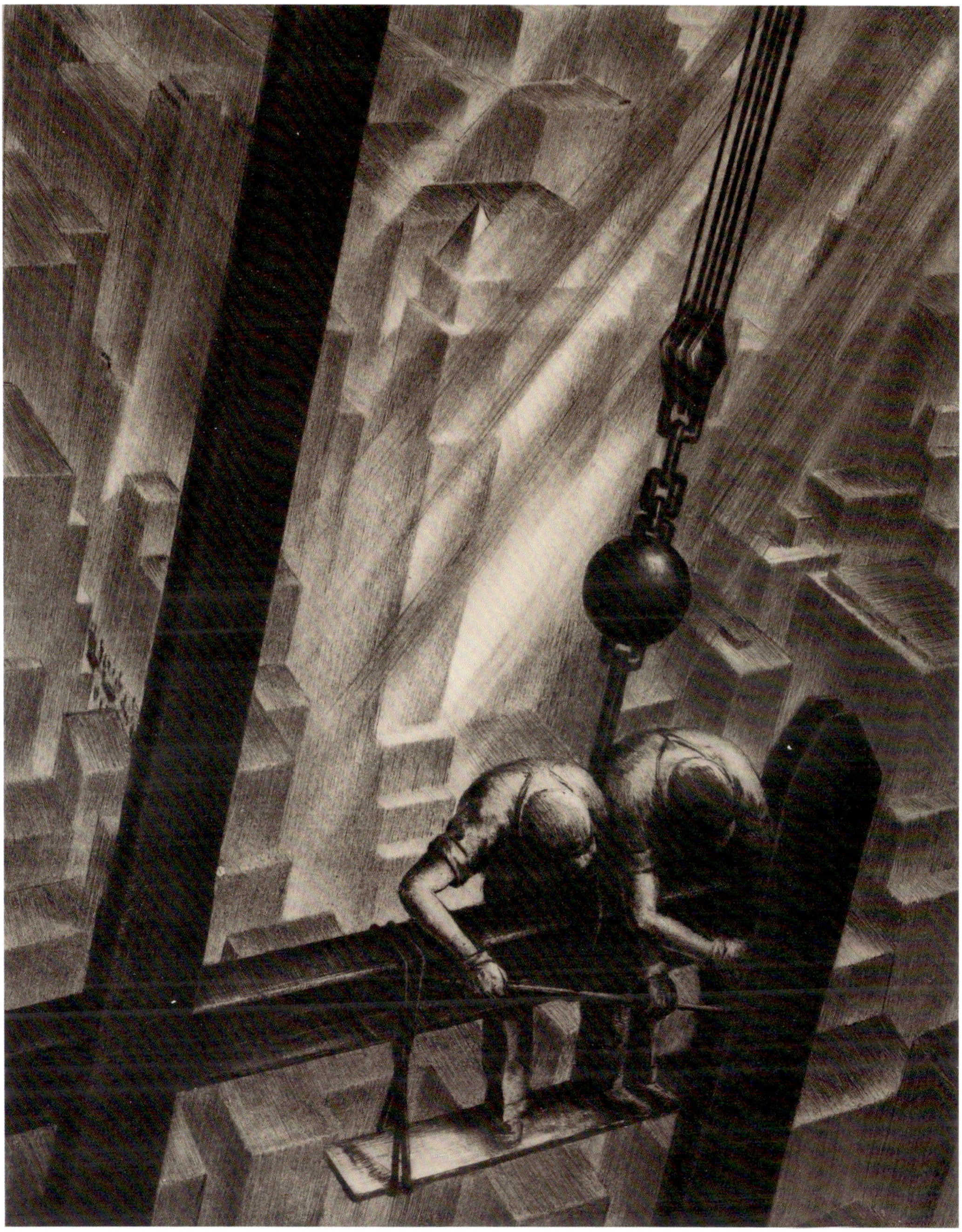

Samuel L. Margolies, *Men of Steel*, 1940. Drypoint. Crystal Bridges Museum of American Art, Bentonville, Arkansas, 2012.295.

such as *Footlight Parade* (1933) and the pin-up in the skintight bathing suit that Earl Moran sketched for Brown & Bigelow, America's largest calendar maker. Moran's pastel was so popular that the company used it to market a variety of commercial products, including a five-pound box of chocolates. Likewise, the covers of immensely popular pulp magazines in the 1930s often featured provocative, half-naked images of women whose hour-glass figures and red lips were fetishized by their mostly male readers.

Even when women were depicted as fully clothed workers, they were not heroized. Ann Rosener's photographs of women spot welding engine parts at the Willow Run Bomber Plant, a Michigan factory constructed by Ford for the mass production of military aircraft from 1942 to 1945, documented how keen sight and fine motor skills, not muscular bravado, were critical to American manufacturing. Norman Rockwell's *Rosie the Riveter*, which appeared on the cover of the *Saturday Evening Post* on May 29, 1943, spoofed both the "mythic regime" of manly labor and wartime demands placed on women workers previously rejected but now urgently recruited to do "men's jobs." Although Rockwell based his working woman on the monumental (and similarly androgynous) figures of prophets and sibyls that Michelangelo painted for the ceiling of the Sistine Chapel, his Rosie is pictured "at rest, not riveting"—note the ham sandwich she holds in her left hand.[20] More comic than heroic, she is stripped of her workplace agency—a prescient critique of the lower wages women were paid during the war (65 percent less than men in comparable jobs) and justification for how, when the war ended, they were once again exhorted to give up jobs to men.[21]

Norman Rockwell, *Rosie the Riveter*, 1943. Oil on canvas. Crystal Bridges Museum of American Art, Bentonville, Arkansas, 2007.178.

The gendered terms of these and other visual culture sources fed the

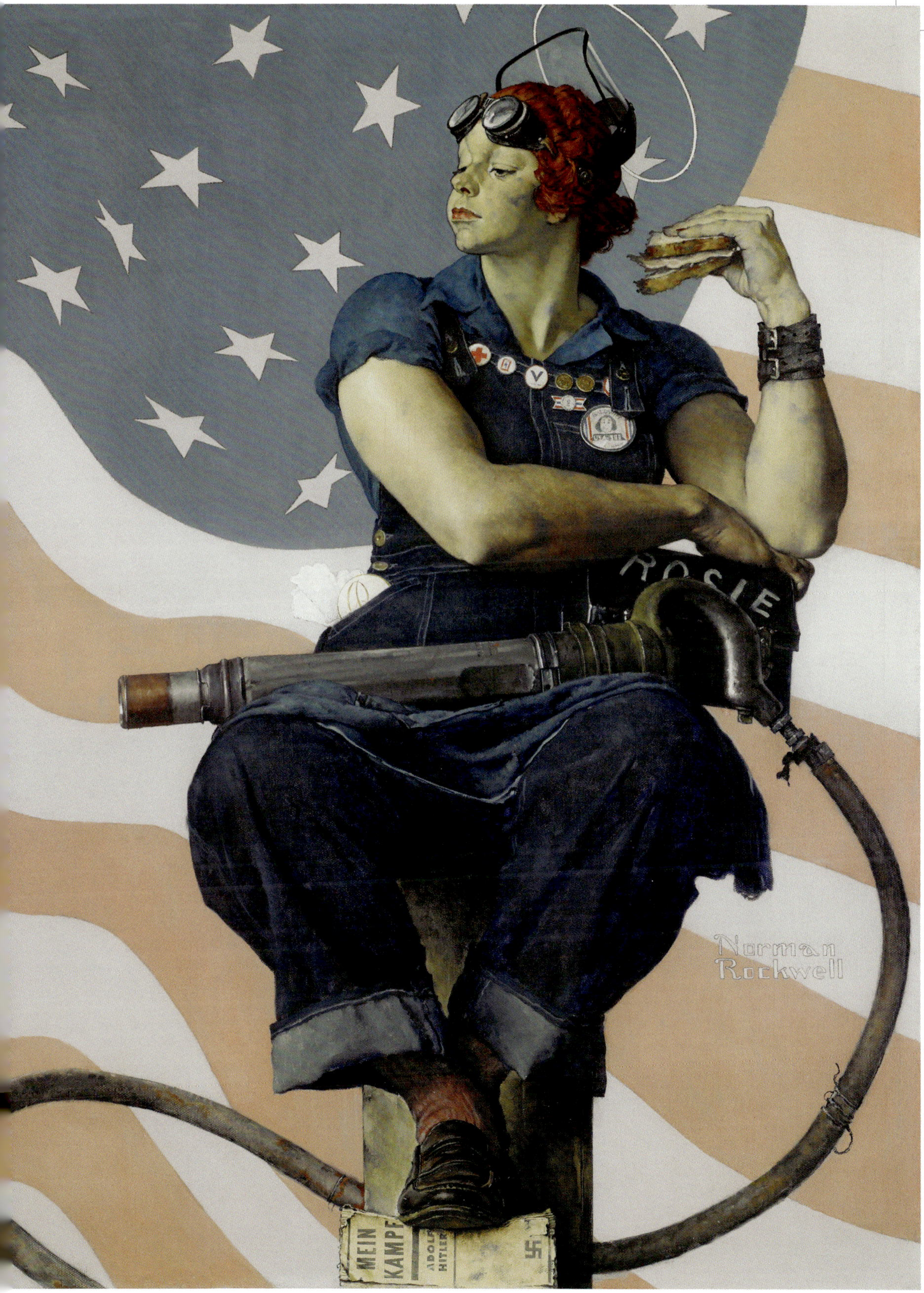
ROSIE
Norman
Rockwell
MEIN
KAMPF
ADOLF
HITLER

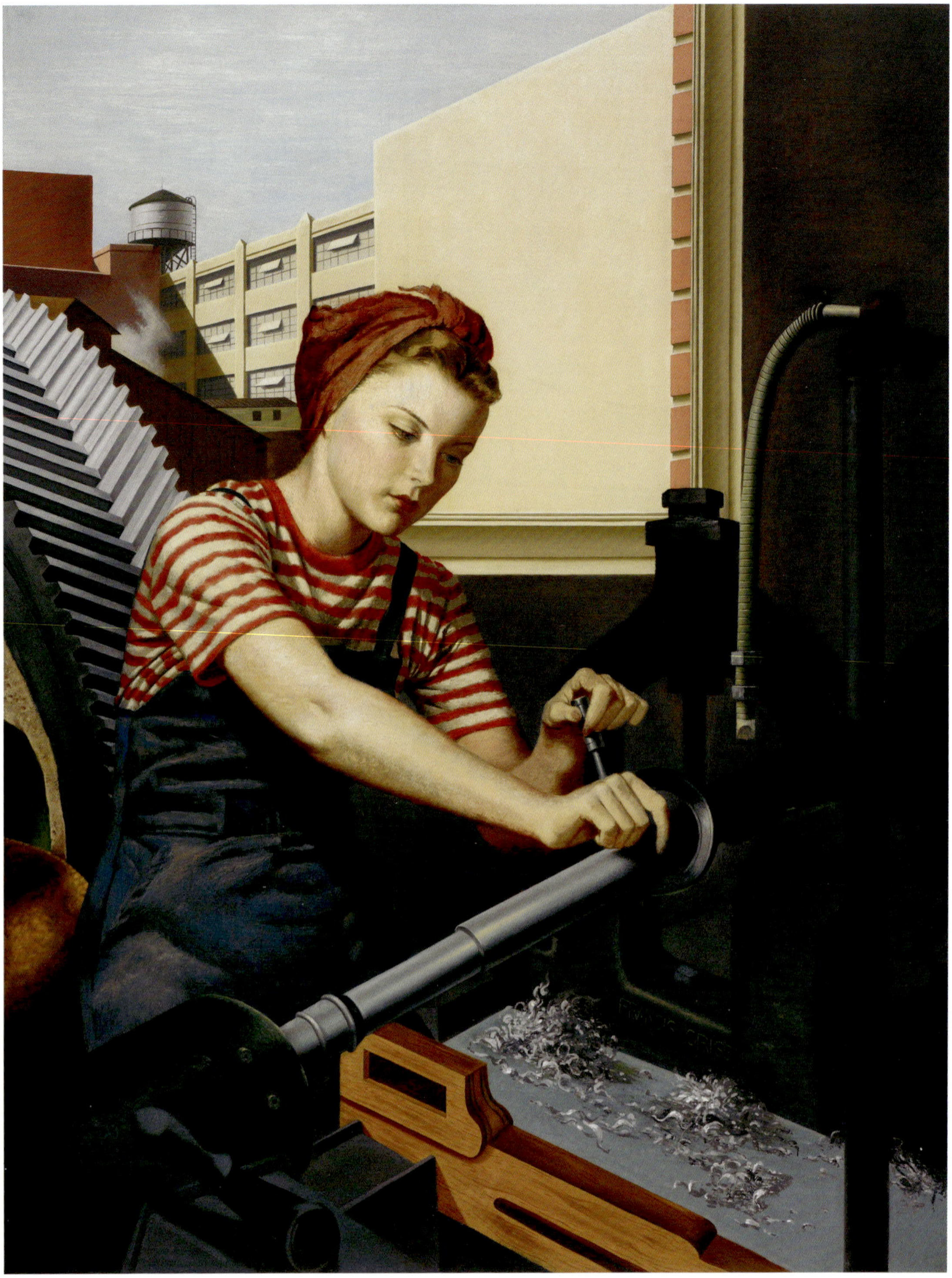

Francis Criss, *Day Shift*, 1943. Oil on canvas. Crystal Bridges Museum of American Art, Bentonville, Arkansas, 2007.182.

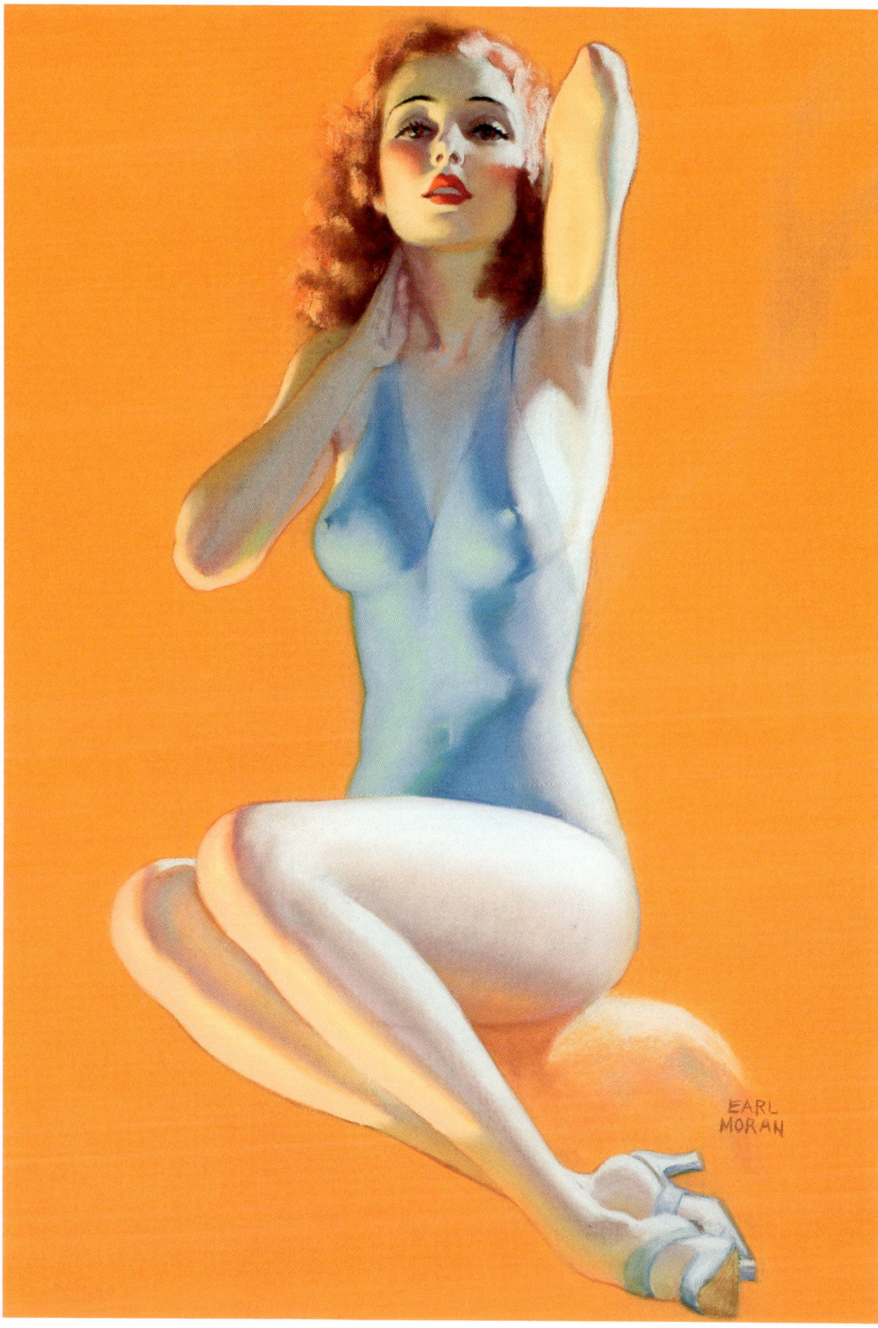

Earl Moran, *Golden Hours*, circa 1930s. Pastel on board. Collection of Jim Halperin, courtesy of Heritage Auctions (HA.com).

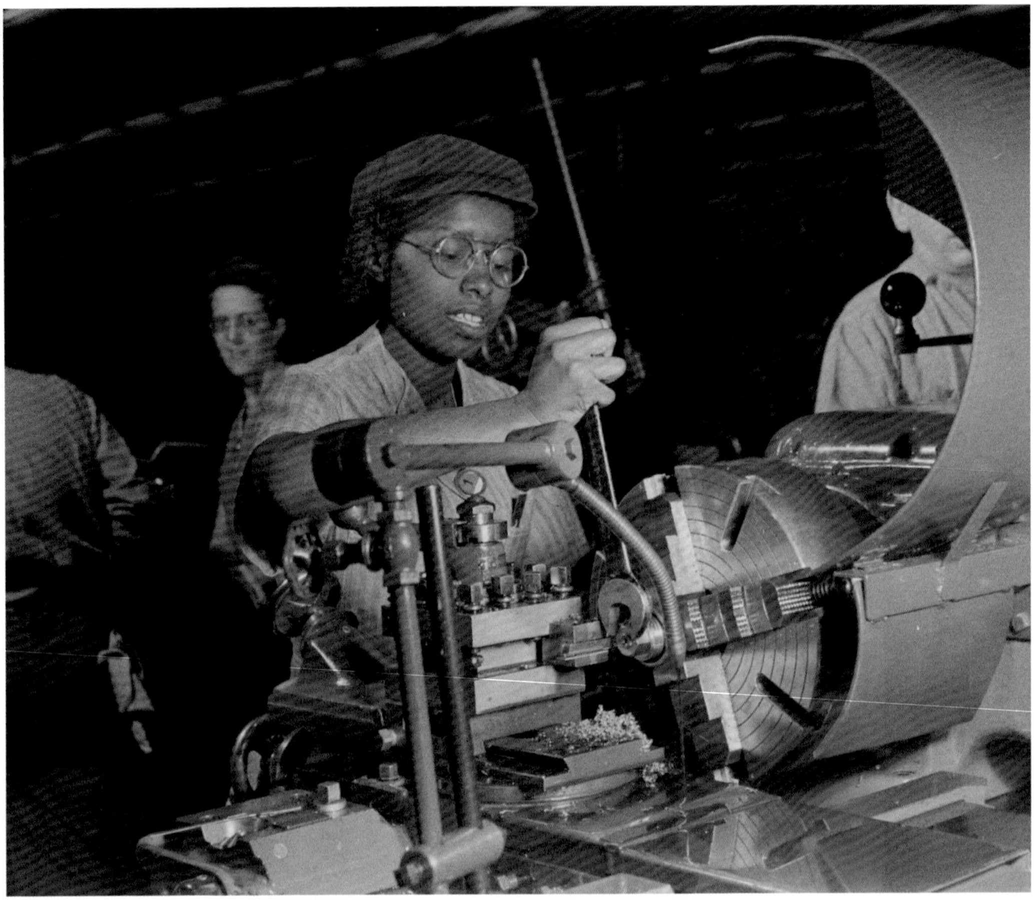

Ann Rosener, *D-007013—Women in war. Supercharger plant workers. Plant foremen point to 20-year-old Annie Tabor as one of their best lathe operators, despite her lack of previous industrial experience. Employed by a large Midwest supercharger plant, this young woman machines parts of aircraft engines. Like many other young Negro girls, she had known only,* 1942. Photograph. *Prints and Photographs Division, Library of Congress, Washington, DC.*

look and the work of the comic book superheroes who emerged in the late 1930s. Superman was styled as a handsome, manly crime fighter who used his superpowers to fight injustice and "become a powerful force for good." His day job as Clark Kent, mild-mannered reporter at the *Daily Planet*, was a ruse. Batman, a.k.a. Bruce Wayne, was based on the Shadow, a pulp magazine character who was also a wealthy playboy by day and a crime fighting vigilante at night. And Wonder Woman, invented by psychologist William Moulton Marston and drawn by artist Harry G. Peter, was fashioned as a bondage culture pin-up: a slinky, kinky "real woman character" who was repeatedly bound, gagged, and chained, and

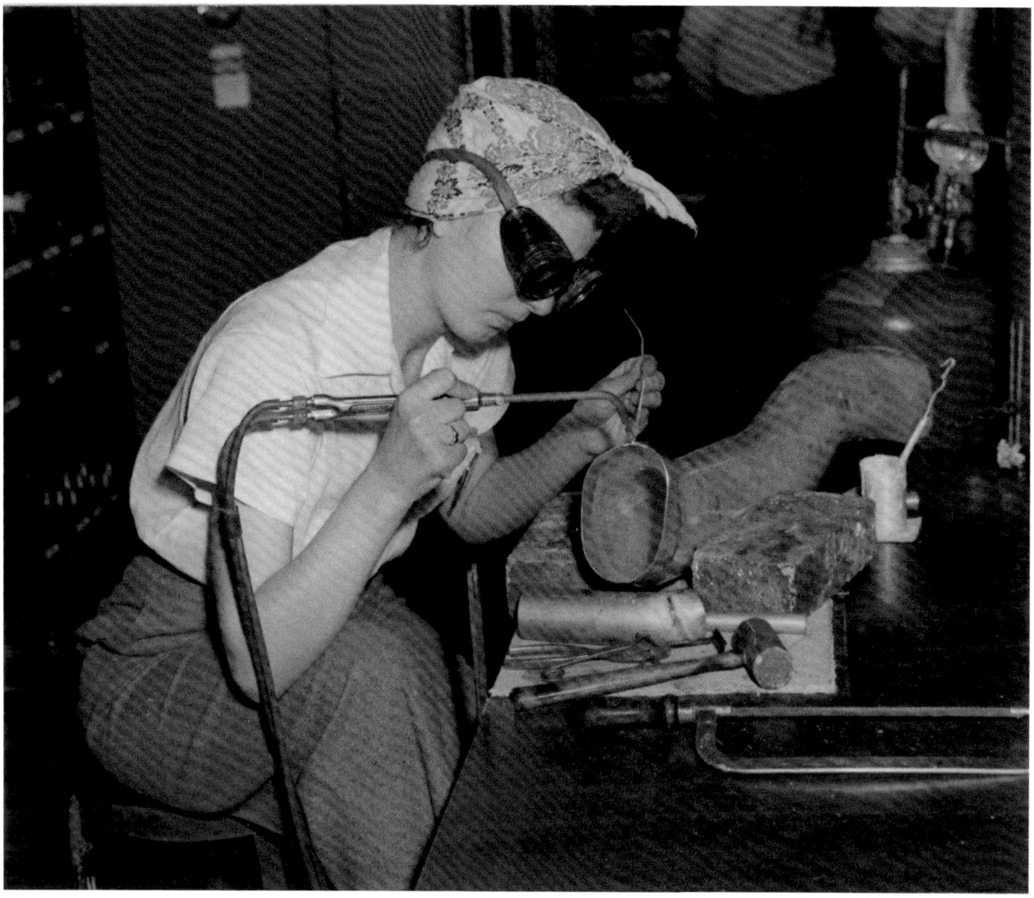

as such, said Marston, corresponded to "a great many readers' erotic fantasies."[22] Born an Amazonian goddess on an island of women, Wonder Woman assumed a secret identity in the original comics as Diana Prince, a secretary in US military intelligence. For all three superheroes, work was an alibi, a cover for their real jobs as problem solvers and planet savers. For the Depression-era audiences who first embraced them to their millions of fans today, comic book superheroes are magical beings who harness their special powers to fix things and restore order. However preposterous, they embody wishful national fantasies about saviors and miracles saving the day.

Ann Rosener, *D-005688—Production. Willow Run bomber plant. Steady of eye and hand, women workers at the great Willow Run bomber plant are among those throughout the country who are relieving serious shortages of skilled workers by doing such semi-skilled jobs as the one shown here. She's welding parts of the cooling system direct to the supercharger. Ford plant, Willow Run,* 1942. Photograph. *Prints and Photographs Division, Library of Congress, Washington, DC.*

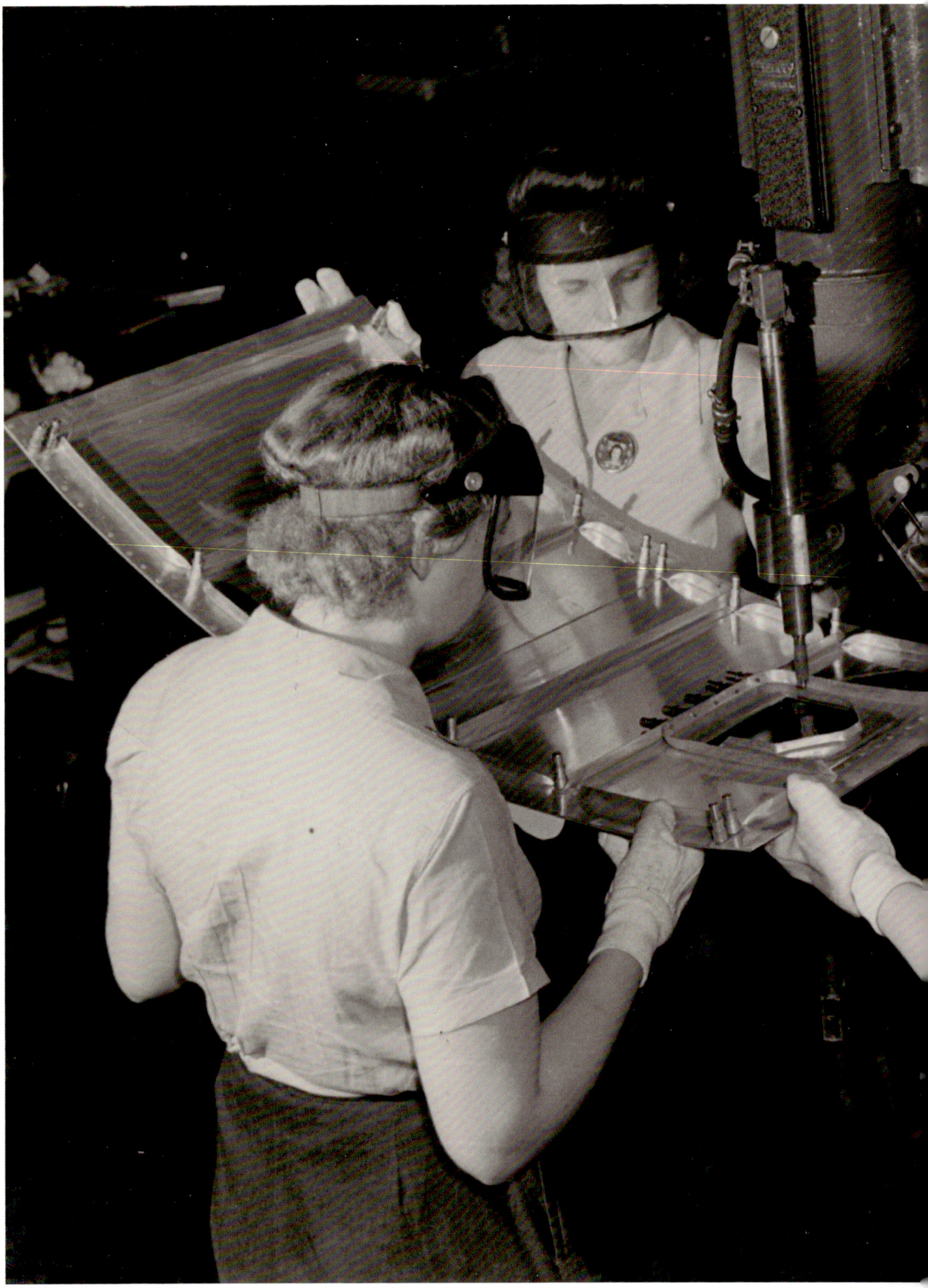

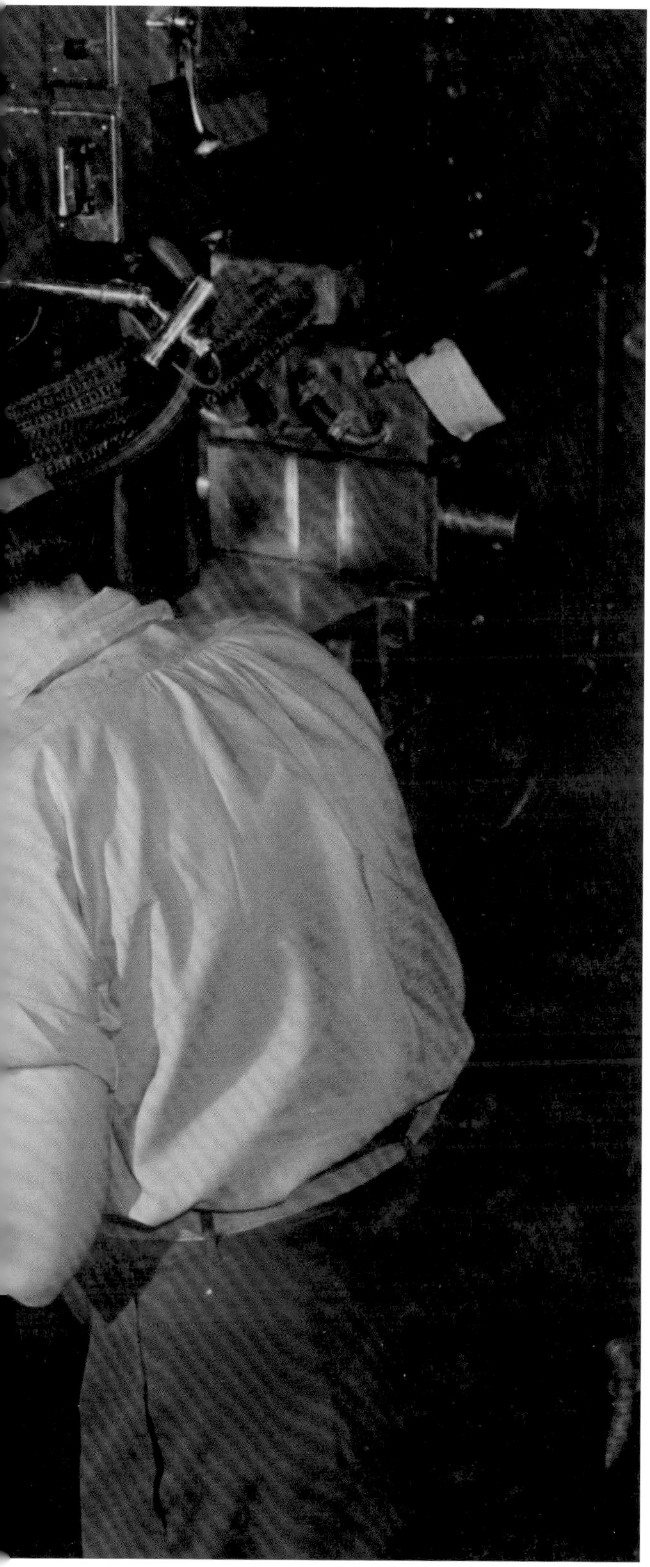

Ann Rosener, *D-005684—Production. Willow Run bomber plant. Spot welding parts for the nacelle of an aircraft engine. These women work in the largest one-story building in the works, the giant bomber plant at Willow Run, Michigan. Ford plant, Willow Run*, 1942. Photograph. *Prints and Photographs Division, Library of Congress, Washington, DC.*

ERIKA DOSS

Erika Doss (PhD, University of Minnesota) is a professor in the Department of American Studies at the University of Notre Dame. Her wide-ranging interests in American art and visual culture are reflected in the breadth of her publications, including *Benton, Pollock, and the Politics of Modernism: From Regionalism to Abstract Expressionism* (1991, which received the Charles C. Eldredge Prize), *Spirit Poles and Flying Pigs: Public Art and Cultural Democracy in American Communities* (1995), *Elvis Culture: Fans, Faith, and Image* (1999), *Looking at* Life *Magazine* (editor, 2001), *Twentieth-Century American Art* (2002), *The Emotional Life of Contemporary Public Memorials: Towards a Theory of Temporary Memorials* (2008), *Memorial Mania: Public Feeling in America* (2010), and *American Art of the 20th–21st Centuries* (2017). The recipient of several Fulbright awards, Doss has also held fellowships at the Stanford Humanities Center, the Georgia O'Keeffe Museum Research Center, and the Smithsonian American Art Museum.

Notes

1 Mel Ramos quoted in Mark Weidenbaum, "The Naked Eye," *Sactown*, June–July 2012, http://www.sactownmag.com/June-July-2012/The-Naked-Eye/index.php?cparticle=4&siarticle=3.

2 David Jenison, "Superheroes Like to Party with Jacky Tsai," *Prøhbtd*, November 8, 2017, https://prohbtd.com/superheroes-like-to-party-with-jacky-tsai.

3 Seth J. Frantzman, "Terra Incognita: Superhero Movies and the Decline of America," *Jerusalem Post*, April 29, 2018, https://www.jpost.com/Opinion/TERRA-INCOGNITA-Superhero-movies-and-the-decline-of-America-553035.

4 See, for example, the articles in the symposium "The Politics of the Superhero" in *PS: Political Science and Politics* 47, no. 1 (January 2014): 85–124.

5 Laurence Maslon and Michael Kantor, *Superheroes! Capes, Cowls, and the Creation of Comic Book Culture* (New York: Crown Archetype, 2013).

6 Frantzman, "Terra Incognita."

7 "Nick Fury/Quote," Marvel Cinematic Universe Wiki, FANDOM Movies Community, accessed May 2, 2018, http://marvelcinematicuniverse.wikia.com/wiki/Nick_Fury/Quote.

8 Annika Hagley, "America's Need for Superheroes Has Led to the Rise of Donald Trump," *Guardian*, March 28, 2016, https://www.theguardian.com/commentisfree/2016/mar/28/america-superheroes-donald-trump-brutal-comic-book-ideal; see also Annika Hagley and Michael Harrison, "Fighting the Battles We Never Could: 'The Avengers' and Post-September 11 American Political Identities," *PS: Political Science and Politics* 47, no. 1 (January 2014): 120–24; and Marc DiPaulo, *War, Politics, and Superheroes: Ethics and Propaganda in Comics and Film* (Jefferson, NC: McFarland & Company, 2011).

9 Daniel T. Rodgers, *The Work Ethic in Industrial America, 1850–1920* (Chicago: University of Chicago Press, 1974), xi–xiii.

10 Erika Doss, *American Art of the 20th and 21st Centuries* (New York: Oxford University Press, 2017), 96–97.

11 Erika Doss, "Toward an Iconography of American Labor: Work, Workers, and the Work Ethic in American Art, 1930–1945," *Design Issues* 13, no. 1 (Spring 1997): 53–66; and Erika Doss, "Looking at Labor: Images of Work in 1930s American Art," *Journal of Decorative and Propaganda Arts* 24 (2002): 230–57.

12 Louis Lozowick, *William Gropper* (East Brunswick, NJ: Associated University Presses, 1983), 50–52.

13 Marissa Vigenault, "The Politics of Labor in William Gropper's *Construction of a Dam*," 2014, May 1, 2018, https://www.academia.edu/8167297/_The_Politics_of_Labor_in_William_Gropper_s_Construction_of_a_Dam._Sheldon_Museum_of_Art_Lincoln_NE._April_2014. See also the discussion of Thomas Hart Benton's similarly aspirational depiction of an integrated work force in his 1930 mural *America Today* in Erika Doss, *Benton, Pollock, and the Politics of Modernism: From Regionalism to Abstract Expressionism* (Chicago: University of Chicago Press, 1991), 70–87.

14 Laura Hapke, *Labor's Canvas: American Working-Class History and the WPA Art of the 1930s* (New Castle: Cambridge Scholars, 2008), 53.

15 Exhibition label for Tyrone Comfort, *Gold Is Where You Find It*, 1934, in *1934: A New Deal for Artists,* Smithsonian American Art Museum, Washington, DC, 2009.

16 Helen Langa, *Radical Art: Printmaking and the Left in 1930s New York* (Berkeley: University of California Press, 2004), 91.

17 See, for example, David Brody, *Workers in Industrial America: Essays on the Twentieth Century Struggle* (New York: Oxford University Press, 1980); and Stanley Vittoz, *New Deal Labor Policy and the American Industrial Economy* (Chapel Hill: University of North Carolina Press, 1987).

18 Alice Kessler-Harris, *Out to Work: A History of Wage-Earning Women in the United States* (New York: Oxford University Press, 2003), 256.

19 Barbara Melosh, *Engendering Culture: Manhood and Womanhood in New Deal Public Art and Theater* (Washington, DC: Smithsonian Institution Press, 1991), 4.

20 Melissa Dabakis, "Gendered Labor: Norman Rockwell's *Rosie the Riveter* and the Discourses of Wartime Womanhood," in *Gender and American History Since 1890*, ed. Barbara Melosh (London and New York: Routledge, 1993), 185, 196–98.

21 Susan M. Hartmann, *The Homefront and Beyond: American Women in the 1940s* (Boston: Twayne, 1982), 21.

22 William Moulton Marston quoted in letter to Maxwell Charles Gaines, as noted in Jill Lepore, "The Surprising Origin Story of Wonder Woman," *Smithsonian.com*, October 2014, https://www.smithsonianmag.com/arts-culture/origin-story-wonder-woman-180952710/. See also Jill Lepore, *The Secret History of Wonder Woman* (New York: Vintage, 2015).

MEN OF STEEL, WOMEN OF WONDER

ISSUE 01

THE HEROES WE KNOW

BART BEATY

MEN OF STEEL, WOMEN OF WONDER

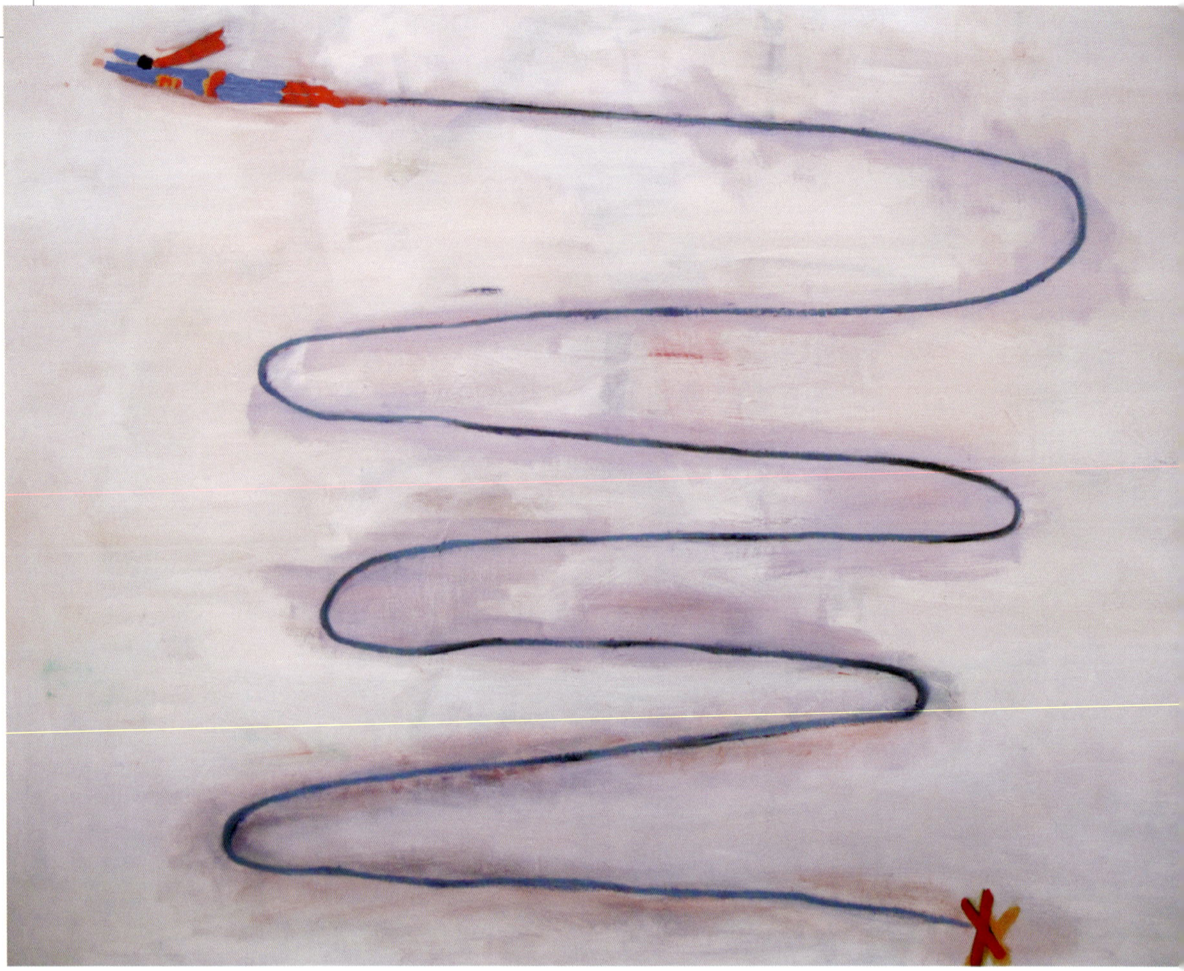

Superman can fly in my paintings, *which is more a symbol of freedom than of might. I chose him for his stacked colors: red then blue then red again with bright yellow belt and insignia. His flying gives me permission to place him anywhere in the rectangle and to draw flight lines in a cloudless sky.*

He's a modern savior: part human, part super; reminding us that we need heroes who will respond to our calls for help. I think of Superman as genderless, willing, and ever-vulnerable.

—KATHERINE BRADFORD

The Spectacular Banality of the Superhero

BART BEATY

When I teach the history of comics in the university classroom, one of the most important lessons that I impart to my students is an awareness of how much drawing styles matter in the creation of meaning. In comics, it is true to say, drawing is a form of writing—it determines how we interpret characters and empathize with their stories. When comic book characters become so ubiquitous in our culture that they attain an iconic status, they have often passed through the pens of multiple artists, who have etched their personalized and often highly idiosyncratic take on their subjects. Those stylistic differences between cartoonists are as identifiable to connoisseurs of the comic book as fingerprints are to investigators.

One exercise that I routinely use to stress these distinctions is to simply ask my students to draw a figure as familiar as Batman. A class with dozens of students will produce a wide array of images with varying levels of detail, technical ambition, and effort. Usually there is only one thing that all students will include in their sketches: the pointy little ears on Batman's cowl. Indeed, given how well known the face-covering mask and cape combination is in the land of the superhero, for many students the *only* required element in an image of Batman is the ears.

Which leads me to wonder: What is the minimal visual unit of Superman or of Wonder Woman? There seems to be no single iconic symbol, like Batman's cowl, that defines either of them. For Superman, the strongest contenders would be the red cape or the stylized *S*, but what would either be without the long, blue underwear? Wonder Woman's tiara or bracelets perhaps might suffice, but are they more defining than the eagle logo or the white stars on her blue bathing suit?

In truth, it is the cacophonous combination of the symbols

Katherine Bradford, *Long Flight*, 2012. Oil on canvas. Collection of Corby and Alexi Reese.

themselves, the riot of bold primary colors, that come together to signify otherworldliness and unyielding righteousness. Neither Superman nor Wonder Woman lurks in the night like Batman or crawls on buildings like Spider-Man. Both characters descend from the sky in all their glittering gaudiness, striking fear in their enemies while dazzling their adorers. They are creatures of the light.

Men of Steel, Women of Wonder stitches together contradictory takes on these superheroic figures, seeing them as equal parts spectacular and banal. The works in this show set about the process of elevating the waitress while bringing the crime fighter firmly back down to earth. How do the artists on display here regard supermen and wonder women? One common thread weaves around the legacies of escapism that have characterized American popular culture for well over a century; another takes a microscope to the politics of populism. Superman, in particular, is the product of a Depression-era politics where "truth, justice, and the American way" was a phrase that might be uttered unironically. The artists in this show reject such simple populism in asking, *Whose truth*? *What justice*? and *Which America*?

Both Superman and Wonder Woman were created during an explosive moment in American history when economic depression devastated working-class communities, ideological battles lurched inexorably onto real battlefields, and the United States was forced to take on the mantle of leading global democracy. Envisioned as icons of peaceful and progressive American values, their red, blue, and gold costumes were not simply functions of the limited color palettes enabled by four-color printing. A refugee from Krypton, a planet ravaged by climactic disaster, and a princess from a hidden kingdom emerge into our world

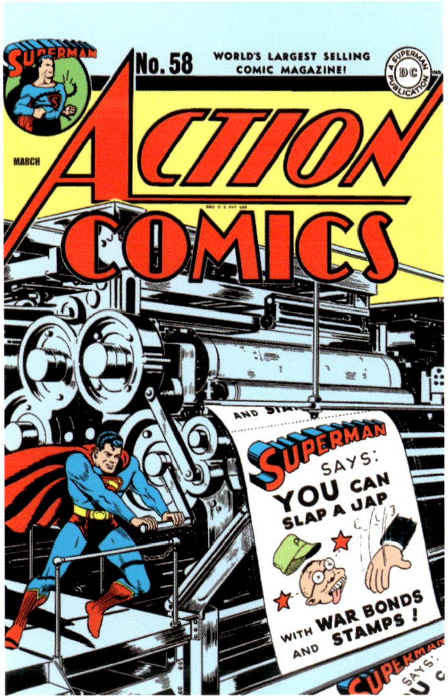

Jack Burnley, cover of *Action Comics* #58, March 1943. © DC Comics.

beautiful and benevolent figures. As the United States steeled itself for war against fascism and genocide, it—and its allies—struggled to excise its own intolerant and xenophobic values. The superhero, as a patriotic ideal, frequently struggled to stay on the side of righteousness.

Who is Superman? It should be a simple question to answer, but the journey from innovative action hero to cultural icon is much more complicated than we might assume for such a seemingly one-dimensional character. Take a look at the Superman story included in the copy of *Action Comics* #1 (June 1938) on display in the exhibition. As the very first Superman story, it may not align with what you have come to know about him. On the first page alone, we learn that Superman was raised on Earth in an orphanage (no mention of Jonathan and Martha Kent here). He has the power to leap one-eighth of a mile, but he does not have the power of flight. He can lift a steel beam with one hand, run faster than an express train, and nothing less than a bursting shell can penetrate his skin. Yet he is not impervious to danger; he has neither x-ray vision nor heat vision nor super-breath nor many of his other miraculous powers. All of these would come later, in the 1950s, as new writers and artists sought to spice up the character for the atomic age.

In the beginning, Superman was an overnight success borne out of years of frustrating failure. Co-created by writer Jerry Siegel and artist Joe Shuster, a pair of Jewish kids who grew up in Cleveland, the concept had been floated without success to nearly every publisher in New York. Originally, Siegel and Shuster had imagined Superman as the star of a daily newspaper strip. The American newspaper strip occupied prized print real estate for four decades, becoming one of the most lucrative forms of entertainment in the United States by the time of the Great Depression. Editors knew that serial strips—like *Little Orphan Annie* and *Dick Tracy*, with their constant cliff-hangers—helped to create a loyal readership, and syndicators helped to make cartoonists likes Milton Caniff and George McManus among the highest-paid cultural producers of the age. The syndicated daily strip was a dream job—a highly visible spot working in trusted local papers read by millions. Of course, they were also scarce—only the best material was offered to local editors, and two Jewish kids from Cleveland with an oddball concept about a caped hero did not clear the bar.

As the story goes, Siegel and Shuster bounced around New York publishing houses desperate for a buyer before they encountered a receptive buyer in Malcolm Wheeler-Nicholson, whose National Allied Publications was one of a small handful of comic book publishers dotting the landscape at the time. He snapped up the rights to the character for $130, and the sample daily strips were snipped and stretched into comic book page format and run as the lead feature in a new magazine named *Action Comics*. That original thirteen-page Superman story has little to do with the character as we imagine him today. In his first adventure, Superman is a crime solver who saves an innocent man from wrongful execution, while Clark Kent, reporter for the *Daily Star*, covers everything from incidents of domestic abuse to corruption

Siri Kaur, *Christopher (phone)*, 2006. Chromogenic print. Courtesy of the artist.

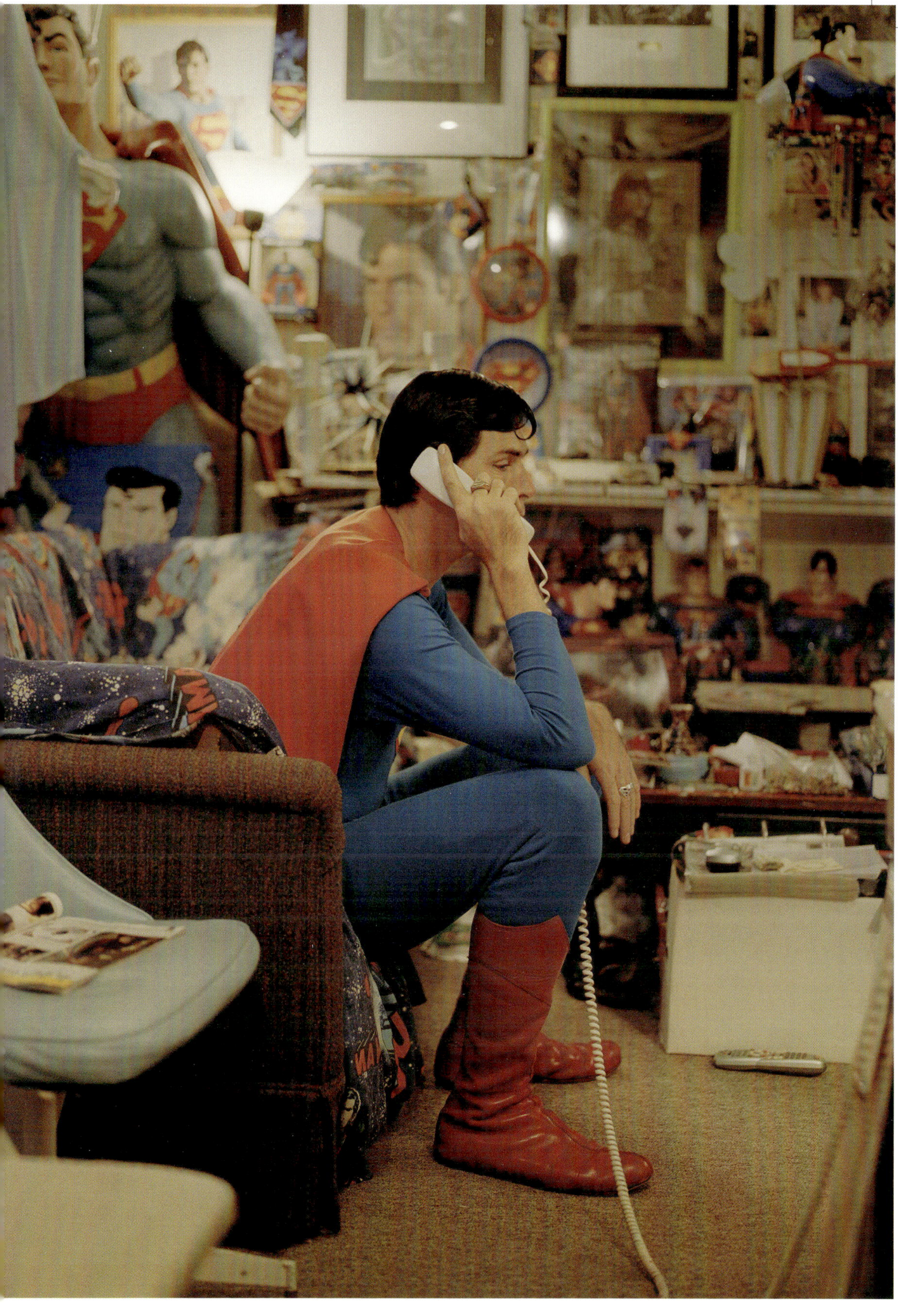

What I had been trying to do since 1958 was to spontaneously develop a story as I painted the picture, a psychological narrative. Good or bad, friendly or hateful, didn't matter to me because I simply enjoyed using my imagination. By the time I painted this picture I had already used Superman, Donald Duck, and toilets a number of times, so the resemblance between my Superman and the real Superman is pretty loose. However, using these cultural icons as subject helped me to connect with the art world, and I'll always be grateful for that. I occasionally revisit Superman, most recently in Superman Discovers God in the Asteroid Belt *(2016).*

—PETER SAUL

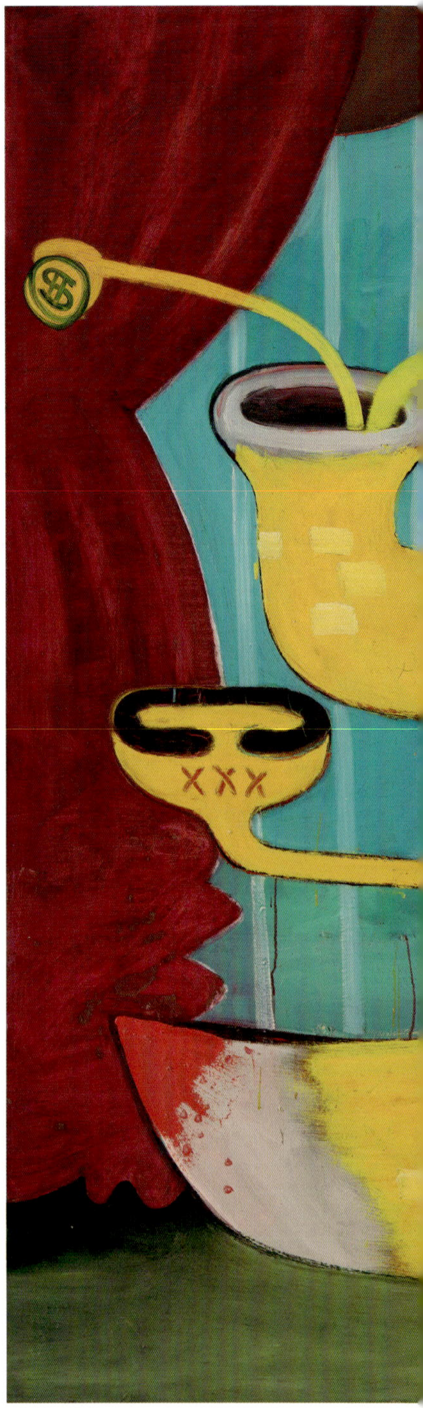

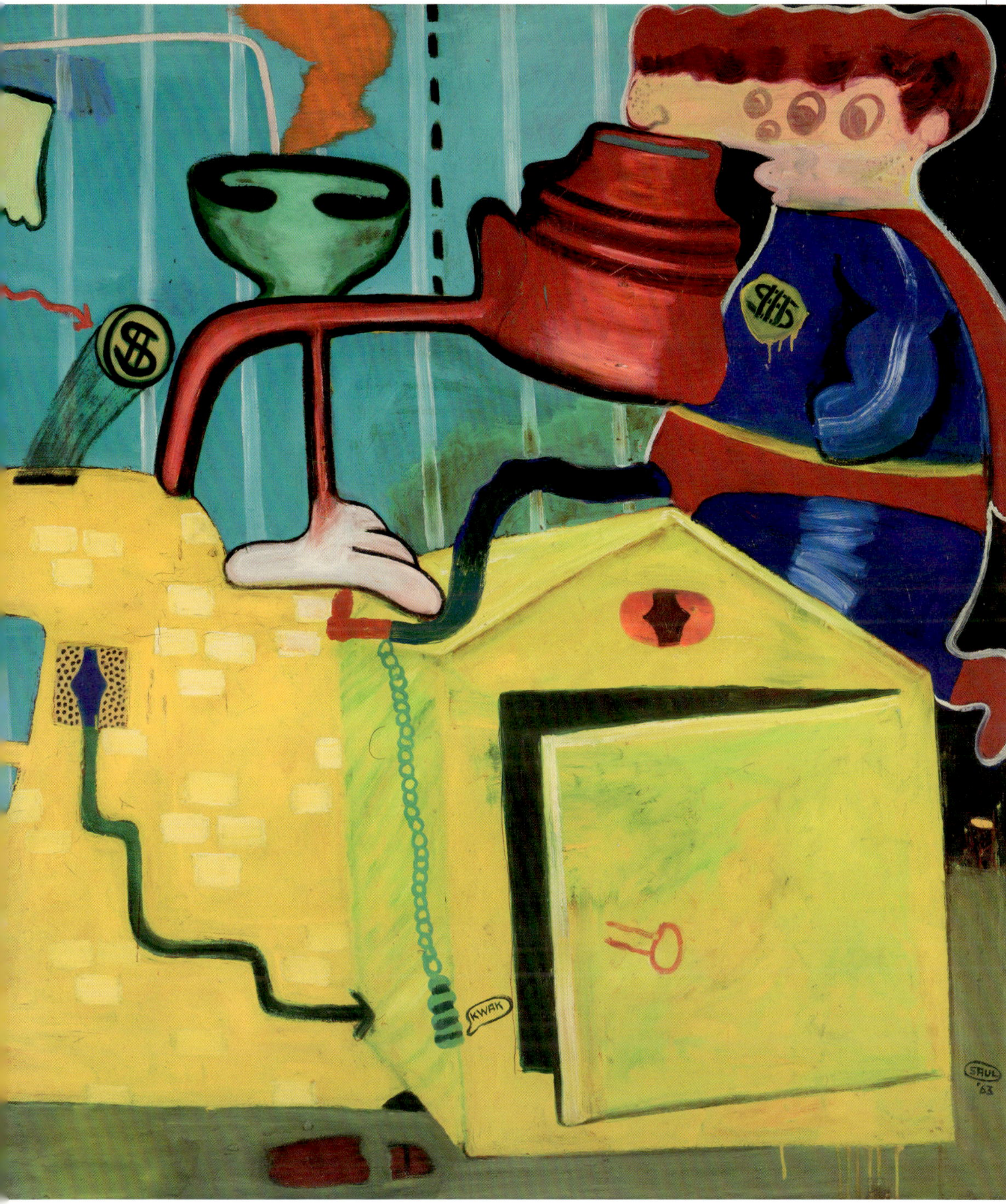

Peter Saul, *Superman Versus the Toilet Duck*, 1963. Oil on canvas. Crystal Bridges Museum of American Art, Bentonville, Arkansas, 2012.497.

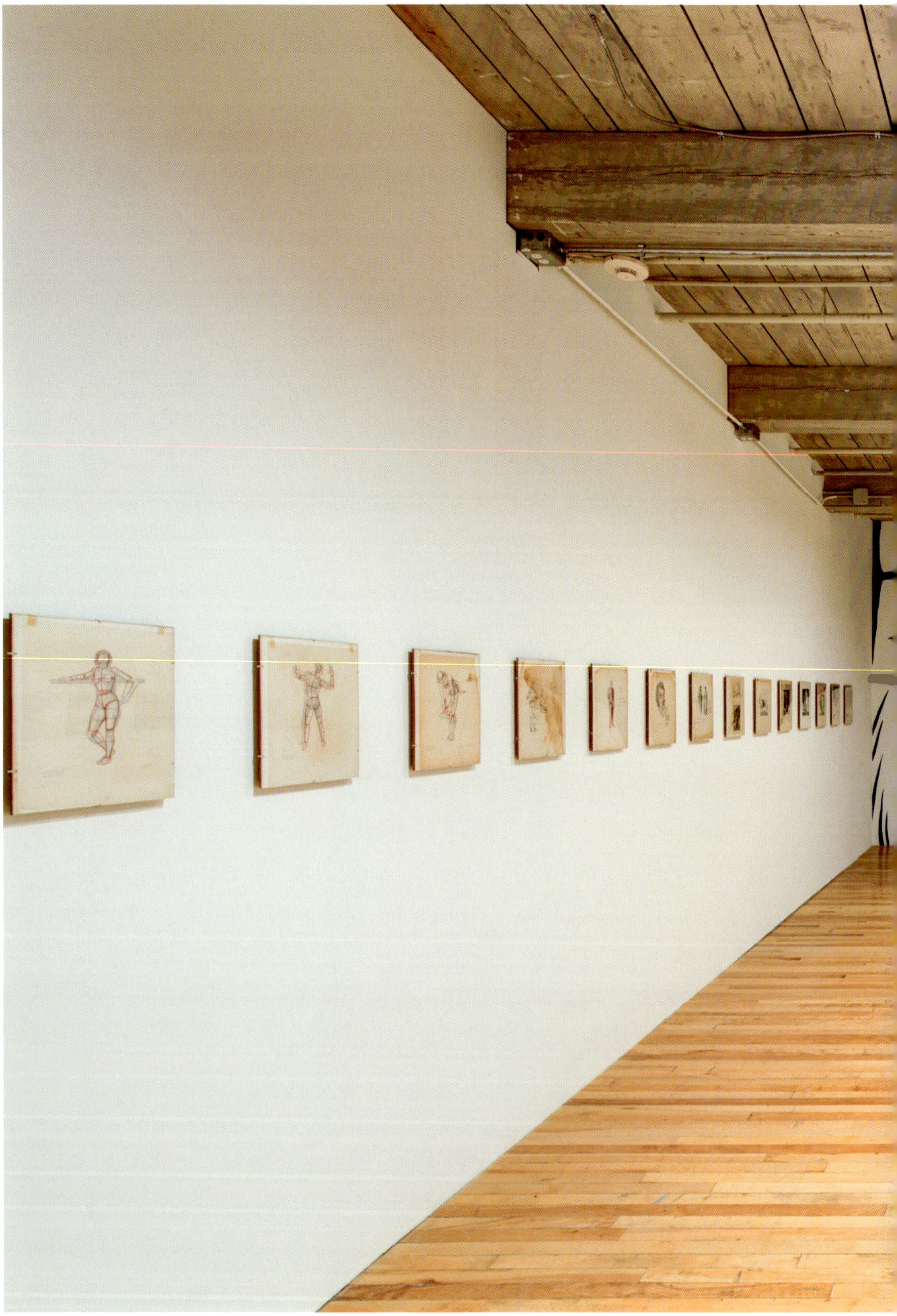

Jim Shaw, *The Issue of My Loins*, 2015. Installation. Courtesy the artist + Simon Lee Gallery, London + Hong Kong + Blum + Poe Los Angeles/New York/Tokyo.

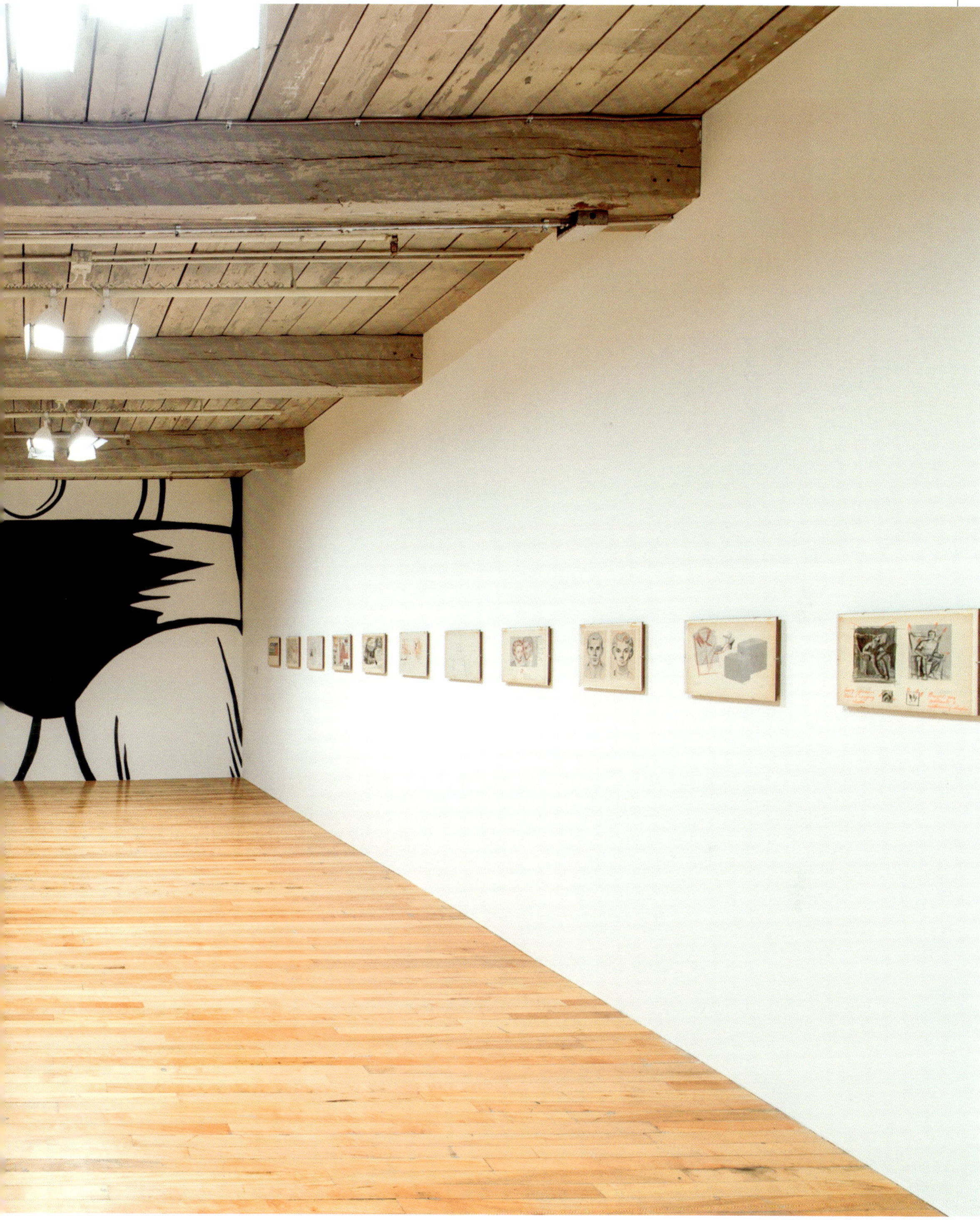

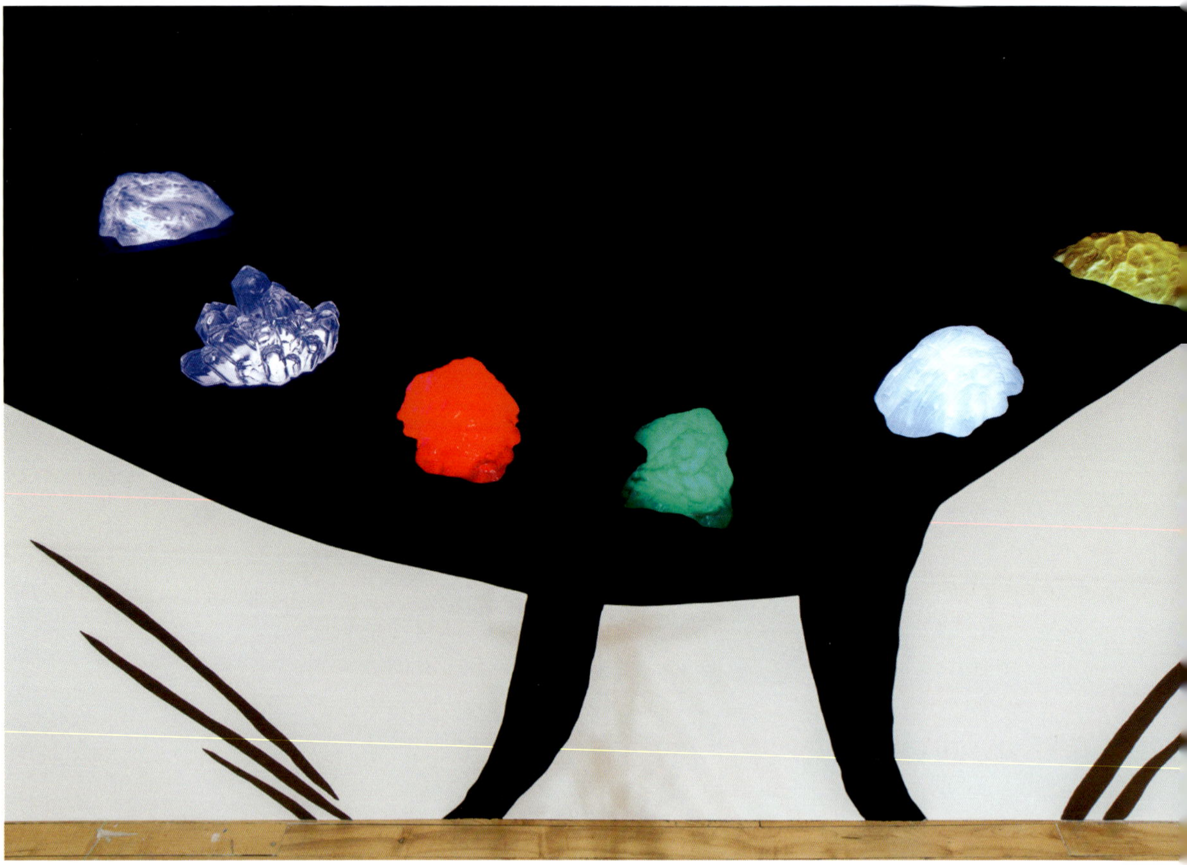

If my dreams are any guide to my subconscious, then Superman and the DC characters have become lodged in a deep vein of my core identity, along with many other mass culture characters. I never identified with Superman. I think he was more of a father figure, especially the wide-waisted version concocted by Wayne Boring (in case DC lost its copyright battle with Siegel and Shuster) that I grew up with. One rather traumatic episode of the TV show had him losing all his powers after being tricked into a freezing chamber by some crooks. I remember being shaken to my core at age eight or nine by that "castration" fantasy. **—JIM SHAW**

in Washington, occasionally transforming into Superman to menace criminals (and help his paper get a scoop).

The young creators seemed to want to shoehorn in every idea in their heads in the very first adventure. It was clear that no one at National Allied Publications felt they had a slam dunk either. Superman shared the first issue of *Action Comics* with seven other purveyors of action and adventure, including the boxer Pep Morgan, Zatara the Master Magician, and the improbably named Sticky-Mitt Stimson. Initially the publisher regarded Superman as no big deal; he appears on the cover of only three of the first ten issues of *Action Comics*. Nonetheless, his rise in the public imagination was genuinely meteoric: a previously unsaleable *Superman* daily newspaper strip by Siegel and Shuster began syndication through the McClure Syndicate on January 16, 1939, (less than a year after his first comic book appearance), and that same year, the covers of *Action Comics* promised "Superman! Appearing in this issue and every issue." The character leapt out of the anthology series and into his own eponymous title, *Superman*, in 1939. Crossover success quickly followed when *The Adventures of Superman* began airing on the Mutual Broadcasting System in February 1940.

It was the radio show, not the comic book, that granted us the phrase "Faster than a speeding bullet. More powerful than a locomotive. Able to leap tall buildings in a single bound!" It was also the radio show that first came up with the idea of kryptonite as a mineral that can weaken and even kill the otherwise indestructible Superman. As gaps began to spring up around his differing appearances in varying media, it became clear that Superman was not a fixed character with unvarying

Jim Shaw, *The Issue of My Loins*, 2015. Installation. Courtesy the artist + Simon Lee Gallery, London + Hong Kong + Blum + Poe Los Angeles/New York/ Tokyo.

aspects; increasingly he became the expression of an idea more than the reflection of a consistently thought-out fictional character.

Over time Superman's supporting cast grew. Spin-off comic books launched in the 1940s focused on Superboy and his adventures in Smallville, and in the 1950s these spin-off comic books were joined by *Superman's Girlfriend, Lois Lane* and *Superman's Pal, Jimmy Olsen*. All through this period, artists and writers struggled to find new ways to construct exciting tales about a hero whose roster of exceptional abilities had grown to absurd proportions, making him all but invincible unless you happened to have some kryptonite lying around. (There are, remarkably, twenty-two distinct types of kryptonite—each of which has distinct effects on Superman and his powers!)

Many of the iconic elements of Superman were developed not by his creators, but by his inheritors. After a fractious relationship with DC Comics, Siegel and Shuster left the company—and the character—in 1948 at the end of their ten-year contract; they assigned the rights to the publisher and moved on (although, in the decades that followed, several lawsuits would see them and their families attempt to regain some of what they sold).

For many, the dominant image of Superman has not been the one drawn by Shuster but the likeness created by Wayne Boring, one of several artists who took over the character in 1948 and who drew Superman into the 1960s. The Superman of Mel Ramos, for example, with his pensive expression and ironically undramatic pose, strongly recalls the costuming and facial features deployed by Boring in the 1950s: the red trunks, boots, and cape on a blue bodysuit, and the yellow only in the belt and crest. More directly, Jim Shaw's drawings in this exhibition are

Mel Ramos, *Superman*, 1962. Oil on canvas. Fine Arts Museums of San Francisco; Museum purchase, Dr. Leland A and Gladys K. Barber Fund and American Art Trust Fund.

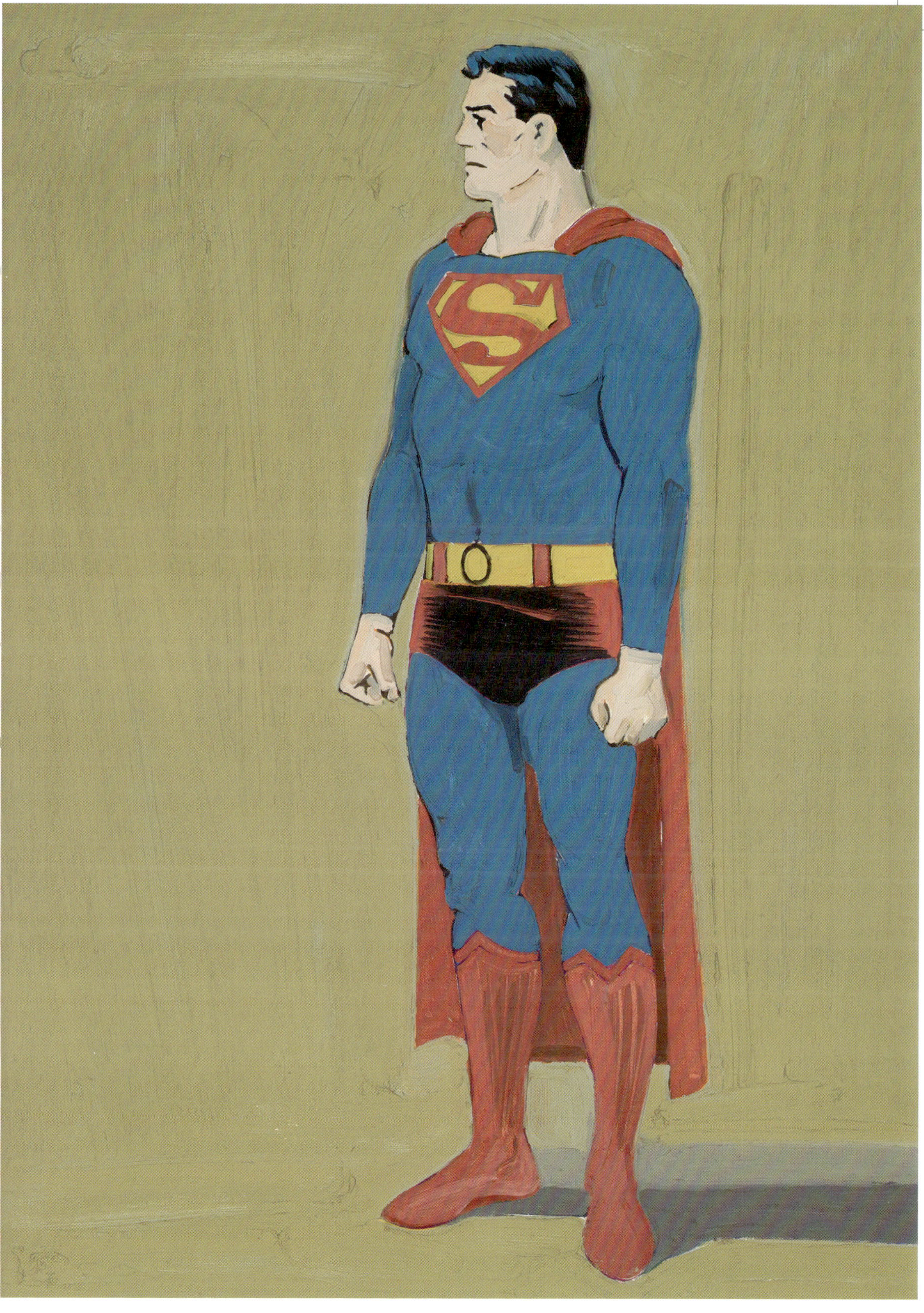

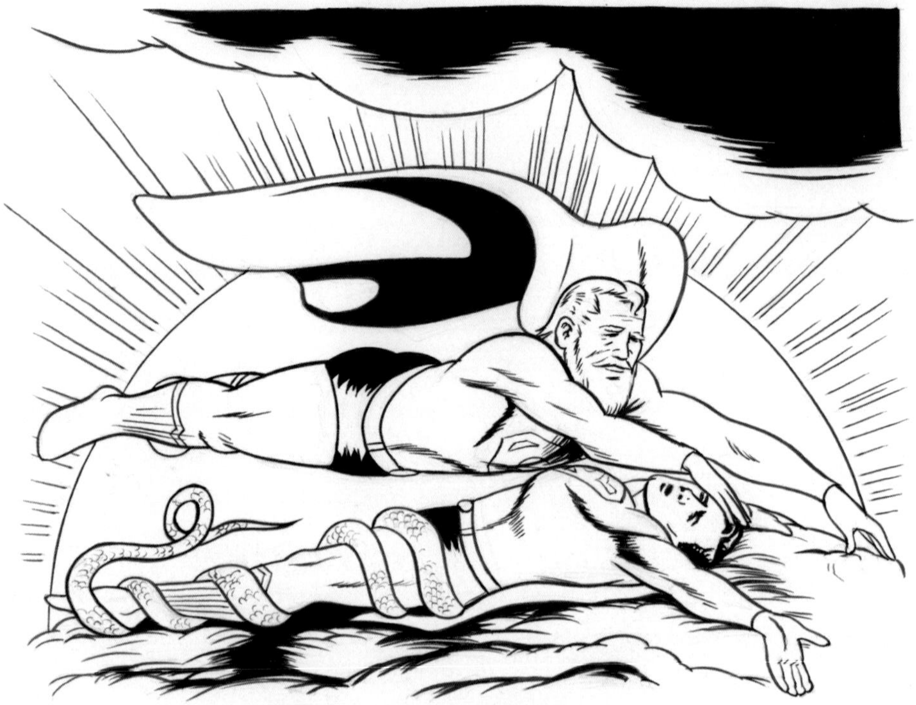

Jim Shaw, *Blake/Boring*, 2010. Ink on paper. Lent by Keith Fox and Tim Keyes.

titled *Blake/Boring*. They combine the Biblical imagery of English poet William Blake with the particularistic drawing style of Minnesotan Wayne Boring to deeply ironic effect. The fact that the Superman ideal is not only Boring's but also, to a large extent, boring, makes its crass obviousness much more supple and quixotic than its originators intended.

While more than one hundred artists have published Superman stories for DC Comics since 1938, the Superman drawn by Wayne Boring remains the urtext for the artists in this exhibition. It is Boring's postwar Superman, with his primary-colored costume and suburban dad next door imagery that is so generative for the artists in the exhibition. Several works here respond directly to the expanded Superman mythos that entered the comic books during the 1950s. Mike Kelley's Kandor sculptures reference the Kryptonian city first introduced into the Superman mythos in 1958, while both Raymond Pettibon's fascist Superman and Llyn Foulkes's *Where Did I Go Wrong* critique the seemingly stable image of Superman as an unproblematically middle-class white savior of the conformist superhero next door. By the 1960s, the angst-free Superman had become supremely uncool; the man in the red flannel cape, and as several of the pieces on display in this exhibition attest, the simple act of altering Superman's whiteness or realigning his sexuality can create profoundly important new understandings of the character.

The unexpected success of Superman spawned literally dozens of knockoffs and imitators, including many from the same publisher that would eventually join him in his crime-fighting adventures: Batman and Robin, the Green Lantern, the Flash, among many others. Perhaps surprisingly, Wonder Woman was not created as a simple gender-bending Superman. While other female superheroes (Bulletgirl, Mary Marvel, and Miss Fury among them) were rushed onto newsstands before her, Wonder Woman represented a genuinely innovative approach to the superhero genre.

Wonder Woman's creator could hardly have been further removed from the upstart kids who had developed Superman. While the early comic book industry, which was a low-paying and low-prestige profession, was dominated by fresh-out-of-high-school talent who wrote and drew monthly adventures as a way to break into the entertainment industry, Wonder Woman's creator, writer William Marston, was a Harvard-educated psychologist who was best known for attempting to develop and popularize the technology behind the lie detector. He was forty-eight years old when Wonder Woman debuted in *All-Star Comics* #8. In a 1940 interview, he praised the educational potential of comic books in a piece that caught the eye of Max Gaines, the publisher of two of the companies that would eventually comprise DC Comics. Gaines hired Marston for his editorial advisory board, which was intended to

Superman has become more than a comic book character. For most Americans, he represents an ideal moral compass, his greatest superpower being the hope and heroism his presence inspires. Referencing Barkley Hendricks' Icon for my Man Superman (Superman Never Saved Any Black People)—Bobby Seale, *1969, my painting,* Nunna My Heros, *2011, is a commentary on the enduring absence of Superman. In the Black community where issues like oppression, poverty, violence, and other traumas persist, Superman's nonappearance is glaring. My character subverts the Superman ideal by becoming his hero.* **—FAHAMU PECOU**

Fahamu Pecou, *Nunna My Heros: After Barkley Hendricks' 'Icon for My Man Superman,' 1969*, 2011. Acrylic, gold leaf, and oil stick on canvas. Nasher Museum of Art at Duke University; Gift of Marjorie and Michael Levine.

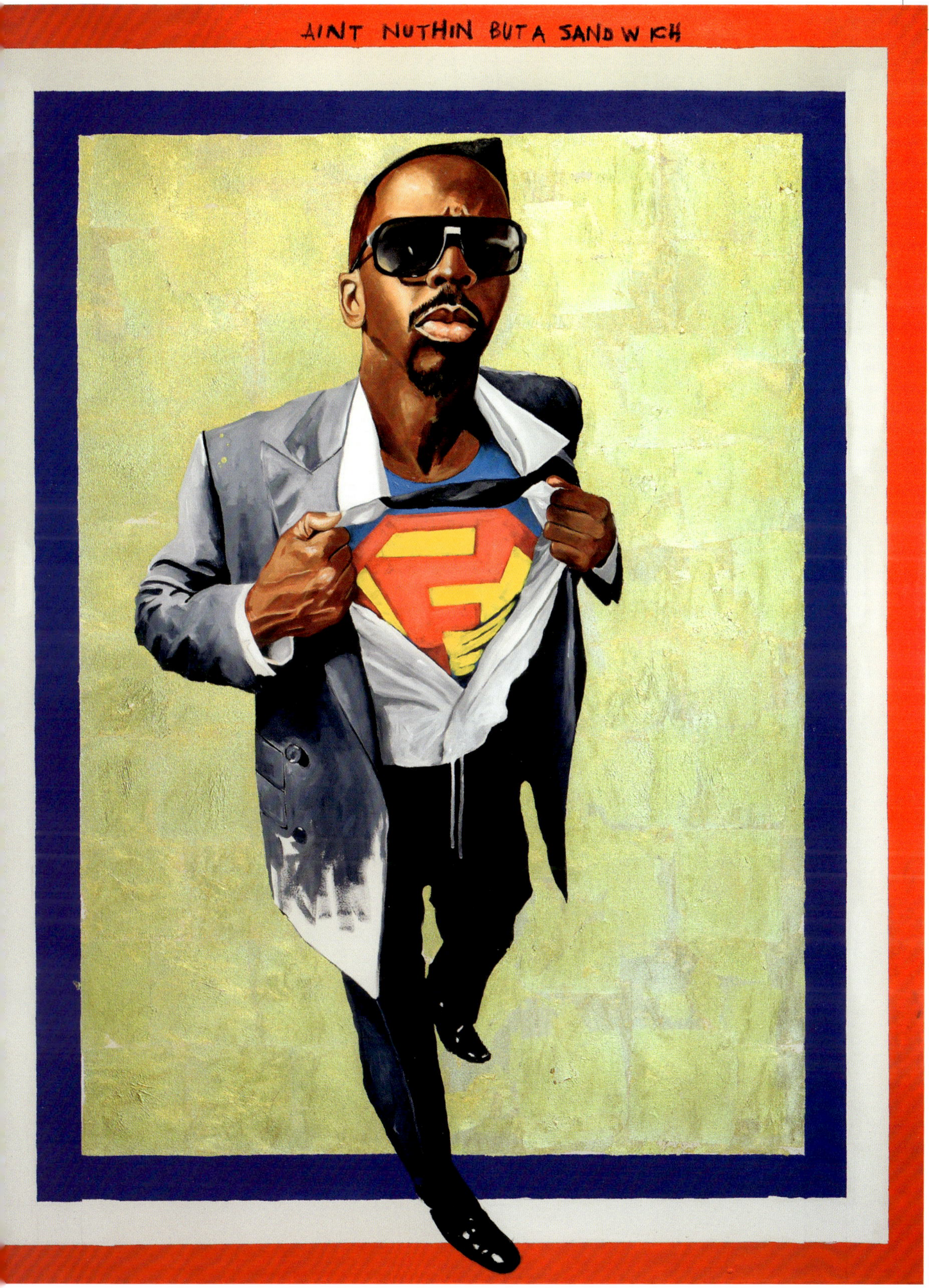
AINT NUTHIN BUT A SANDWICH

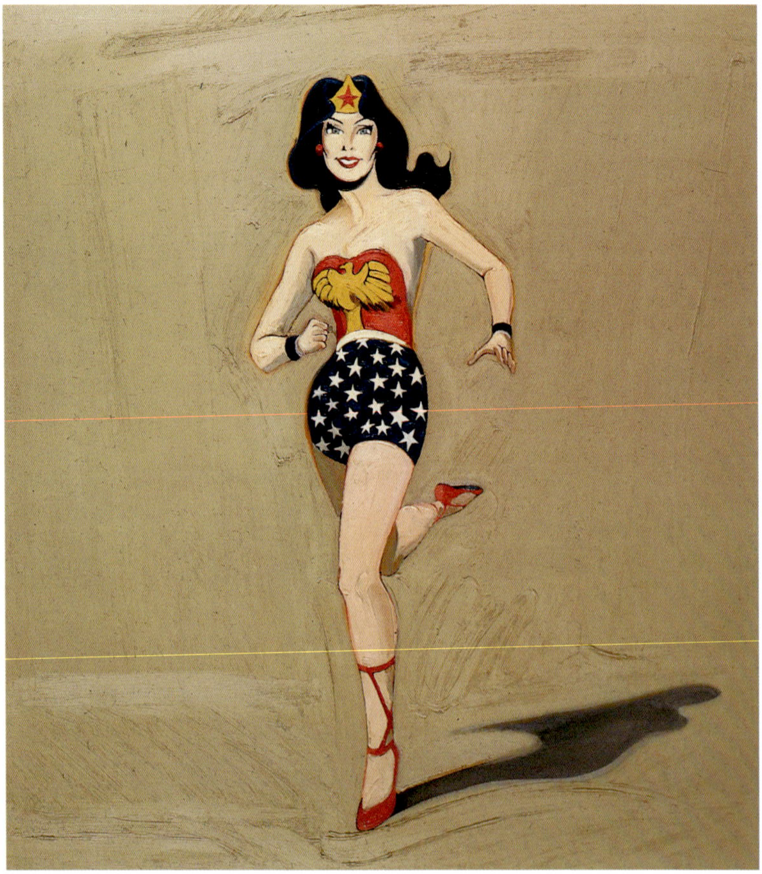

I'm a collector of comic books, and I don't read them so much anymore but they provide visual stuff for me to use. When I was younger, I started collecting them, and that grew into six or seven boxes of these things. Wonder Woman and Superman—when I painted those pictures it was like I was a little kid. As the years have gone by, things have changed, and people have taken these pictures for much different reasons. I'm flabbergasted by how much interest they have. They never were important pieces, they were just pieces I did. It's beyond me that they were so popular, but I'm happy for it. **—MEL RAMOS**

help ward off complaints from parents that the comic books published by Gaines and his colleagues were corrupting their children. It was Marston's wife, Elizabeth, who suggested the development of a female superhero who battled crime with love rather than with her fists, so he pitched the idea to the publisher. After a try-out appearance, Wonder Woman took the lead in the newly launched *Sensation Comics* beginning in 1942.

As she made her comics debut almost exactly coincidental with the belated entry of the United States into the Second World War, it is not surprising that Wonder Woman was originally styled as a patriotic crime fighter. She shares a red, blue, and yellow color scheme with Superman, but her star-spangled blue skirt and red tunic held steady for decades, even after the skirt was dropped for a more form-fitting costume resembling a bathing suit. Over the years, Wonder Woman has been transformed even more dramatically than Superman. Originally an Amazonian warrior fighting evil in "Man's World" on behalf of her beloved Steve Trevor, her origins were shifted to take on a Hellenic lineage in the 1960s under writer Robert Kanigher when she was described as "beautiful as Aphrodite, wise as Athena, strong as Hercules, and swift as Hermes." In the 1970s she briefly lost her powers, opened a boutique, and became a private investigator. The 2000s saw a return to Greek mythology as the basis for many of her stories. By the time of the 2017 movie, her competing origin stories had become synchronized so that she was the daughter of Queen Hippolyta, a legendary Amazonian from Greek mythology.

Throughout it all, Wonder Woman has been defined by a visual style that is readily on display in this exhibition. Among the hallmarks

Mel Ramos, *Wonder Woman*, 1962. Oil on canvas. Rochelle and Darren Leininger Family Collection.

Growing up in the 1980s, superheroes were the true gods of the airwaves next to glam rock-and-rollers, and Wonder Woman was tops. Fast forward to my first week in Los Angeles: walking down Hollywood Boulevard, I saw Superman standing on the corner. His tarnished uniform hung loose. But there was glee in his face. He took me back to when I was Wonder Woman, to the unflattering nude stockings and sequined embroidery that transformed me for Halloween. I knew that when he looked in the mirror he WAS Superman, just as I was Wonder Woman and everything was perfect. Even if the costumes are dingy and the makeup cheap, dressing up as these superheroes that we worshipped in childhood carries a powerful magic that I want to revisit in my work.

—SIRI KAUR

Siri Kaur, *Wonder Woman*, 2013.
Chromogenic print.
Courtesy of the artist.

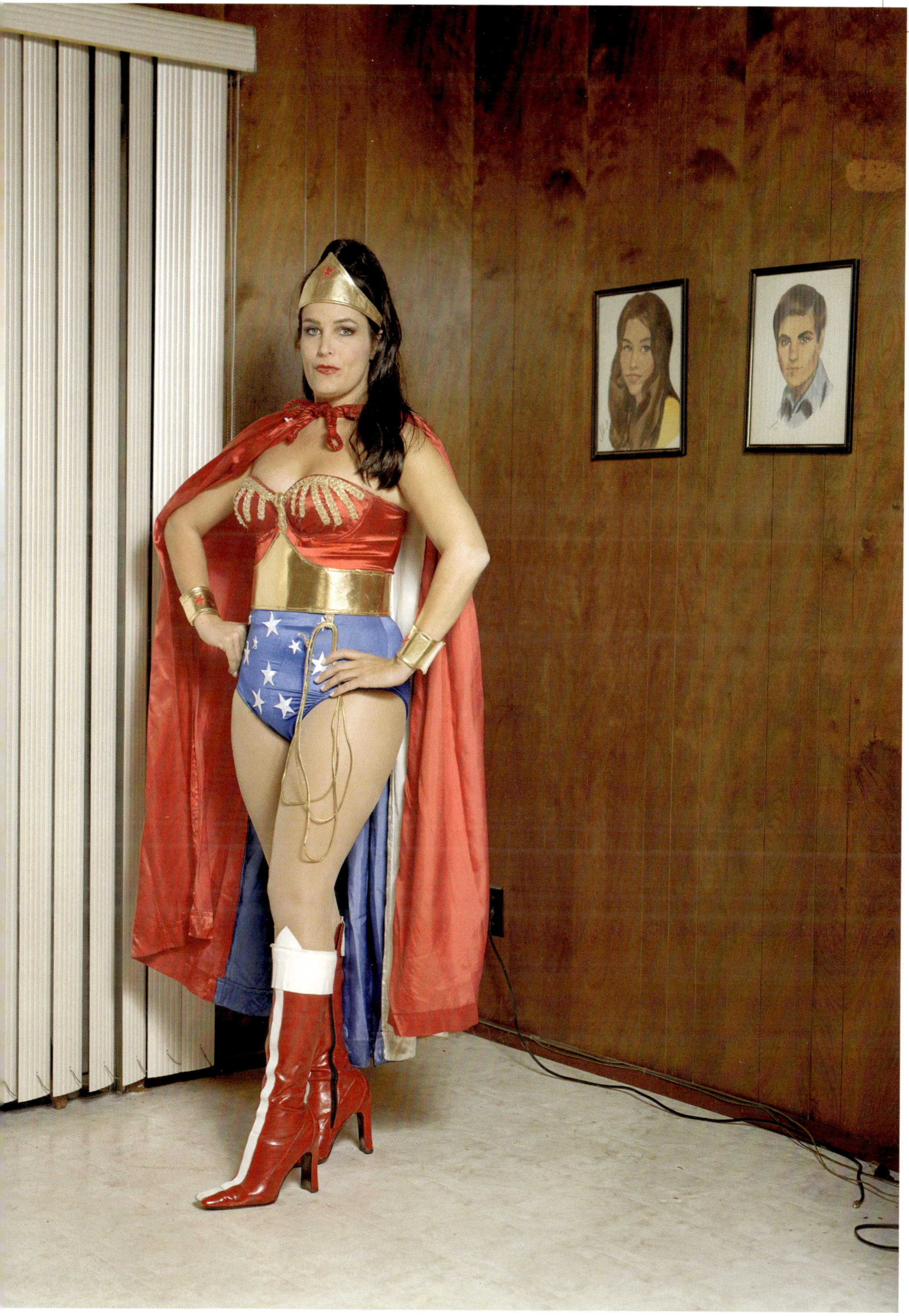

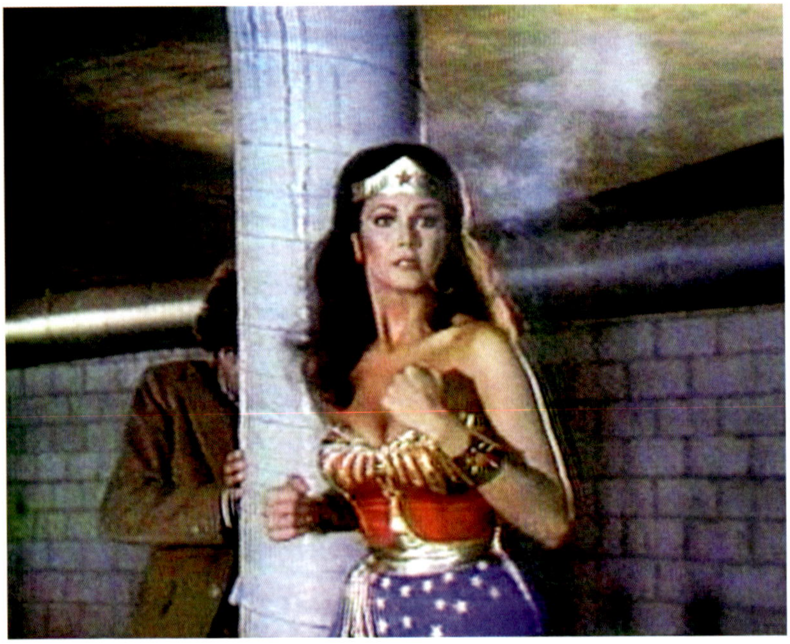

of Wonder Woman are the golden tiara and wrist bracelets that featured so prominently in the 1970s television series (and therefore also in Dara Birnbuam's *Technology/Transformation: Wonder Woman*). Indeed, it is the look and style of Lynda Carter from the short-lived *Wonder Woman* television series of the mid-1970s that sets the standard for the character more than it is the style of the comic books. Works in this exhibition by Siri Kaur, Mary Beth Edelson, and Sarah Hill are among those that most concretely reference the televisual version of Wonder Woman. This is not surprising given that Wonder Woman only emerged as a significant cultural icon in the 1970s. While Superman and Batman were the subjects of multiple forms of cross-media promotion, including film and radio, beginning in the 1940s, Wonder Woman's success was much more limited. Not even a daily comic strip caught hold in her early years; it ran only for a little more than one year in 1944 and 1945, a notable failure given the standards of the time. In a postwar era in which a multitude of comics targeted young female readers, Wonder Woman did not particularly stand out and her title was never especially noteworthy. Romance comics, humor comics, even comic books featuring Betty and Veronica outshone Wonder Woman in the early part of her story.

Dara Birnbaum, *Technology/Transformation: Wonder Woman*, 1978. Video. Collection of the artist.

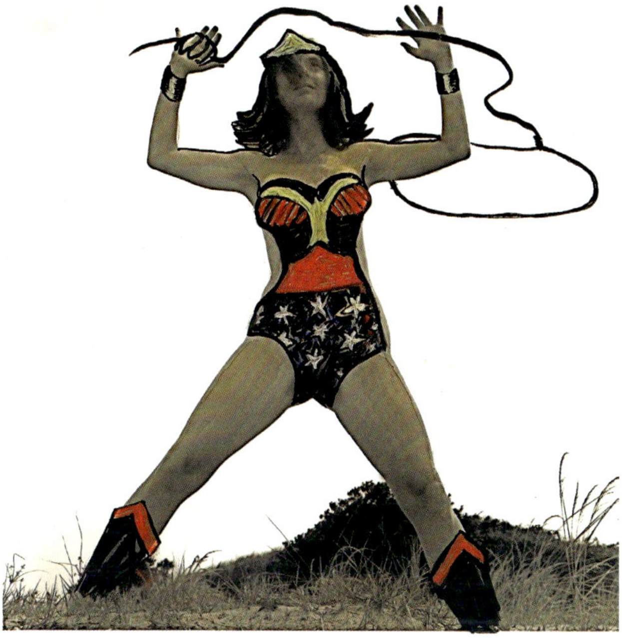

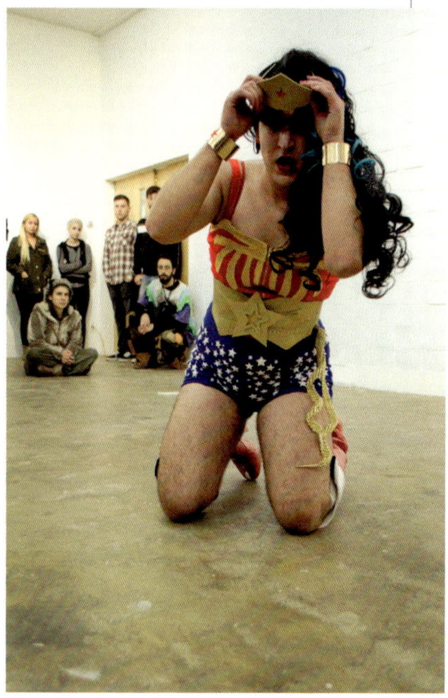

All that changed in 1972, when Gloria Steinem launched *Ms. Magazine* and put Wonder Woman on the very first cover. While it was meant as an appeasement to the magazine's backer, Warner Communications (which by that point, was also the owner of DC Comics), Steinem nonetheless set about to reclaim the character as the icon of second wave feminism. She could have just as easily picked Rosie the Riveter—whose own iconicity begins to blur into Wonder Woman's as many of the artists in this exhibition so ably demonstrate. However, at the height of demonstrations against the war in Vietnam, Rosie must have seemed an inopportune choice.

By the early seventies, Wonder Woman's heroism was far from assured. In the comic books, her character had been stripped of her exceptional powers and become a boutique-owning supersleuth. In her efforts to reassert the character's spectacular origins, Steinem inadvertently became the catalyst for DC Comics to cancel a six-part "Women's Lib" story in which Wonder Woman comes to the aid of an abortion clinic. Yet she also helped cement the image of Wonder Woman in popular culture when she edited a volume of 1940s Wonder Woman stories by Marston and artist Harry Peter in 1977. By that time, the now-cult classic television series starring Lynda Carter had been on and off

← Mary Beth Edelson, *To the Rescue*, 1973. Oil and ink on silver gelatin print. Collection of Amy Gold and Brett Gorvy.

↑ Sarah Hill, *They Wonder*, 2015. Public Communication: Performing Knowledge of the Body. Suplex, BLUE orange Contemporary, Houston, Texas.

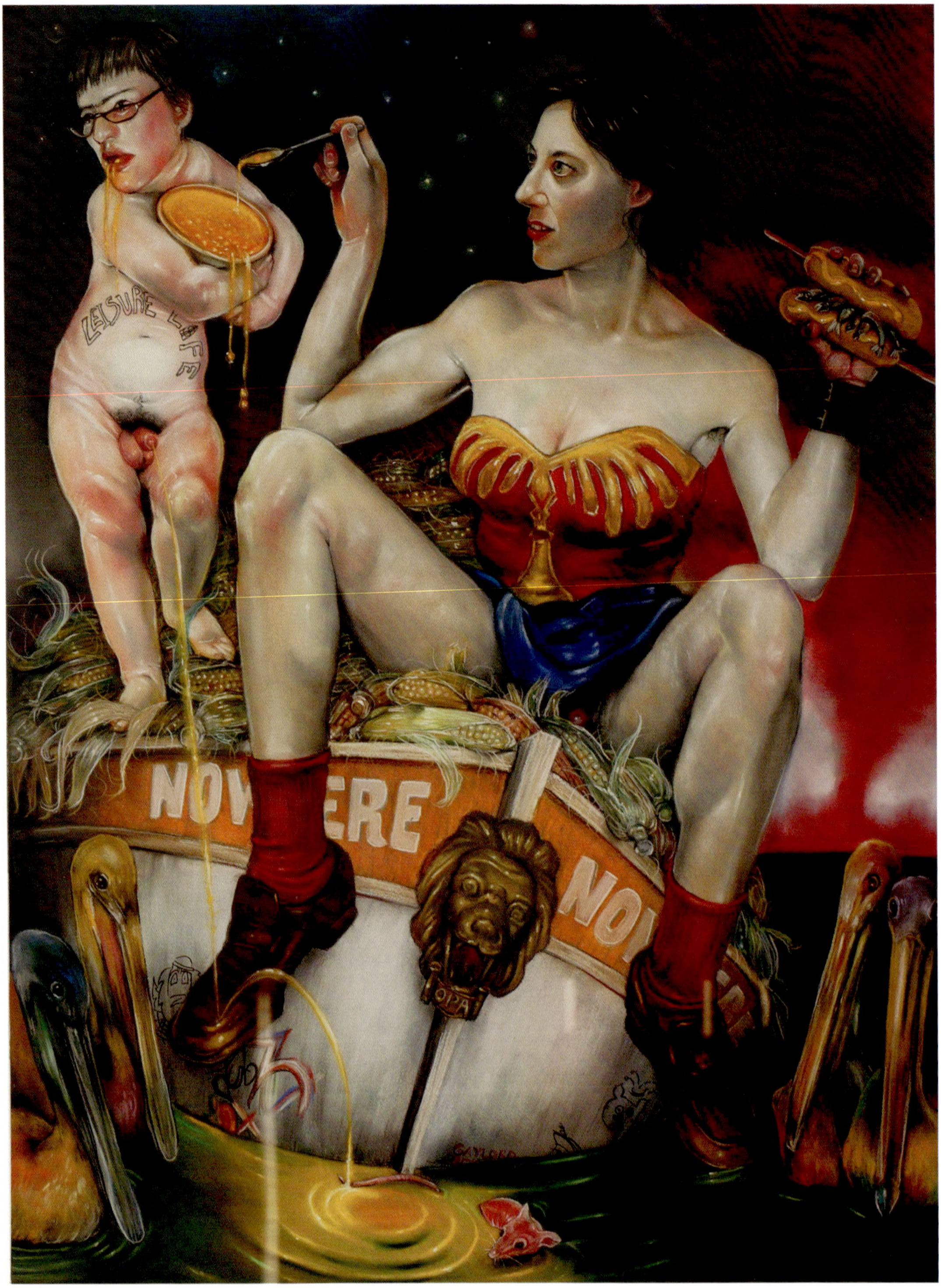
LEISURE LIFE
OPA

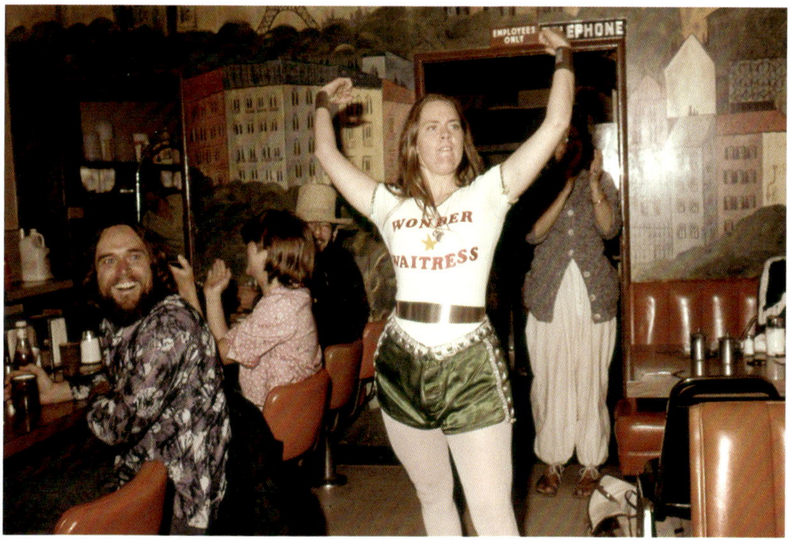

the air for two years. It is that version, more than any comic book style, that is most evident in the exhibition. Carter's Wonder Woman was part Barbie Doll, part Mary Tyler Moore, and everything young girls craved in the hypersexualized, quasi-feminist popular culture of the seventies.

As second-wave feminism gave way to postfeminism and gender politics embraced new forms of intersectional feminism, Wonder Woman and Rosie the Riveter found increasingly common ground. The goddess and the laborer are no longer dialectical versions of femininity but embodiments of the spectacular and ordinary elements necessary to survive in a world where poverty and violence remain gendered. Their wartime roles minimized, they now stand together as icons of empowered working women, exhorting other women to join them as they fight for gender justice. Jamie Wildman-Webber of the artist collective The Waitresses, with her biceps flexed and fists pumped in the 1978 performance *Wonder Waitress*, recalls both Diana and Rosie, while other works in the exhibition remind us of the everyday heroics of any woman working minimum wage service jobs or breaking gender barriers in mechanical and technology sectors.

Wonder Woman's is a complicated feminism, to be sure, rooted more in postfeminism than in the inclusive and diversity-driven potential of intersectionality. Renée Cox draws attention to the all-consuming whiteness of feminine power, transforming Wonder Woman's all-American costume into a pan-African emblem of resistance to cultural colonialism. Most striking to me in this exhibition is the iconic relationship between

↑ The Waitresses, *Wonder Waitress* vignette, April 1978. Documentary photograph, 7-day, site-specific, Conceptual Performance Art. © The Waitresses – Jerri Allyn & Anne Gauldin. Photographer Maria Karras.

← Barnaby Whitfield, *Gold Lion's Gonna Tell Me Where the Light Is*, 2007. Pastel on paper. From the collection of James and Maureen Dorment.

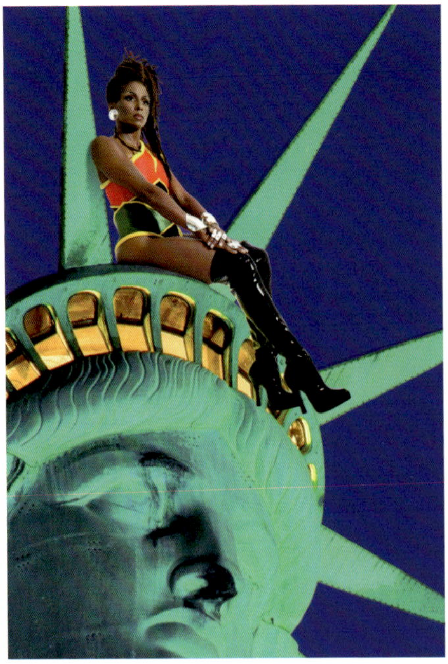

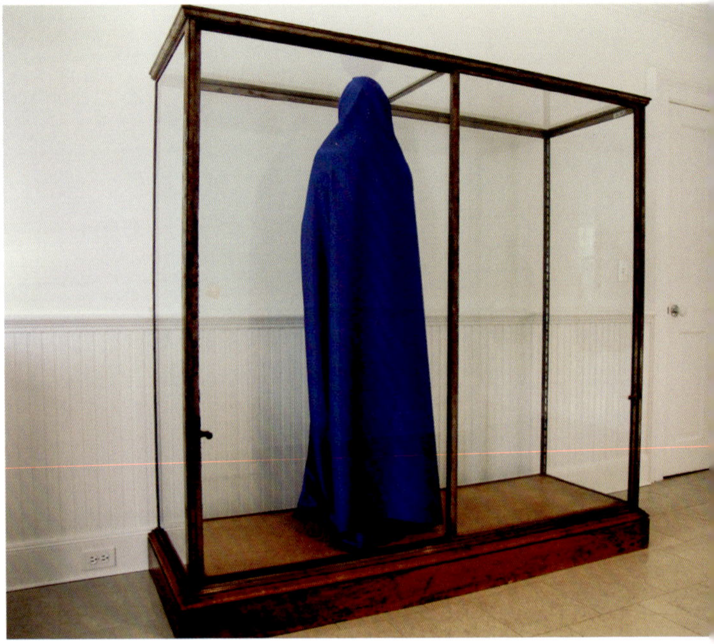

↑ Renée Cox, *Chillin' with Liberty* (from the Rajé Series), 1998. Cibachrome print. Courtesy of the artist.

→ Aphrodite Désirée Navab, *Object of Curiosity* from *Super East/West Woman*, 2002–8. Archival chromogenic prints. Collection of the artist.

the superhero cape and the chador, a traditional Muslim covering, by Aphrodite Désirée Navab. Referencing Superman more than Wonder Woman, the long blue cape is a collision of gender and colonial politics, where neither culture emerges as victor and the invisible woman regains her agency. Indeed, the image of Wonder Woman roaming the skies in her invisible jet—a turbo-powered room of her own, is present by the very absence of any woman's body here.

Some critics argue that superheroes are the closest thing that American culture has come to creating mythic figures that genuinely represent the United States in the industrial (and now postindustrial) age. Tempting as this line of argument might be, the reality is that myths are not the trademarked property of WarnerMedia, Inc. The reality is that Superman and Wonder Woman are not myths but they are symbols. They are ideas about heroism, about patriotism, about service and self-sacrifice that are reducible to a small handful of iconic visual elements rather than to the sometimes overly complicated elements of the competing narratives in which they have starred for more than eight decades. Blue tights and red trunks. A star-spangled skirt. A stylized *S*. Thigh-high red boots. These are the starting points for the artists in this exhibition who mobilize these sometimes-tired elements in the service of entirely new ideas and ideals.

BART BEATY

Bart Beaty has written, edited, and translated more than a dozen books about comics. His monographs include: *Fredric Wertham and the Critique of Mass Culture* (2005), *Canadian Television Today* (with Rebecca Sullivan, 2006), *Unpopular Culture: Transforming the European Comic Book in the 1990s* (2007), David Cronenberg's *A History of Violence* (2008), *Comics Versus Art* (2012), *Twelve-Cent Archie* (2015; second edition 2017), and *Greatest Comic Book of All Time* (with Benjamin Woo, 2016). He is the editor of the seven volumes of the *Critical Survey of Graphic Novels* (2012; second edition 2018), and co-editor of *How Canadians Communicate: Contexts of Canadian Popular Culture* (2010), *The French Comics Theory Reader* (2014), and the forthcoming *Comics Studies Guidebook* (with Charles Hatfield, 2018). As translator, he has published three volumes: Thierry Groensteen's *The System of Comics* (2007), Jean-Paul Gabilliet's *Of Comics and Men* (2010), and Thierry Smolderen's *The Origins of Comics* (2014). He is a professor of English at the University of Calgary.

MEN OF STEEL, WOMEN OF WONDER

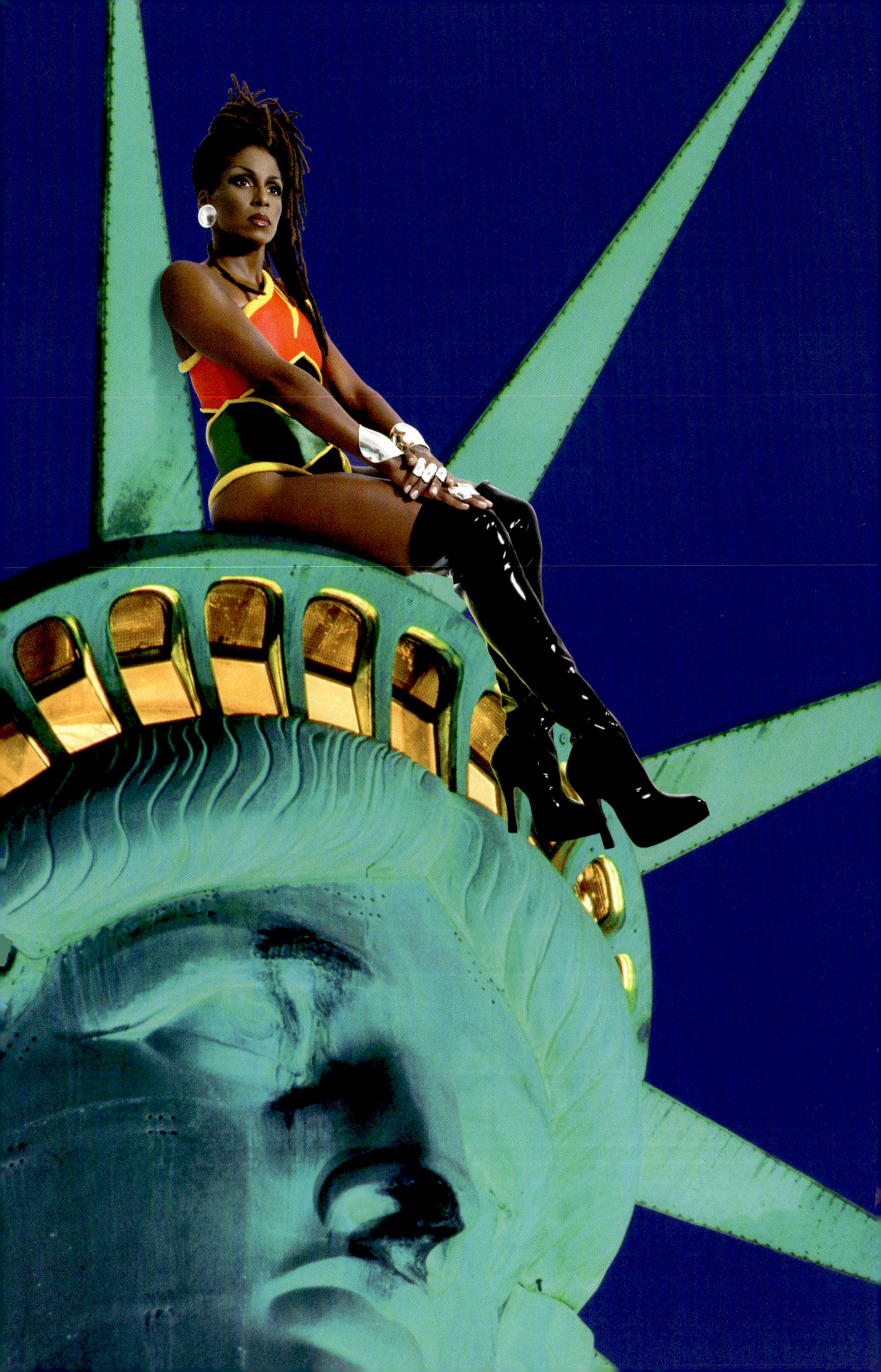

MEN OF STEEL WOMEN OF WONDER

Modern American Superheroes in Contemporary Art

ALEJO BENEDETTI

Crystal Bridges Museum of American Art The University of Arkansas Press | Fayetteville | 2019

CONTENTS

ISSUE

00

ZERO ISSUE

MEN OF STEEL, WOMEN OF WONDER

FOREWORD

Growing up my two brothers and I would frequently take on the personas of various superheroes in some amazing adventure. My older brother was always Superman and my younger brother and I were relegated to playing Plastic Man or other supporting characters. (I personally loved being Plastic Man.) For me, thinking of Superman evokes fond childhood memories, but while my thoughts center on role-playing with my brothers, for many people—including artists—superheroes evoke vastly different emotions and perspectives.

Men of Steel, Women of Wonder was designed to examine art-world responses to Superman and Wonder Woman, responses that range from endearing tributes to cringing critiques. Themes of national identity, American values, social politics, and even humanity itself are called into question in this exhibition as artists use the influence of these superheroes on American pop culture to draw connections to real-world issues. In this exhibition, several works from the Crystal Bridges permanent collection can be found alongside works on loan from artists, museums, and collectors from around the world.

Crystal Bridges Museum of American Art opened in 2011 with a vision of education and transformation through art. It is a place where all are welcome, even superheroes from Krypton and Paradise Island (now known as Themyscira)—the places from which Superman and Wonder Woman, for reasons of war and displacement, immigrated to the United States to become iconic symbols of American democracy. What could be a better way for an American art museum to pay tribute to our superheroes than by showcasing artists who use them to reflect on American identities at their best and at their worst? It is through heritage and artistic possibility that we can do our part to fight for truth, justice, and the American way.

Ever since Crystal Bridges Assistant Curator Alejo Benedetti began working on *Men of Steel, Women of Wonder*, it seems that our entire staff has found a way to feel like kids again, accessing their love of superheroes anew as they discover different perspectives through the eyes of the exhibition artists. We look forward to welcoming visitors of all ages and walks of life to *Men of Steel, Women of Wonder*, whether they've been with Superman and Wonder Woman for the past eighty years or are just learning their names. We know they will come away with a greater understanding of these intriguing characters and of the American spirit, as seen through the eyes of the artists in the show.

ROD BIGELOW
Executive Director & Chief Diversity and Inclusion Officer
Crystal Bridges Museum of American Art

ACKNOWLEDGMENTS

I've long had a fascination with superheroes. They adorn my desk at work, have played a surprisingly large role in my art history career, and find their way into my normal life on nearly a daily basis. It's a crazy, beautiful, and magnificent world to live in, and so the opportunity to organize a show around two icons like Superman and Wonder Woman is, in short, a dream project. Crystal Bridges continually proves itself to be a breeding ground for these types of opportunities, and what is even more amazing is the unbelievable amount of support that accompanies the projects we conceive. Everyone from artists, lenders, sponsors, and colleagues leaned into their geekiness to help make this project a reality. It's been the greatest joy to watch a small passion project become such an amazing to-do, and I want to pause for just a moment to thank some of the heroes that shaped, refined, and helped realize this vision.

I want to start by thanking all of the living artists in the exhibition who let me pick their brains about their works, talked to me about Superman and Wonder Woman, and generously spent time answering the question *Why Superman/Wonder Woman?* These artists include: Laylah Ali, Emma Amos, Laurie Anderson, Dara Birnbaum, Katherine Bradford, Enrique Chagoya, Michael Ray Charles, Papo Colo, Renée Cox, Mary Beth Edelson, Siamak Filizadeh, Llyn Foulkes, Margaret Harrison, Sarah Hill, Steven Paul Judd, Siri Kaur, Simon Monk, Aphrodite Désirée Navab, Fahamu Pecou, Raymond Pettibon, Dulce Pinzón, Pope.L, Valentin Popov, Robert Pruitt, Mel Ramos, Vincent Ramos, Peter Saul, Jim Shaw, Roger Shimomura, Rich Simmons, Keiichi Tanaami, Jacky Tsai, the Waitresses, Peter Williams, Barnaby Whitfield, and Jason Bard Yarmosky. This show is all about heroes, and I've always thought that curators are really just artist superfans in khakis. It's been a pleasure working with art world heroes I've admired for years and meeting new ones whose adventures are just unfolding—for whom I hope this show is just one small stepping stone in their soon-to-be well known origin stories.

I also would like to thank the lenders to this exhibition: the Fine Arts Museums of San Francisco; the Rochelle and Darren Leininger Family Collection; the Nasher Museum of Art at Duke University; Alexi and Corby Reese; Simon Lee Gallery; Maureen Dorment; Louis K. and Susan P. Meisel; Jim Halperin and Heritage Auctions; the Library of Congress; the Smithsonian American Art Museum; the Westmoreland Museum of American Art; the #Menelik Woolcock Collection: Zewditu Menelik, Aron Daniel, Adrian Woolcock; David Lewis Gallery; the Mike Kelley Foundation; the Walker Art Center; Roozbeh Taeed; Mel Casas Family Trust; Koplin Del Rio Gallery; Oliver Cole Gallery; Julia L. Lanigan; The Art of Emprise, Emprise Bank, Wichita, KS; Los Angeles County Museum of Art; Modernism Inc.; Barbara Karp Shuster; Amy Gold and Brett Gorvy; Ronald Feldman Gallery; Alida Anderson Art Projects; Mitchell-Innes & Nash; Ryan Lee Gallery; Alan Hergott and Curt Shepard. Thank you for letting us live with your artworks for the run of the show. It's no small gesture to lend these works, and we're forever grateful for your generosity.

This exhibition would not have been possible without the generous support of our exhibition sponsors: Stout Executive Search, Rhianon DeLeeuw and Joshua Mahoney, Esther Silver-Parker, and Deborah Wright, the Arkansas Humanities Council, and the National

Endowment for the Humanities. It's not just superpowers that get a show like this off the ground, and your financial support helped us reach new heights with this show.

The idea for this catalog was born out of an awareness of the comic source material, a love of that format, and a desire to nod to those origins in this publication. I'm tremendously appreciative of D. S. Cunningham and the entire team at the University of Arkansas Press, who listened to a crazy idea, saw its potential, and helped put together something that we are immensely proud to call our publication. An enormous thank you goes out to Diane Carroll, director of communications at Crystal Bridges, for coordinating this partnership and guiding this collaboration.

I thank Bart Beaty, Erika Doss, and Andrianna Campbell for their fantastic and insightful contributions to the catalog. Each brought their unique voice to the publication and presented new, thoughtful scholarship to a topic brimming with possibility. Each essay approaches these characters and artworks from a different angle, and each brilliantly provides new insight into how we should think about these familiar characters and their roles in society.

I am thrilled beyond belief that *Men of Steel, Women of Wonder* will have a life past Crystal Bridges as it travels first to the San Antonio Museum of Art in my home state of Texas and then to the Addison Gallery at Phillips Academy in Andover, Massachusetts—the alma mater of another comic hero, Tony Stark. These heroes protect all of America, they can't be contained in one place, and traveling to different institutions allows the message of the show and these iconic heroes to spread across the United States.

Exhibitions and catalogs have many moving pieces and take teamwork to get off the ground. Nothing gets accomplished at this museum without a team of incredible superheroes. Huge thanks go to the *Men of Steel, Women of Wonder* team at Crystal Bridges: Moira Anderson, senior museum educator, public programs; Catherine Hryniewicz, project manager, exhibitions; Jessi Mueller, exhibition designer; Anna Vernon, creative director; Jennifer de Martino, head of collections management; Melanie Fox, associate registrar, exhibitions and loans; Teagan Piazza, collections assistant; Leesha Alston, registrar of exhibitions; and everyone on the collections management team who assisted with this project. A special thank you goes to my main partner in crime on this project, interpretation manager Stace Treat, whose love of these characters rivals my own and whose role as sounding board, cheerleader, and collaborator more than earns him the title of Superman in his own right.

Thank you to the entire Crystal Bridges curatorial team for assisting throughout the process and for being the early audience and advocates for this project, especially my two curatorial mentors, Chad Alligood and Lauren Haynes, whose sage wisdom and direction from the beginning to the end of the project kept me on the right path. Thank you to Robin Groesbeck, director of exhibitions and interpretation, and Margi Conrads, director of curatorial affairs for advocating for this project early in the process. Thank you to two summers' worth of interns in Emma Osle and Alex Jones for agreeing to be geeks with me for a few months and for always being willing to tackle anything I threw your way. Thank you to Rod Bigelow, executive director and chief diversity and inclusion officer, for his support of this exhibition. And thank you to Meg, who was the first to hear about this idea and who—with this project and everything—helps me find my hidden super strength.

Finally, I would like to thank the board of directors and all of the amazing supporters of Crystal Bridges for allowing me to do the work I love. There aren't many places where you feel encouraged to follow your passion and then find support at every step along the way. For that I am eternally grateful.

ALEJO BENEDETTI

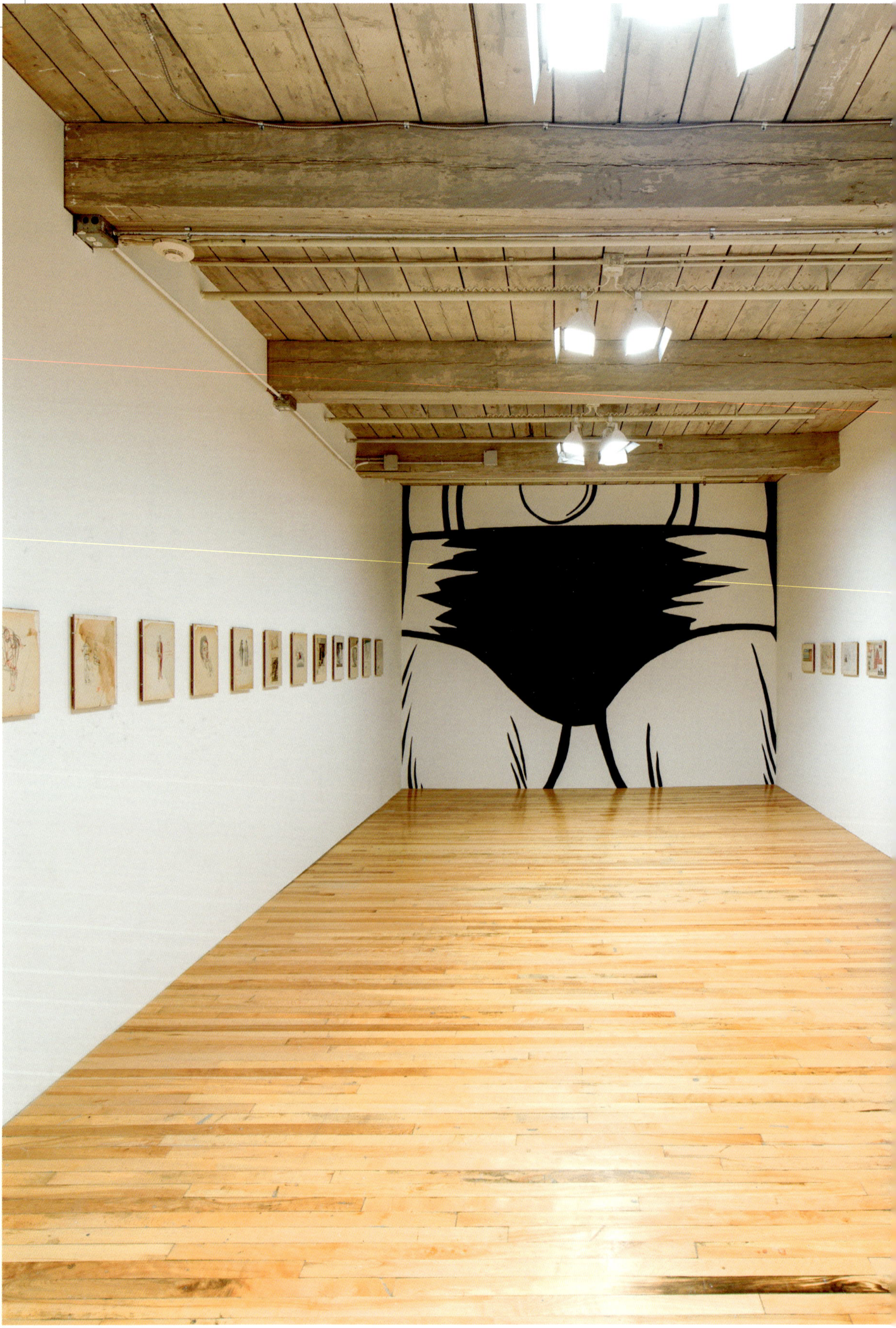

Of Waistbands and Journeys

An Introduction

ALEJO BENEDETTI

Zero Issue

For me it starts with underwear. Underwear, a belt, and the realization that even after eight decades, thousands of comics, multiple film franchises, and millions of dollars spent on costumes, the Man of Steel still has not discovered the secret of waistbands in keeping up his briefs. Now it's not really underwear, and the belt is more for show than a way to keep anything up—the creators were actually referencing the costumes of circus strongmen, a point that Grant Morrison explained in his book *Supergods*.[1] However, what it symbolized for me was something bigger—that Superman is such a prevalent figure that we don't even question some of his more glaring quirks. And it got me thinking—if a bright-yellow belt and what looks like red undies go unnoticed, what other attributes about our heroes have we simply accepted without question?

The societal perception of Superman and Wonder Woman is that they are the faultless defenders of truth, justice, and the American way. They are the better versions of ordinary Americans, instilled with values admired by the country at large. Americans need not fear any threat because the star-spangled crime fighters are always on the lookout. But they aren't always perfect. They don't always save the citizen in peril, their iron-clad moralities can vary from one issue to another. Superman has done things that are sexist, Wonder Woman has at times been racially insensitive. Over the course of eighty years, hundreds of writers guided the actions and adventures of these characters, responding to trends and norms in mass culture—which means sometimes these heroes did or said things that today we find cringeworthy.

In spite of this, they remain beloved characters with cult followings,

Jim Shaw, *The Issue of My Loins*, 2015. Installation. Courtesy the artist + Simon Lee Gallery, London + Hong Kong + Blum + Poe Los Angeles/New York/ Tokyo.

track records of adapting to the times, and a history of standing up against powerful forces for what was right. They respond to critique and to the many calls to action society throws their way. Therefore, it should come as little surprise that artists—the other watchdogs of culture—continue gravitating toward these characters. And it is not just the niche, nerdy artists. It is art-world heavyweights like Laurie Anderson, Jim Shaw, Renée Cox, Pope.L, and Enrique Chagoya. These are prominent voices and art stars who use these characters because they understand the importance of these heroes. The works gathered for this show tell stories in parable—using the familiarity of the Amazon Princess and Man of Steel as gateways into difficult conversations about the present moment. To this end, the show breaks out thematically—grouping works together by focusing on salient messages and arranging these groupings into a compelling narrative that gradually breaks down and reexamines these two recognizable characters.

This connection to storytelling is critical to this show. After all, these heroes first existed as characters in serial comic books with ever-unfolding adventures. Since Superman and Wonder Woman were born of comics, we wanted to pay homage to the characteristics of the print medium in this publication. To do this we broke the catalog into individual issues. The acknowledgements, director's foreword, and this introduction comprise the first section, our "Zero Issue." This title nods to the backstory issue in comics, often written later to set the stage before the adventure actually begins. The other four issues in this box set, numbered 1–4, follow the thematic progression of the exhibition. Each issue consists of reproductions of the works in that section, accompanied by a hundred-word blurb from the corresponding living

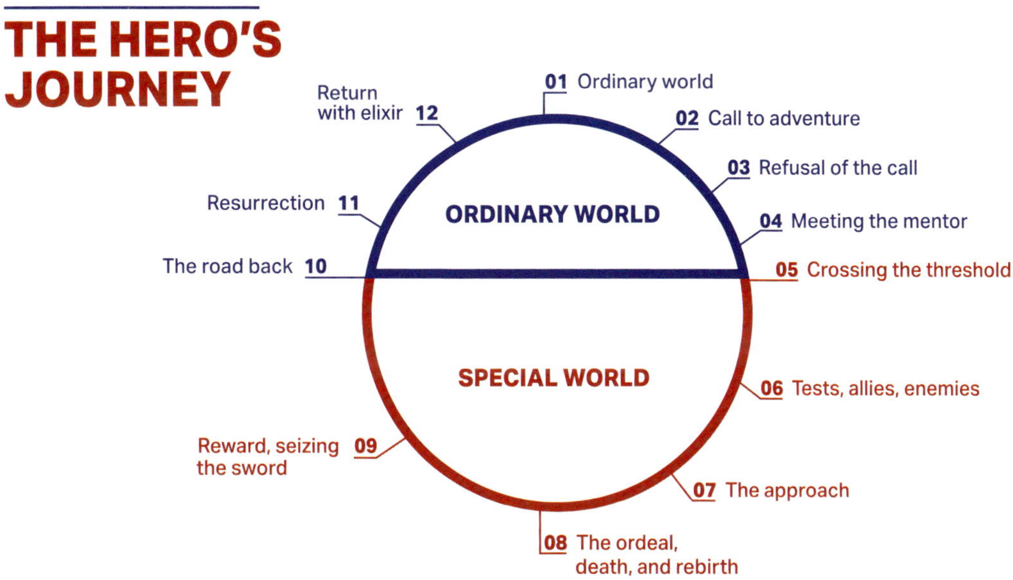

Graphic of the hero's journey by Anna Vernon.

artists who answered the question "Why Superman / Wonder Woman" by email. In each issue, an essay from a contributing scholar dives more deeply into a particular aspect of that section's theme.

The numeric progression of the issues is not just used for the sake of simplicity. It also references the narrative structure fundamental to the Superman and Wonder Woman comics: Joseph Campbell's "Hero's Journey." This same story framework has been the backbone of most hero stories for millennia, leading to what the literary scholar Campbell calls "the hero of a thousand faces" and the idea that all heroes complete a similar adventure. As illustrated in the hero's journey graphic, a hero starts in the ordinary world, but answers the call to enter the "special world" where he goes on an adventure, ultimately leading him back—after a series of tests and challenges—to where he started.[2] However, the adventure always leaves the hero changed, returning with newfound wisdom—what Campbell calls "the elixir."[3] With *Men of Steel, Women of Wonder*, we wanted to create a similar experience as people walk through the space. Here the adventure is an exploration of these beloved heroes. As visitors progress through the galleries or read through the issues, they descend deeper and deeper into this journey of breaking down and reexamining the heroes we've all known for years. The result of this adventure is a new, slightly changed perspective on Superman and Wonder Woman, guided by the artists in the show.

Issue 1: The Heroes We Know

The journey starts in the ordinary world with "The Heroes We Know." Upon first encountering this show we wanted people to realize that these are familiar characters and known points of entry. Greeted by iconic works like *Superman* and *Wonder Woman* by Mel Ramos, visitors first encounter the characters presented in patriotic garb with the perfectly toned muscles and expertly coiffed hair we've come to expect. The section also includes photographs by Siri Kaur showing impersonators dressed in cheap costumes; Fahamu Pecou's self-portrait nod to his art-world hero through a visual quotation of Barkley Hendricks's 1969 self-portrait, *Icon for My Man Superman (Superman Never Saved Any Black People—Bobby Seale)*; and a Katherine Bradford painting that speaks to how iconic Superman's boots and cape are in popular culture.

This opening section functions as an introduction to the show to come, but it's grounded very much in the world of the familiar and the everyday. We call our moms wonder women; send our kids to school with Superman lunch boxes; and weirdly all know about kryptonite, even when identifying a real stone like amethyst might be a struggle. The mythologies of Superman and Wonder Woman are woven into our social fabric, and this first section identifies some of the ways artists explore those connections in their work. To this end, the catalog features an essay written by the comic scholar Bart Beaty, whose past work examines the ways the art and comic worlds collide and occasionally overlap. His essay delves into how these characters function as symbols, analyzing how certain iterations of the heroes became the prevailing versions referenced throughout popular culture.

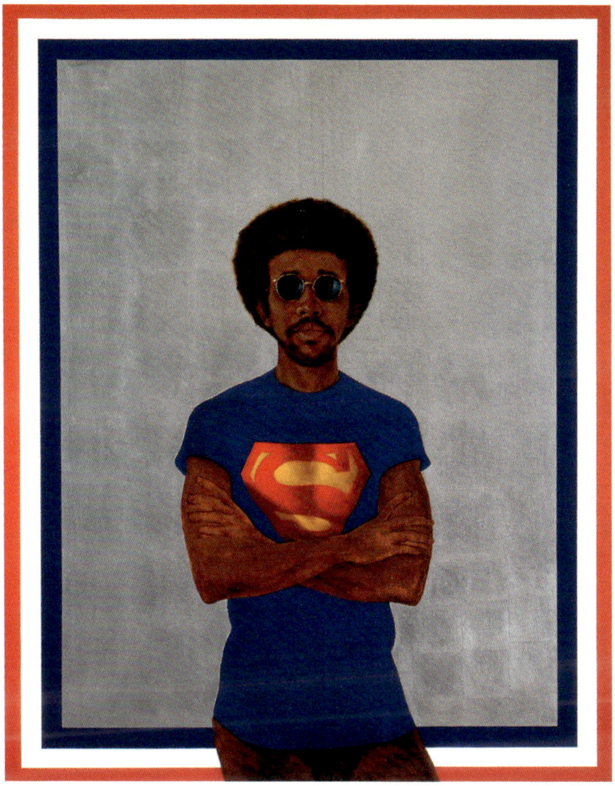

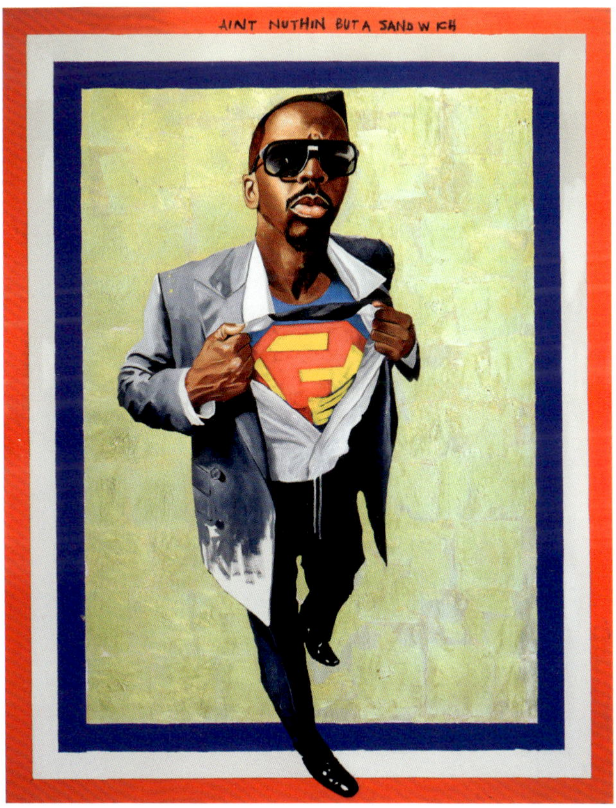

↑ Barkley Hendricks, *Icon for My Man Superman (Superman Never Saved any Black People—Bobby Seale)*, 1969. Oil, acrylic, and aluminum leaf on canvas. Collection of Liz and Eric Lefkofsky.

← Fahamu Pecou, *Nunna My Heros: After Barkley Hendicks' 'Icon for My Man Superman,' 1969*, 2011. Acrylic, gold leaf, and oil stick on canvas, Nasher Museum of Art at Duke University. Gift of Marjorie and Michael Levine.

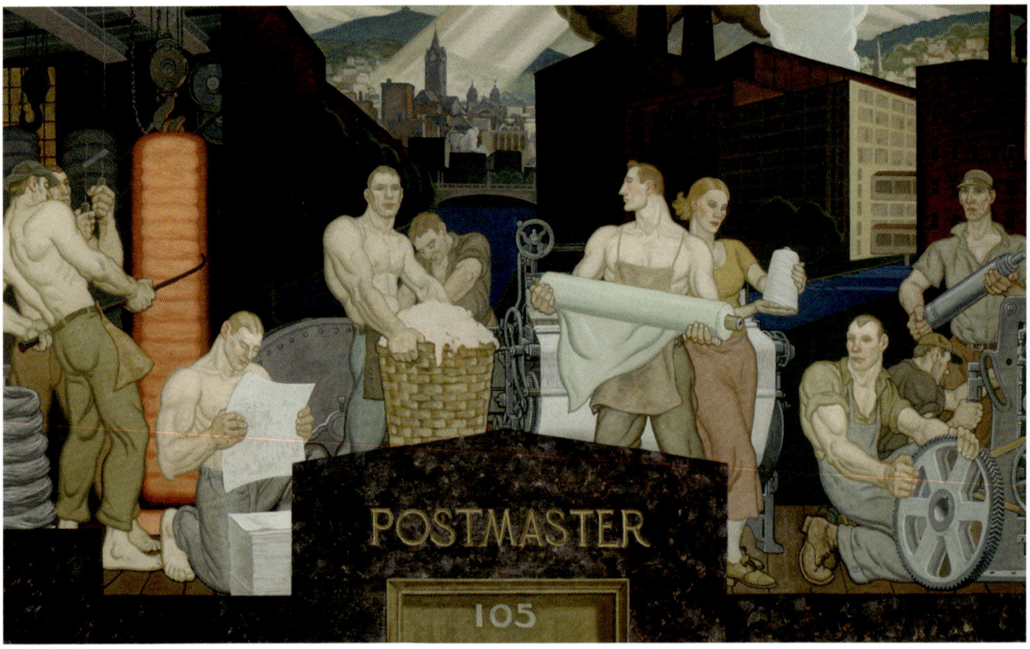

Aiden Lassell Ripley, *Industries of Holyoke*, 1935. Oil on plywood panel. The Westmoreland Museum of American Art; Bequest of Richard M. Scaife (2015.88).

Issue 2: Origin Stories

From the familiarity of the first section, we invite visitors to answer the call of adventure and enter the special world—one in which they reexamine the heroes they thought they knew. In "Origin Stories" we don't recount Superman's escape from Krypton and adolescence in Kansas or relay how Wonder Woman left a utopian island of women to accompany General Steve Trevor back to the United States. Instead, we wanted to challenge guests to reassess why these characters even came into existence by placing both into their respective cultural contexts. In both cases these were heroes born of crisis. The debut of Superman occurred during the height of the Great Depression in 1938. At that time, Franklin D. Roosevelt's New Deal created opportunities for American men to go back to work helping rebuild America through able-bodied action. The New Deal also funded artists to create murals and prints, often featuring muscular, broad-chested men. When viewers look at a mural study like *Industries of Holyoke* or a print like *Men of Steel* by Samuel L. Margolies, they start to understand how the herculean abilities of Superman could easily emerge as the superheroic extension of New Deal values. Wrap all of those sentiments in a tight-fitting blue suit, underwear, and a chunky belt similar to that worn by the circus

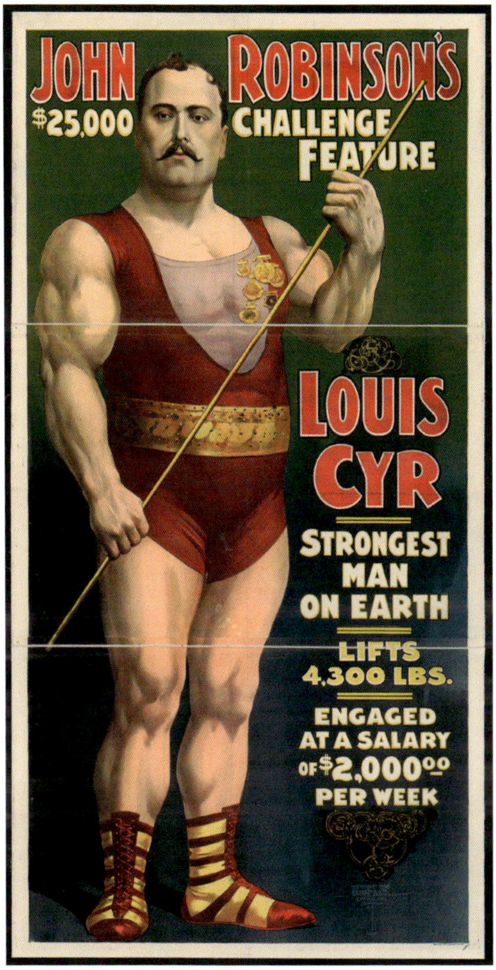

Courier Lithography Company, *John Robinson's $25,000 Challenge Feature – Louis Cyr, strongest man on earth, lifts 4300 lbs.*, 1898. Chromolithograph. *Prints and Photographs Division, Library of Congress, Washington, DC.*

strongman in the Courier Lithography Company's print, and suddenly the world's first superhero is born.

Wonder Woman burst onto the scene three years later, in December of 1941, the same month the United States joined World War II. From the very outset, Diana Prince was a member of the US military, working by day as a secretary but stepping away to fight hand-to-hand against Nazis as Wonder Woman. As women filled vacant factory jobs, these American "Rosies" found a champion in Wonder Woman, doing the superheroine equivalent of supporting the war effort. As with Norman Rockwell's *Rosie the Riveter* (featured in the show holding a riveting gun while wearing lipstick and painted nails), Wonder Woman was powerful, but was also expected to remain beautiful and feminine. Her

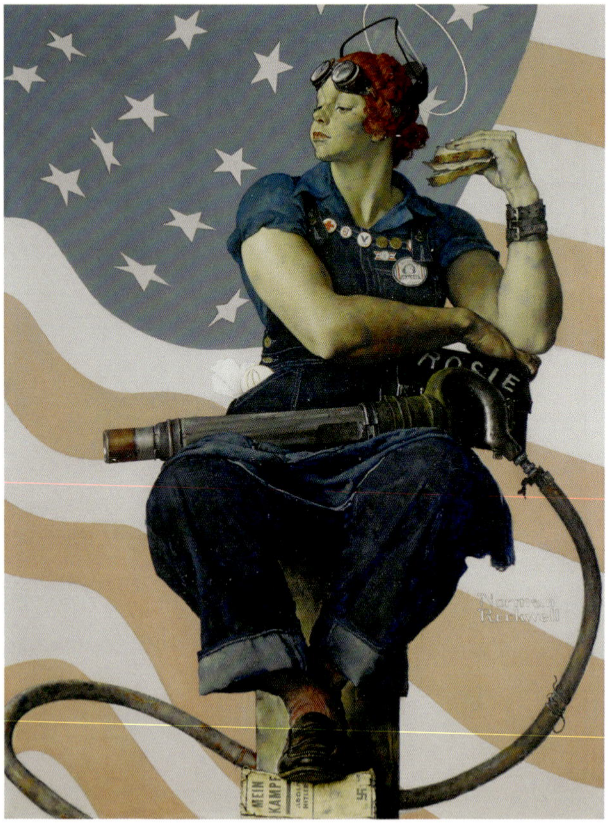

↑ Norman Rockwell, *Rosie the Riveter,* 1943. Oil on canvas. Crystal Bridges Museum of American Art, Bentonville, Arkansas. 2007.178

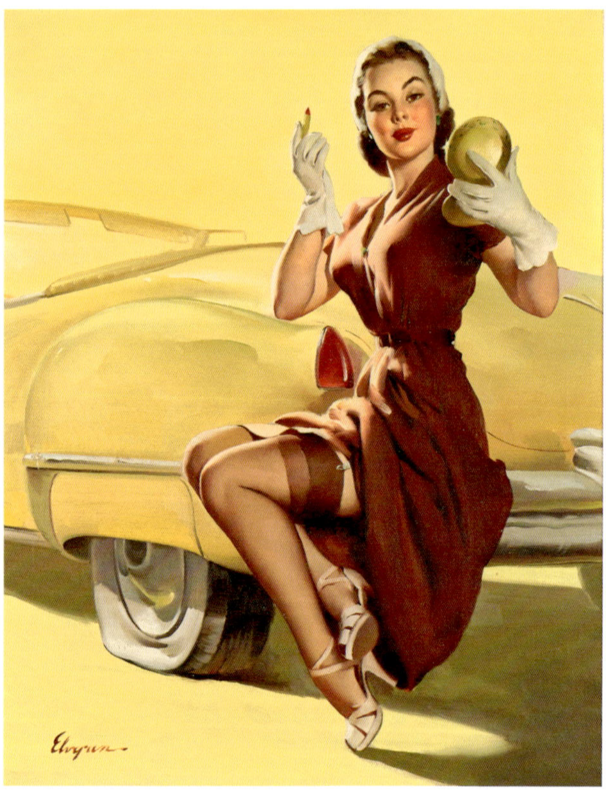

→ Gil Elvgren, *Jill Needs Jack*, 1950. Oil on canvas. Courtesy of Louis K. and Susan P. Meisel.

creator, William Moulton Marston, based her in part on pin-up girls like those of Earl Moran or Gil Elvgren. He believed that a woman's sexuality was one of her strongest sources of power—a belief that Wonder Woman continues to tussle with today.

To drive these origin stories home, this section culminates with the only two comics in the exhibition: the first cover appearances of both characters, *Action Comics* #1 and *Sensation Comics* #1. The catalog essay for this section, written by art historian and visual culture scholar Erika Doss, explores the real-world origins of these characters in detail. Her essay navigates the current obsession with superheroes and traces that thread back into history while providing in-depth analysis of artwork from the section.

Issue 3: Glimpsing Humanity

Having established the origins of these characters, the exhibition then moves on to "Glimpsing Humanity." In this section we build on the idea that, in order to overcome the nation's hardships, America created its own mythology with Superman and Wonder Woman as its version of Zeus and Hera. Here we wanted guests to question how they could possibly connect to these fictional American gods who embody the best midcentury values of our nation and whose abilities so exponentially exceed those of an average human.

To do this, the section is broken into two halves. The first deals with the notion that these godlike characters are effectively all-powerful beings to be admired and possibly even feared. Valentin Popov deifies both characters in his icon paintings, while Jim Shaw inverts this point

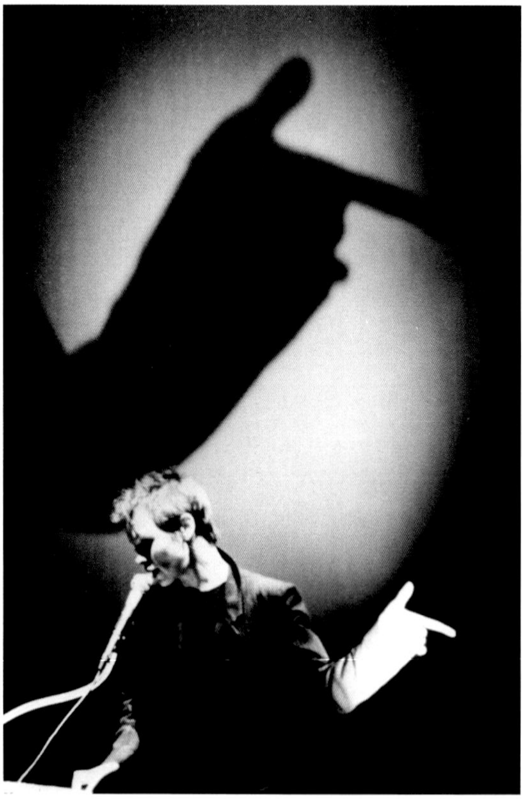

by casting Superman as Satan in scenes culled from William Blake's illustrations of *Paradise Lost*. Alternatively, Laurie Anderson removes the religious connection but preserves the power with her crossover music video / video work *O Superman*, which hauntingly casts the Man of Steel as a proxy for Soviet-era government power.

The second half of the section deals with the vulnerability of these heroes, inviting guests to consider what it means when artists remove certain abilities or highlight already-existing character flaws. Here the artist Mike Kelley prompts consideration of the internal struggle faced by Superman in *Superman Recites Selections from 'The Bell Jar' and Other Works by Sylvia Plath*, while Jason Bard Yarmosky presents his grandmother—who was living with Alzheimer's at the time—in a Wonder Woman costume, drawing attention to mental health, youthful beauty, and how society defines bravery. This second half of the section is also the focus of my catalog essay. In it I take a closer look at the value of finding the vulnerabilities in these characters and how artists prodding those perceived weaknesses actually make the heroes stronger.

Laurie Anderson, Laurie Anderson performing *O Superman*, 1982.

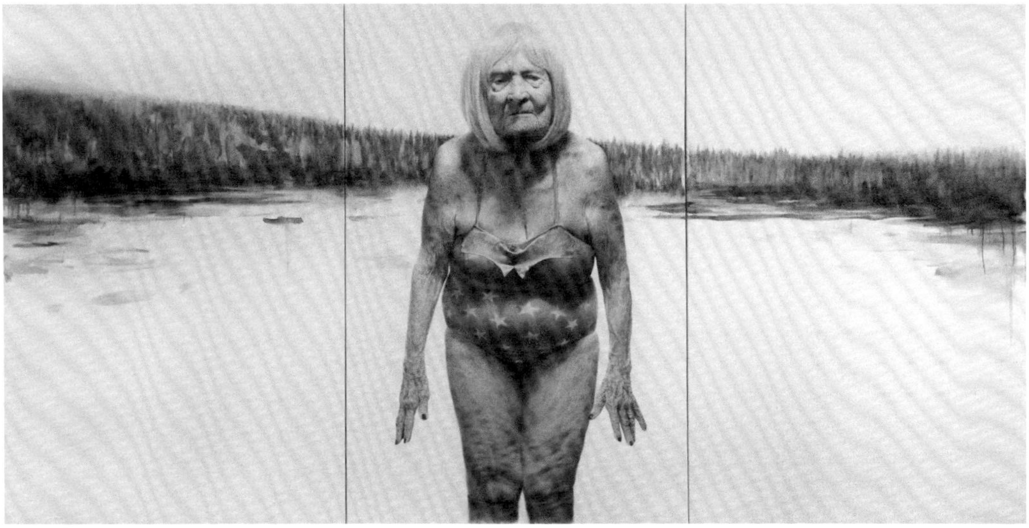

Issue 4: Defender of Innocents

The final section of the show focuses on the jobs these characters were called to do. From the opening pages of their respective comics, they both existed to help defend the defenseless. Therefore, when designing the progression of this exhibition, we knew we wanted to dedicate the most space to examining this, the callings of Superman and Wonder Woman. In each of the section's groupings, viewers encounter artists either implicating Superman and Wonder Woman for their shortcomings or using them as champions for their causes.

The first grouping, "Comic Whitewash," takes its name from the Mel Casas painting featuring Superman alongside other white heroes, driving home the idea that these "defenders of all" are often merely perpetuating a white savior narrative—a longstanding trope in which people of color need to be saved by a white protector. The artists in this whole grouping address a lack of representation, noticeable through the dearth of heroes of color and from the fact that historically white superheroes have often saved other white characters. For some, racial injustice is the focus, but the artist still admires the hero, as is the case with Emma Amos, who paints herself in Wonder Woman attire but also carries an alter-ego T-shirt change that would disguise her as an objectified brown woman. Alternatively, Peter Williams creates The N-Word, a black hero with all of the powers of Superman, but one who is not given the same leeway to perform vigilante justice as his white counterpart.

Jason Bard Yarmosky, *Wintered Fields*, 2016. Oil on canvas. Courtesy of the artist.

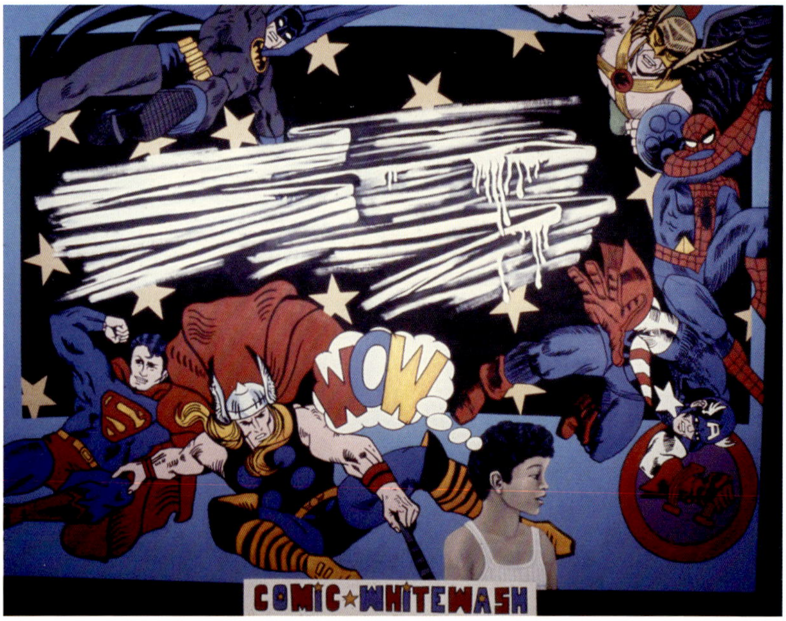

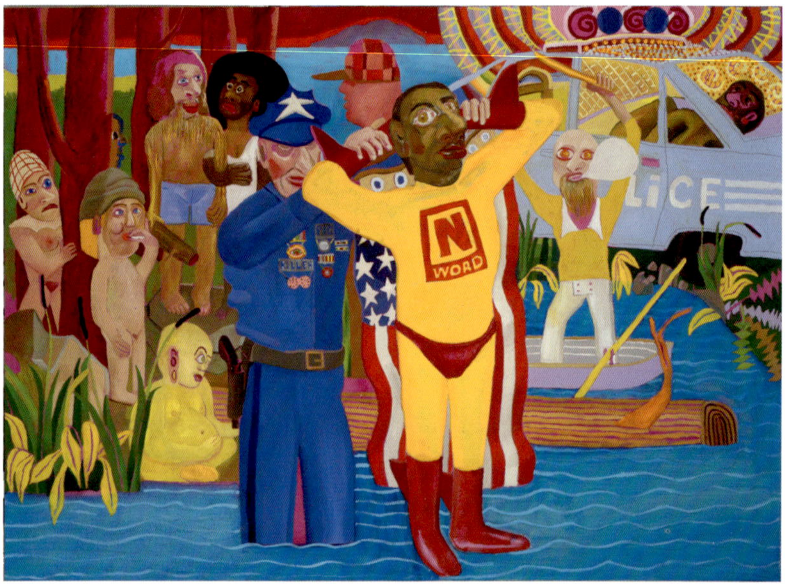

↑ Mel Casas, *Humanscape 70 (Comic Whitewash)*, 1970. Acrylic on canvas. Mel Casas Family Trust.

→ Peter Williams, *Duck Soup, a Comedy*, 2016. Oil on canvas. Courtesy of the artist.

With works like those by Renée Cox, the previous grouping bleeds into one focused on gender norms and sexuality. While some would credit Wonder Woman as a symbol of feminist pride, others see her and Superman as straight, cisgender reinforcements of an existing binary patriarchal system. Addressing some of these concerns, this subsection features works by the artist collective the Waitresses, who latched onto Wonder Woman as a champion of their feminist fight around

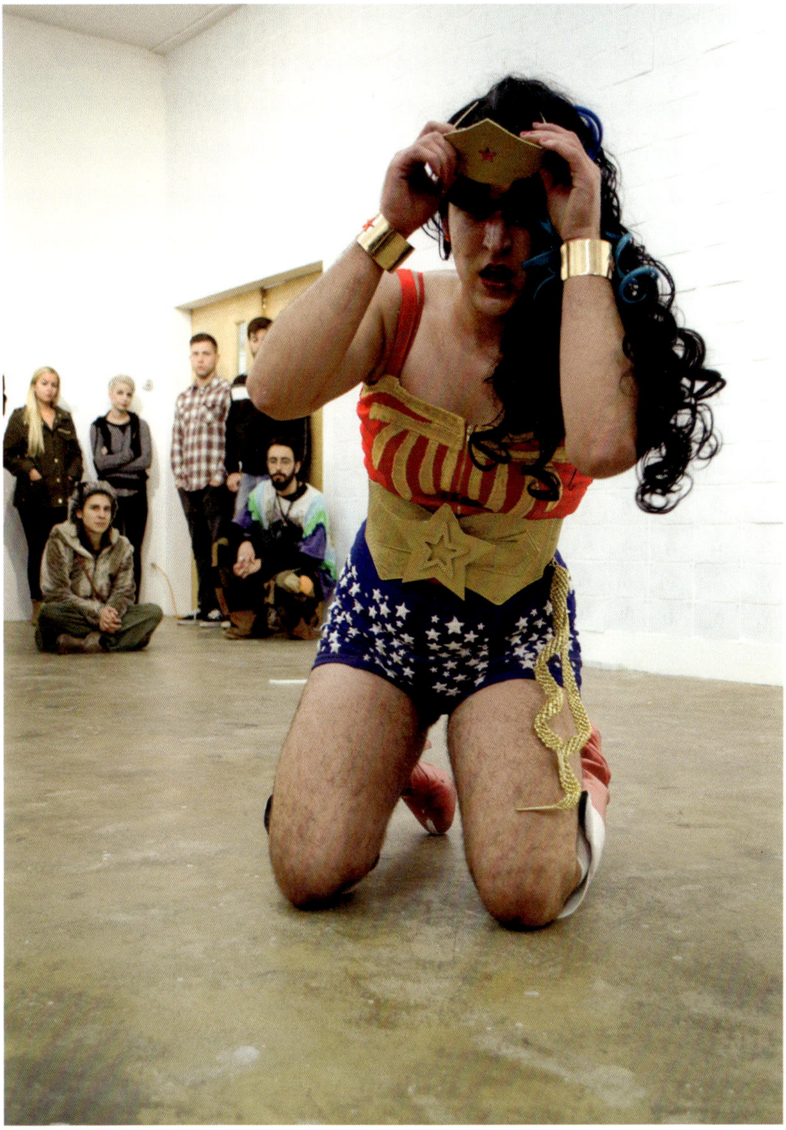

themes of work, money, sexual harassment, and stereotypes of women. Additionally, in this grouping there is a work by the artist Sarah Hill called *They Wonder*. This work nods to Dara Birnbaum's important 1978 *Technology/Transformation: Wonder Woman* (also included in this subsection) and features Hill spinning to the point of collapse, speaking to the exhaustive nature of constantly performing while navigating societal expectations as a transgender person.

Sarah Hill, *They Wonder*, 2015. *Public Communication: Performing Knowledge of the Body*. Suplex, BLUE orange Contemporary, Houston, Texas.

The following subsection, *Aliens Among Us*, builds upon the idea that both characters are illegal immigrants. Wonder Woman comes to the United States from the island of Themyscira. Superman is literally an alien—having escaped from another planet as it was exploding—also making him a refugee. Many artists, particularly Latinxs, have explored this element of the characters in light of current debates regarding immigration. Vincent Ramos gravitated toward the Wonder Woman portrayed by Lynda Carter, who millions idolized without knowing her Mexican American heritage. In *Barbed Wire, Chain Link, & the Lasso of Truth*, Ramos places the actress beyond a fence, alluding to the current border wall debate. Taking a different approach, Enrique Chagoya presents Superman pulling back a Pilgrim's costume to reveal his logo to an Aztec god in *Crossing I*. Chagoya reminds viewers that colonizers were also powerful illegal aliens, inviting a slightly different outlook on Superman's lonely alien narrative.

The final room places these characters on a global stage in a grouping called "American Ambassadors." The perspectives in this room come from international artists, immigrants, and native-born citizens, all of whom portray Superman and Wonder Woman as beacons of American ideals and expectations. The artists use these characters as American archetypes useful in the exploration of multiple layers of individual, cultural, and national identity—at times almost more like amalgamations of all of American culture as opposed to unique, stand-alone characters. The Iranian artist Siamak Filizadeh created a series relocating a classic Persian hero, Rostam, to present-day Tehran and casting him as a beefy quasi-Superman, surrounded by American kitsch. Aphrodite Désirée Navab was also born in Iran but fled as a child during the Islamic Revolution. She later created Super East/West Woman, a character who blurs Navab's own dual identity as Iranian American, boldly declaring her presence with her brilliant blue chador. Alternatively,

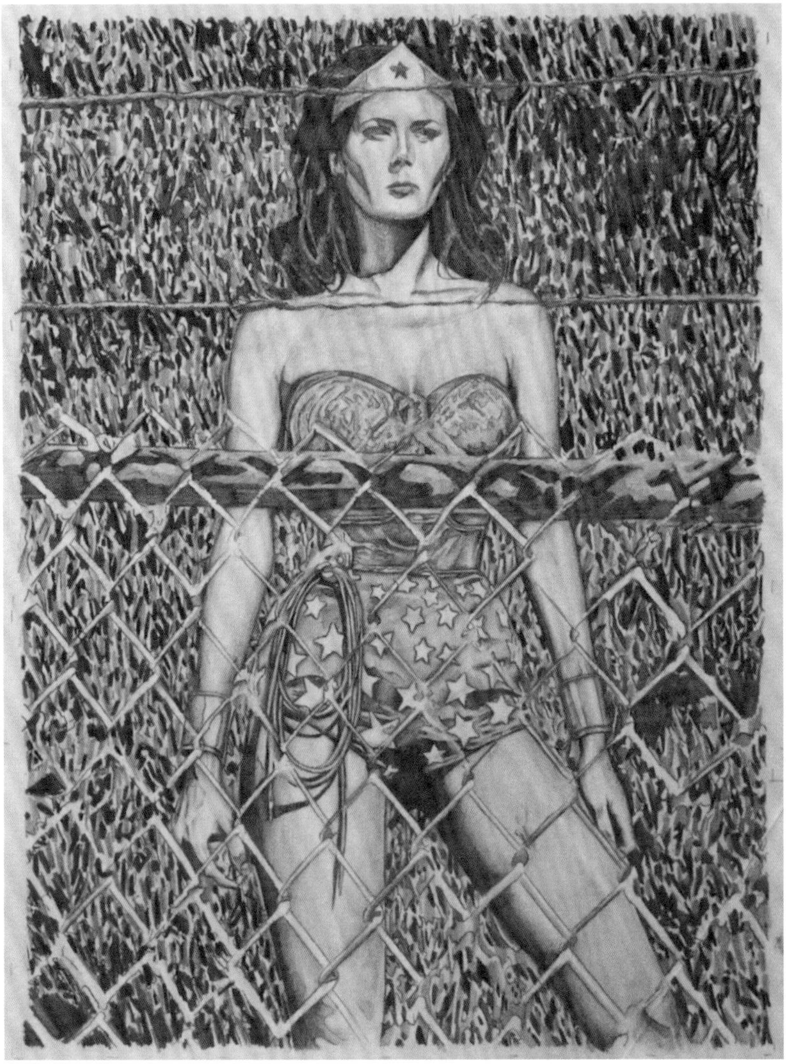

Vincent Ramos, *Barbed Wire, Chain Link, & the Lasso of Truth*, 2016. Graphite and carbon on paper. Courtesy of the artist.

Roger Shimomura was born in Seattle to Japanese American parents and places himself in the work *American vs. American #2* as a stereotypical Asian character in martial arts robes punching out Superman. While the title reminds viewers that both are American, Shimomura pries at the perception around what values and features society associates with Americanness. The themes explored in this large, final grouping of works form the basis of art historian Andrianna Campbell's essay. Her text explores the inherent paradox associated with the democratic goals of Superman and Wonder Woman by analyzing artworks from the exhibition that delve into issues of tolerance, representation, and liberty.

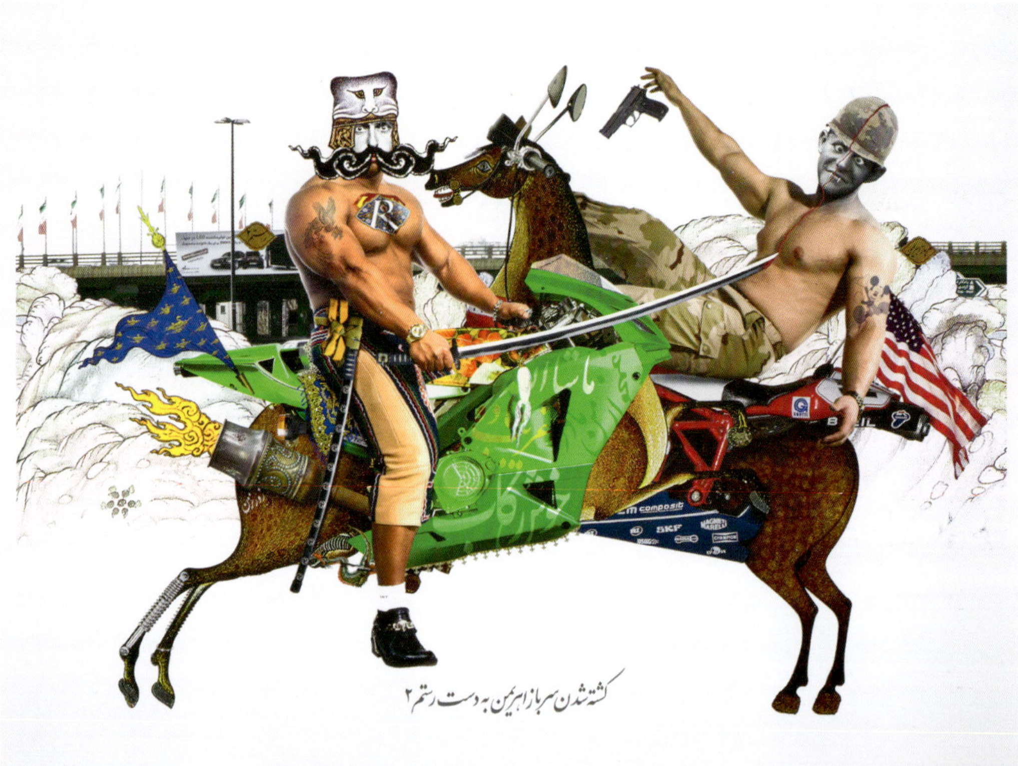

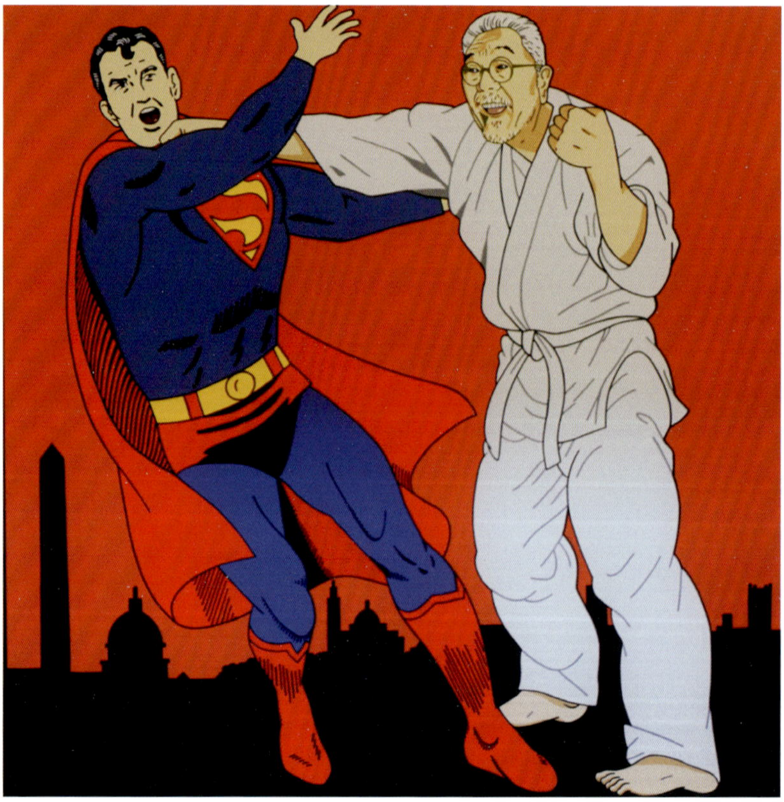

↑ Siamak Filizadeh, *The Soldiers of Evil Are Killed by Rostam II*, Rostam II Series, 2009. Edition 3/5. Digital print on canvas. Los Angeles County Museum of Art. Purchased with funds provided by the Karl Loring Trust and Art of the Middle East.

→ Roger Shimomura, *American vs. American #2*, circa 2012. Acrylic on canvas. Courtesy of the artist.

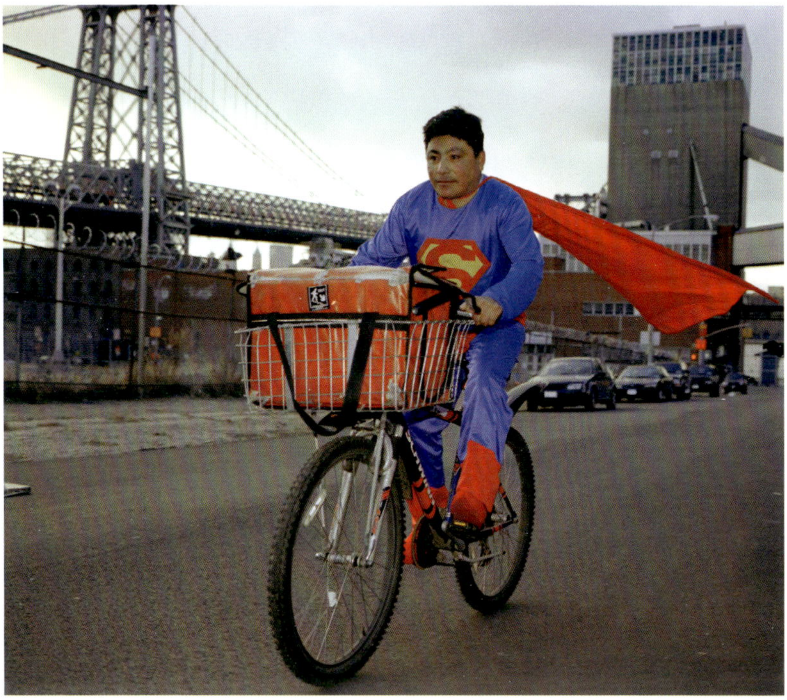

Bonus Issue: The Return

But of course, ending with "Defender of Innocents" does not resolve the narrative in the way Joseph Campbell would propose finishing the Hero's Journey. A well-known trope of mainstream comics is their longevity. *Action Comics* featuring Superman just celebrated its one thousandth issue. If it resolved after every narrative arc with a return home for Superman, we wouldn't have decades of adventures.[4] Indeed, Brett M. Rogers identifies the comic genre as unique in that it never fully resolves itself in light of the hero's journey—typically stopping just short of "the return"—allowing for ongoing stories.[5] In the exhibition and catalog alike we cut the narrative off without a conclusion section as a deliberate reference to the comic medium. When visitors leave the "special world" of the galleries, however, *they* do complete the hero's journey. Back in the ordinary world where they started, they are now equipped with the knowledge gained on their journey. The next time they encounter references to Superman or Wonder Woman in their daily lives, they won't look at them quite the same way. They have the elixir and their perceptions are forever changed.

Dulce Pinzón, *Noe Reyes from Puebla works as a delivery person in Brooklyn, New York. He sends $500 a week.* 2005–2010. Archival c-print from analog image. Courtesy of the artist.

Notes

1 Grant Morrison, *Supergods: What Masked Vigilantes, Miraculous Mutants, and A Sun God From Smallville Can Teach Us About Being Human* (New York: Spiegel & Grau, 2012).

2 Joseph Campbell, *The Hero With a Thousand Faces*, 3rd ed. (New York: Pantheon Books, 1949; Novato, CA: New World Library, 2008).

3 Campbell.

4 Though his home planet of Krypton was destroyed, there are moments throughout the comics when Superman symbolically "returns" when he visits the shrunken capital city of Kandor (which he keeps in a bell jar in his Fortress of Solitude along with all of its inhabitants) or when he returns to Smallville, Kansas—his adopted home where he was raised by Jonathan and Martha Kent.

5 Brett M. Rogers, "Heroes UnLimited: The Theory of the Hero's Journey and the Limitation of the Superhero Myth," in *Classics and Comics*, ed. George Kovacs and C. W. Marshall (New York: Oxford University Press, 2011), 79.

WORKS IN EXHIBITION

The Heroes We Know

MEL RAMOS, *Superman*, 1962. Oil on canvas, 40 × 30 in. *Fine Arts Museums of San Francisco; Museum purchase, Dr. Leland A. and Gladys K. Barber Fund and American Art Trust Fund.*

MEL RAMOS, *Wonder Woman*, 1962. Oil on canvas, framed: 50 × 44 in. *Rochelle and Darren Leininger Family Collection.*

PETER SAUL, *Superman Versus The Toilet Duck*, 1963. Oil on canvas, 63 × 78 ¾ in. *Crystal Bridges Museum of American Art, Bentonville, Arkansas, 2012.497.*

SIRI KAUR, *Christopher (phone)*, 2006. Chromogenic print, 60 × 45 ½ in. *Courtesy of the artist.*

SIRI KAUR, *Wonder Woman*, 2013. Chromogenic print, 60 × 45 ½ in. *Courtesy of the artist.*

FAHAMU PECOU, *Nunna My Heros: After Barkley Hendricks' 'Icon for My Man Superman,' 1969*, 2011. Acrylic, gold leaf, and oil stick on canvas, 63 × 49 ½ in. *Nasher Museum of Art at Duke University; Gift of Marjorie and Michael Levine, 2012.8.1.*

KATHERINE BRADFORD, *Long Flight*, 2012. Oil on canvas, 68 × 80 in. *Collection of Corby and Alexi Reese.*

JIM SHAW, *The Issue of My Loins*, 2015. Installation, 120 × 300 in. Courtesy the artist + Simon Lee Gallery, London + Hong Kong + Blum + Poe Los Angeles/New York/Tokyo.

BARNABY WHITFIELD, *Gold Lion's Gonna Tell Me Where the Light Is*, 2007. Pastel on paper, 40 × 30 in. *From the collection of James and Maureen Dorment.*

Origin Stories

WOMEN OF WONDER

NORMAN ROCKWELL, *Rosie the Riveter*, 1943. Oil on canvas, framed: 52 × 40 in. *Crystal Bridges Museum of American Art, Bentonville, Arkansas, 2007.178.*

FRANCIS CRISS, *Day Shift*, 1943. Oil on canvas, framed: 38 × 29 in. *Crystal Bridges Museum of American Art, Bentonville, Arkansas, 2007.182.*

HUGO GELLERT, *Free Man's Duties I*, 1943. Screen Print, framed: 20 × 16 in. *Crystal Bridges Museum of American Art, Bentonville, Arkansas, 2012.124.*

ANN ROSENER, D-*005684—Production. Willow Run bomber plant. Spot welding parts for the nacelle of an aircraft engine. These women work in the largest one-story building in the works, the giant bomber plant at Willow Run, Michigan. Ford plant, Willow Run,* 1942. Photograph, Negative 4 × 5—matted 9 ½ × 12 in. *Prints and Photographs Division, Library of Congress, Washington, DC.*

ANN ROSENER, D-007013—*Women in war. Supercharger plant workers. Plant foremen point to 20-year-old Annie Tabor as one of their best lathe operators, despite her lack of previous industrial experience. Employed by a large Midwest supercharger plant, this young woman machines parts of aircraft engines. Like many other young Negro girls, she had known only,* 1942. Photograph, 9 ¼ × 12 in. *Prints and Photographs Division, Library of Congress, Washington, DC.*

ANN ROSENER, D-*005688—Production. Willow Run bomber plant. Steady of eye and hand, women workers at the great Willow Run bomber plant are among those throughout the country who are relieving serious shortages of skilled workers by doing such semi-skilled jobs as the one shown here. She's welding parts of the cooling system direct to the supercharger. Ford plant, Willow Run,* 1942. Photograph. 1942. Photograph, 9 ¼ × 12 in. *Prints and Photographs Division, Library of Congress, Washington, DC.*

GIL ELVGREN, *Jill Needs Jack*, 1950. Oil on canvas, 24 × 30 in. *Courtesy of Louis K. and Susan P. Meisel.*

EARL MORAN, *Golden Hours*, circa 1930s. Pastel on board, 38 ½ × 27 ½ in. *Collection of Jim Halperin, courtesy of Heritage Auctions (HA.com).*

MEN OF STEEL

COURIER LITHOGRAPHY COMPANY, *John Robinson's $25,000 Challenge Feature – Louis Cyr, strongest man on earth, lifts 4300 lbs.*, 1898. Chromolithograph, 81 ½ × 42 ¼ in. *Prints and Photographs Division, Library of Congress, Washington, DC.*

TYRONE COMFORT, *Gold Is Where You Find It*, 1934. Oil on canvas, 40 ⅛ × 50 ⅛ in. *Smithsonian American Art Museum, Transfer from the US Department of the Interior, National Park Service.*

AIDEN LASSELL RIPLEY, *Industries of Holyoke*, 1935. Oil on plywood panel, 30 ½ × 50 ¼ in. *The Westmoreland Museum of American Art, bequest of Richard M. Scaife, 2015.88.*

JAMES EDWARD B. ALLEN, *The Skyman*, 1932. Etching, 15 ⅛ × 10 ¾ in. *Crystal Bridges Museum of American Art, Bentonville, Arkansas, 2012.37.*

HERSCHEL LEVIT, *Take it Away*, 1940. Lithograph, 19 × 12 ⅝ in. *Crystal Bridges Museum of American Art, Bentonville, Arkansas, 2012.255.*

SAMUEL L. MARGOLIES, *Men of Steel*, 1940. Drypoint, 16 1/16 × 11 ½ in. *Crystal Bridges Museum of American Art, Bentonville, Arkansas, 2012.295.*

HARRY STERNBERG, *Riveter*, 1935. Color screen print, 11 ¼ × 11 ¼ in. *Crystal Bridges Museum of American Art, Bentonville, Arkansas, 2012.406.*

Action Comics #1–24 Bound Volumes (DC, 1938–40) [Volume #1]. 11 × 8 in. Comic book. *Collection of Jim Halperin, courtesy of Heritage Auctions (HA.com).*

Sensation Comics #1–12 File Copy Bound Volume (DC, 1942). 11 × 8 in. Comic book. *Collection of Jim Halperin, courtesy of Heritage Auctions (HA.com).*

Glimpsing Humanity

ULTIMATE POWER

VALENTIN POPOV, *St. Superman*, 2009. Oil on wood block with eighteenth-century 24 karat gold-plated oclad, framed: 19 × 17 × 4 in. *Courtesy of the artist and Modernism Inc. San Francisco.*

VALENTIN POPOV, *St. Wonder Woman*, 2009. Oil on wood block with eighteenth-century 24 karat gold-plated oclad, framed: 19 × 17 × 4 in. *Courtesy of the artist and Modernism Inc., San Francisco.*

JIM SHAW, *Blake/Boring*, 2010. Ink on paper, 9 × 12 in. *Lent by Keith Fox and Tom Keyes.*

JIM SHAW, *Blake/Boring*, 2010. Ink on paper, 12 × 9 in. *Lent by Keith Fox and Tom Keyes.*

JIM SHAW, *Blake/Boring*, 2010. Ink on paper, 12 × 9 in. *Courtesy the artist + Simon Lee Gallery, London + Hong Kong.*

ROBERT PRUITT, *Heliocentrist*, 2013. Conte, gold leaf, coffee, framed: 72 × 54 in. *#Menelik Woolcock Collection: Zewditu Menelik, Aron Woolcock, Daniel Woolcock, Adrian Woolcock.*

LAURIE ANDERSON, *O Superman (for Massenet)*, 1981. Video, duration: 8:25. *Courtesy of the artist.*

MARY BETH EDELSON, *To the Rescue*, 1973. Oil and ink on silver gelatin print, 10 × 8 in. *Collection of Amy Gold and Brett Gorvy.*

MARY BETH EDELSON, *In Exile,* 1989. Acrylic, fabric, and collage on canvas: 129 × 228 x ¾ in. *The artist and David Lewis, New York.*

MIKE KELLEY, *Kandor 17*, 2007 (edition of 2). Mixed Media with video, sound. Dimensions variable; sculpture: 108 × 61 × 53 in., tank: 60 × 9 in [diam], plus a projected video. *Artworks by Mike Kelley © Mike Kelley Foundation for the Arts. All rights reserved.*

VULNERABILITY

MIKE KELLEY, *Superman Recites Selection from 'The Bell Jar' and Other Works by Sylvia Plath*, 1999. Video, duration: 7:19. *Artworks by Mike Kelley © Mike Kelley Foundation for the Arts. All rights reserved.*

RAYMOND PETTIBON, *No Title, (Do you see...)*, 2015. Ink and acrylic on paper, 22 × 30 in. *Courtesy the artist and David Zwirner.*

LLYN FOULKES, *Where did I go wrong?*, 1991. Oil and mixed media on board, 71 × 54 in. *Collection of Alan Hergott and Curt Shepard.*

LAYLAH ALI, *Untitled*, 2005. Colored pencil, graphite on paper, 11 ⅝ × 8 ¼ in. *Collection Walker Art Center, Minneapolis. Miriam and Erwin Kelen Acquisition Fund for Drawings, 2005.*

LAYLAH ALI, *Untitled*, 2005. Colored pencil, graphite on paper, 11 ⅝ × 8 ¼ in. *Collection Walker Art Center, Minneapolis. Miriam and Erwin Kelen Acquisition Fund for Drawings, 2005.*

JASON BARD YARMOSKY, *Wintered Fields*, 2016. Oil on canvas, 72 × 144 in. *Courtesy of the artist.*

SIMON MONK, *Superman II*, 2013. Oil and alkyd on wood, 23 ⅝ × 19 11/16 in. *Private Collection.*

SIMON MONK, *Bargain Box 3—Box of Superheroes*, 2015. Charcoal on paper, 13 × 15 in. *Courtesy of Alida Anderson Art Projects, Washington, DC.*

Defender of Innocents

COMIC WHITEWASH

POPE.L, *The Great White Way, 22 Miles, 5 Years, 1 Street* (Segment #1: December 29, 2001), 2001–2006. Video, CRT monitor, and resin, edition of 5 plus one AP. *Courtesy of the artist and Mitchell-Innes & Nash, New York.*

MICHAEL RAY CHARLES, *You Need a and You Know It (Forever Free)*, 1994. Acrylic latex, oil wash, and copper penny on paper, 43 × 67 in. *Barbara Karp Shuster.*

EMMA AMOS, *Tightrope*, 1994. Acrylic on linen with Kente borders, 82 × 58 in. *Courtesy of the artist and Ryan Lee Gallery, New York.*

MEL CASAS, *Humanscape 70 (Comic Whitewash)*, 1970. Acrylic on canvas, 72 × 96 in. *Mel Casas Family Trust.*

STEVEN PAUL JUDD, *Siouxperman*, 2014. Serigraph. Edition 25, 12 × 24 in. *Courtesy of the artist.*

STEVEN PAUL JUDD, *Siouxperwoman*, 2014. Serigraph. Edition 25, 12 × 24 in. *Courtesy of the artist.*

PETER WILLIAMS, *Duck Soup, a Comedy*, 2016. Oil on canvas, framed: 50 × 68 in. *Courtesy of the artist.*

ROBERT PRUITT, *SUP*, 2018. Conte charcoal on coffee stained paper, 50 × 38 in. *Courtesy of the artist and Koplin Del Rio Gallery.*

RENÉE COX, *Chillin' with Liberty* (from the Rajé Series),1998. Cibachrome Print, 60 × 48 in. *Courtesy of the artist.*

RENÉE COX, *Eruption* (from the Rajé Series), 1998. Cibachrome Print, 60 × 48 in. *Courtesy of the artist.*

GENDER/SEXUALITY

DARA BIRNBAUM, *Technology/Transformation*, 1978. Video, Run time: 5:50. *Collection of the artist.*

RICH SIMMONS, *Between the capes*, 2014. Mixed media, 48 × 30 in. *Collection of the artist and Oliver Cole Gallery–Miami.*

RICH SIMMONS, *Chrome Reflections*, 2016. Mixed media, 40 × 30 in. *Collection of the artist and Oliver Cole Gallery–Miami.*

SARAH HILL, *They Wonder*, 2014/2015. Performance, Costume/Video documentation, duration: 4 min. *Collection of the artist.*

MARGARET HARRISON, *The Healthier Choice*, 2007. Watercolor and drawing materials, 18 ¼ × 12 ½ in. *Courtesy of the artist and Ronald Feldman Gallery, New York.*

THE WAITRESSES, *Wonder Waitress* vignette from "Ready to Order?" Performed April 27, 1978, Lafayette's Café. Three documentary photographs of seven-day, site-specific, conceptual performance art, 22 × 30 in. © *The Waitresses - Jerri Allyn and Anne Gauldin.*

THE WAITRESSES, *Wonder Waitress,* excerpt from The All-American Waitress Radio Show; Voices: Anne Gauldin, Chutney Gunderson, Jamie Wildperson. Performed March 4, 1981, International Women's Day Program, KPFK-FM Pacific Radio, Hollywood, CA. Audio–digital file. Approximately 2 minutes. © *The Waitresses - Jerri Allyn and Anne Gauldin.*

THE WAITRESSES - ANNE GAULDIN, JERRI ALLYN, *Placemats*, 2018. Open run for audience takeaway, 11 × 17 in. © *2019 The Waitresses - Jerri Allyn, Anne Gauldin.* Men of Steel, Women of Wonder, *Crystal Bridges Museum of American Art, Bentonville, Arkansas.*

ALIENS AMONG US

DULCE PINZÓN, *Noe Reyes from Puebla works as a delivery person in Brooklyn, New York. He sends $500 a week,* 2005–2010. Archival c-print from analog image. 30 × 37 in. *Courtesy of the artist.*

DULCE PINZÓN, *Maria Luisa Romero from Puebla works in a laundromat in Brooklyn, New York. She sends $150 a week,* 2005–2010. Archival c-print from analog image. 30 × 37 in. *Courtesy of the artist.*

ENRIQUE CHAGOYA, *Crossing 1 (El Cruce 1)*, 1994. Acrylic and water-based oil on handmade Mexican Amate paper (handmade paper from the Amate tree), 48 × 72 in. *From the collection of Julia L. Lanigan.*

VINCENT RAMOS, *Barbed Wire, Chain Link, & the Lasso of Truth*, 2016. Graphite and carbon on paper. 21 x 18 in. *Courtesy of the artist.*

VINCENT RAMOS, *March Against Dick*, 2016. Graphite and carbon on paper. 21 x 18 in. *Courtesy of the artist.*

US DEPARTMENT OF ILLEGAL SUPERHEROES. *Illegal Superheroes,* Series 1, (24 of 25) & ICE DISH seal, 2012.

AMERICAN AMBASSADORS

ROGER SHIMOMURA, *American vs. American #2*, circa 2012. Acrylic on canvas, 54 × 54 in. *Courtesy of the artist.*

ROGER SHIMOMURA, *American vs. American*, 2010. Acrylic on canvas, 54 × 54 in. *The Art of Emprise, Emprise Bank, Wichita, Kansas.*

PAPO COLO, *Superman 51*, 1977. Performance, Video documentation of performance. *Collection of the artist.*

APHRODITE DÉSIRÉE NAVAB, *World Summit* from *Super East/West Woman*, 2002–8. Archival chromogenic prints, 22 × 17 in. *Collection of the artist.*

APHRODITE DÉSIRÉE NAVAB, *Landing* from *Super East/West Woman*, 2002–8. Archival chromogenic prints, 22 × 17 in. *Collection of the artist.*

APHRODITE DÉSIRÉE NAVAB, *Object of Curiosity* from *Super East/West Woman*, 2002–8. Archival chromogenic prints, 17 × 22 in. *Collection of the artist.*

KEIICHI TANAAMI, *Comic Strip*, 1967. Collage and photography, 12 ¾ × 18 ⅞ in. *Collection Walker Art Center, Minneapolis, T. B. Walker Acquisition Fund, 2015.*

JACKY TSAI, *Golden Fortune Tree*, 2017 Lacquer carving on wood panel, 39 × 70 ½ in. *Courtesy of the artist.*

SIAMAK FILIZADEH, *The Soldiers of evil are killed by Rostam II*, Rostam II Series, 2009. Edition 3/5. Digital print on canvas, 41 15⁄16 × 55 in. *Los Angeles County Museum of Art, Purchased with funds provided by the Karl Loring Trust and Art of the Middle East: CONTEMPORARY (M.2011.45.11).*

IMAGE CREDITS

Photo: Fine Arts Museums of San Francisco: 59, 78

Photo: Courtesy of the artist: 64, 78

Photo: Crystal Bridges Museum of American Art: Issue Spines, 18, 52–53, 86, 89, 97, 98, 99, 101, 102

Photo: Courtesy of the artist: 51

Photo: Courtesy of the artist: 66

Photo: Nasher Museum of Art at Duke University: Front Cover, 15, 63, 80

Photo: Courtesy the artist: Cover Issue 01, 46

Photo: Simon Lee Gallery: 10, 54–55, 56

Photo: Courtesy of Amelchenko Art Advisory: 70

Photo: Image courtesy of the Prints and Photographs Division, Library of Congress: 17, 84, 85, 104, 105, 106–107

Photo: Courtesy of Louis K. Meisel Gallery, NY: 18, 87

Photo: Courtesy of Heritage Auctions (HA.com): 103

Photo: Smithsonian American Art Museum: 92–93, 94–95

Photo: Westmoreland Museum of American Art: Cover Issue 02, 16, 90–91

© DC Comics: 49, 82, 83, 161

Photo: Courtesy of the artist: 134

Photo: Courtesy of the artist: 118

Photo: Simon Lee: 60, 123, 124, 125

Photo: Courtesy of the artist: 126

Photo: Photo by Chriss Harris, courtesy of Canal Street Communications: 20, 147

Photo: David Lewis Gallery: 69, 120–121, 136

© Mike Kelley Foundation for the Arts. All Rights Reserved/VAGA at ARS, NY: Cover Issue 03, 143, 144

Photo: Courtesy the artist and David Zwirner: 145

© Raymond Pettibon: 145

Photo: David Zwirner: 141

Photo: Walker Arts Center: 138, 139

Photo: Courtesy of the artist: Back Cover, 21, 132–133

Photo: Alida Anderson Art Projects: 122, 129

Photo: Long Gallery: Cover Issue 04, ii, 72, 149, 198, 199, 200

Photo: Courtesy of the artist and Mitchell-Innes & Nash, New York: 202

© Pope.L: 202

Photo: Courtesy of the artist: 204

Photo: © 2018 Emma Amos / Licensed by VAGA at Artists Rights Society (ARS), NY; Courtesy of the artist and Ryan Lee Gallery, New York: 187

Photo: Mel Casas Family Trust: 22, 149, 208

Photo: Courtesy of the artist: 178

Photo: Courtesy of the artist: 179

Photo: Courtesy of the artist: 22, 206–207

Photo: Eleana Del Rio: 158

Photo: Oliver Cole Gallery: 194, 195

Photo: Documentation by Max Fields: 23, 69, 192

Photo: Vince Ruvolo: 148, 196

Photo: © The Waitresses - Jerri Allyn and Anne Gauldin. Photographer Maria Karras: 71, 191

Photo: Courtesy of the artist and Electronic Arts Intermix (EAI), New York: 68, 188, 189

© Dara Birnbaum: 68, 188, 189

Photo: Courtesy of the artist: 27, 169

Photo: Courtesy of the artist: 170–171

Photo: Courtesy of the artist: 172–173

© Enrique Chagoya 1994: 172–173

Photo: Courtesy of the artist: 25, 182

Photo: Courtesy of the artist: 183

Photo: Courtesy of ICE DISH: 174

Photo: Courtesy of the artist: 26, 175

Photo: Courtesy of the artist: 176

Photo: Courtesy of the artist: 209

Photo: Courtesy of the artist: 210

Photo: Edward C. Robison III: Cover Issue 00, 72, 164, 165, 166

Photo: Walker Art Center: 180–181

Photo: Courtesy of the artist: 80–81, 184–185

© Museum Associates/LACMA: 26, 162–163

© Hendricks ©The estate of Barkley L. Hendricks: 15

Photo: Courtesy of the estate of the artist and Jack Shainman Gallery, New York: 15

Photo: The Art Institute of Chicago: 130

Photo: Tim Graham: 130

© Getty Images: 130

Photo: Courtesy of the artist: 142

© 2018 The Andy Warhol Foundation for the Visual Arts, Inc. / Licensed by Artist Rights Society (ARS), New York: 160

Photo: Courtesy of the artist: 177

MEN OF STEEL WOMEN OF WONDER

This publication accompanies the exhibition *Men of Steel, Women of Wonder,* at Crystal Bridges Museum of American Art in Bentonville, Arkansas, on view February 9–April 22, 2019.

The exhibition will travel to:

San Antonio Museum of Art

The Addison Gallery of American Art

In collaboration with

CRYSTAL BRIDGES
MUSEUM OF AMERICAN ART

ART School of Art
University of Arkansas

ACQUAVELLA

Crystal Bridges publications are sponsored by Acquavella Galleries.

Men of Steel, Women of Wonder is an exhibition at Crystal Bridges sponsored as of the publication date by:

stout
Executive Search
Your Placement. Our Passion.

Rhianon DeLeeuw and Joshua Mahony,

Esther Silver-Parker and Deborah Wright.

This project is supported in part by a grant from the Arkansas Humanities Council and the National Endowment for the Humanities.

ARKANSAS HUMANITIES COUNCIL
MAKING CONNECTIONS

Manufactured in Canada

ISBN: 978-1-68226-097-5
eISBN: 978-1-61075-666-2
23 22 21 20 19 5 4 3 2 1

Designer: Liz Lester

∞ The paper used in this publication meets the minimum requirements of the American National Standard for Permanence of Paper for Printed Library Materials Z39.48-1984.

Library of Congress Control Number: 2018960459